D1592199

A Visitor's Guide to

CHEQUAMEGON
National Forest

A Special Place in the
Northern Highlands of Wisconsin

Gary F. Kulibert

Foreword by U.S. Congressman David R. Obey

Explorer's Guide Publishing
Rhinelander, Wisconsin

A Visitor's Guide to
Chequamegon National Forest

First Edition, 1995
Printed in the United States of America

Published by

Explorer's Guide Publishing
4843 Apperson Drive
Rhinelander, WI 54501
715-362-6029

ISBN 1-879432-10-2
LCCN 94-72154

Limits of Liability and Disclaimer of Warranty
This book has been designed to enrich your knowledge and appreciation of the
Chequamegon National Forest. Every reasonable effort has been made to gather the
most current and accurate information. The information presented in this book is
intended only as a general guide and not as an authority on the subject. The publisher
and the author shall have neither liability nor responsibility to any person or entity with
respect to any loss or damage caused, or alleged to be caused, directly or indirectly, by
the information contained in this book.

I would like to acknowledge and thank the hard-working men and women of the Chequamegon National Forest for protecting the natural and environmental resources of the Forest, and for their efforts to provide all of us with the great recreational opportunities that lie within its borders. I would especially like to thank Forest Recreation Planner SUSAN NELSON for coordinating this project and each of the RANGER DISTRICT STAFF for their help.

TABLE OF CONTENTS

FOREWORD

Welcome to the Chequamegon National Forest!

It has been my pleasure to represent northern Wisconsin in the United States Congress for many years. And as I travel around it, almost every year I discover a different spot full of the natural beauty that's a way of life up here. But I have to admit that one of my favorite places is the Chequamegon.

With its miles of trails, scores of lakes and all the creeks and rivers, the Chequamegon truly has something for everyone. If you are looking for some of the most interesting, serene, and beautiful places anywhere in Wisconsin, you'll find them right here in the Chequamegon National Forest. There are snowmobile and hiking trails just waiting to lead you to a new adventure. There are remote areas which are just waiting for you to discover and enjoy. And, there are also a number of areas which will give you a chance to see and experience the diverse management practices displayed in the Chequamegon.

You may also want to stop by a couple of my favorite spots in the Chequamegon, the wooden bridge across the Flambeau River at the Smith Rapids Campground, and the old growth forest in Price County. I'm sure you're going to enjoy your time here and, once again, welcome.

Sincerely,

Congressman Dave Obey

CHAPTER 1

FROM THE BEGINNING
An Historical Overview

As you survey the Forest landscape—with its lowlands and rolling hills all covered with snow, rich greens, or brilliant yellows and reds—imagine, if you will, the vastly different landscape that stretched across this area millions of years ago.

During the Archean Eon, about three billion years ago, the area was a warm, tropical coastal plain, with erupting volcanoes and colonies of bacteria and algae. This was a period of great metamorphosis, as the Earth's crusts were being formed. Tectonic movements created rifts, giving rise to massive mountain ranges—only to eventually erode away and be replaced, again, by seas. Then, more mountains formed as continental plates once again collided.

In Wisconsin, this last continental shift formed the Penokee Range. Over time, the continued onslaught of geological evolution and four continental glaciers eroded these once vast mountains to the landscape that greeted the first visitors nearly 10,000 years ago.

As the glaciers of the last Ice Age began to recede, small bands of nomadic people found their way to this area. They lived off a tundra-like land, hunting bison, wooly mammoth, and other animals living in this harsh environment.

Over the next 8,000 years, the climate grew warmer and drier. Animals accustomed to the cooler climates perished, forests of birch and spruce were replaced by conifers and hardwoods, streams and lakes took their present form, and the nomadic tribes began to establish permanent residence.

These hunter-gatherers continued to evolve, gaining information from the environment and establishing their own cultures. They experimented with different plants and herbs, fashioned pottery, and built homes fit for the rough winters. Commerce between tribes also progressed. Trading of raw materials, such as pipestone and flint, was extensive. Such materials often found their way hundreds of miles from their source.

With the coming of the Europeans in the seventeenth century and the advent of the beaver fur trade, the culture and life-styles of the Native Americans began to change. Over time, the rights to trade with the Europeans became a deadly struggle for supremacy of the region.

This was so with the Huron and Iroquois tribes; the pursuit of furs locked the two tribes in a bitter war. Other tribes, including the Ojibwa (Chippewa), fled to the Great Lakes region, which was already inhabited by the Sioux. After a brief period of peace, the Sioux and Chippewa tribes became hostile rivals. In the ensuing years, many bloody confrontations took place, resulting in the death of many members of the Sioux tribe. Those that did survive were forced west, still holding bitter feelings.

The first European to visit present-day Wisconsin was Jean Nicolet, a French explorer. His goal was to find a short route to the Orient. Instead, he found the Upper Midwest with its riches of fur. He not only opened the land to the fur trade, but also paved the way for European settlements.

Two traders from the newly established French territory in present-day Canada, Medard Chouart des Groseilliers and Pierre-Esprit Radisson, were the first Europeans to enter the Chequamegon Bay area. They were received eagerly by local tribes and returned to France with a large load of furs. French interests in fur trading in the New World were suddenly aroused. Others, such as Jacques Cartier and Samuel de Champlain, continued to explore the Great Lakes and reaches of the St. Lawrence River.

Missionaries followed the early explorers and fur traders. Their goal was to convert the native peoples to Christianity. Unlike the fur traders, missionaries were not received with open arms. Their churches were often burned and they were forced to leave.

During this trading and exploration boom, strong, adventurous men were needed to transport heavy goods and furs across the Great Lakes. These hired "voyageurs" were expected to walk a thousand yards, carrying 200-300 pound bundles on their backs, as well as be able to paddle 35-50 foot canoes from dawn to dusk. Traveling in the wilderness was treacherous and often fatal.

Explorers, fur traders, voyageurs, and missionaries led the way for the mainstream of people wishing to settle, work, and exploit the "New-found land." In the first half of the nineteenth century, discoveries of rich iron-ore deposits lured thousands of people to the Lake Superior area. Lack of transportation made mining slow at first, but as railroads and canals were developed, a mining boom was well on its way. Ashland became known as the Iron Capital. Mining fever triggered land speculation and stock investments. Millions of dollars were spent.

About the same time, logging began to attract fortune seekers. Timber was in great demand for building the cities of the Midwest and East. People of all kinds became lumberjacks here. These were hard working men in a very dangerous profession, coming to the new land with only cross-cut saws and their muscles to harvest the great forests. Although their methods were rudimentary, Wisconsin led timber production for the nation in 1899 with 3.5 billion board feet cut!

By the end of the 1880s, almost all of the white pine forests had been cut and cleared. Sawmill towns had sprung up, with sawmills, planing mills, lumberyards, blacksmith shops, burner barns, tool houses, sleeping shanties, and pumping houses. Railroads contributed their engines, flat cars, roundhouses, turntables, repair shops, and miles of track. They em-ployed hundreds of workers, living in company housing, often with families. These towns left the mark of a great logging era.

Following close behind the loggers were settlers ready to tame the wild land cleared by others. Railroad officials were eager to sell these surplus lands, and with the help of immigration agencies, began to advertise cheap land. Special deals and enticing advertisements drove many immigrants, farmers, lumber barons, and hustlers up north. Settlers could purchase 160 acres with a down payment of fifty cents per acre, if they lived on it, cleared fifteen acres in five years, and added $200 in improvements. By the time these programs ended, 500,000 acres had been totally cleared and 4,000,000 partially cleared. The rocky, nutrient-poor lands were unsuitable for most farming, and after efforts to bring widespread agricultural settlement ended, reforestation became the new priority.

The Chequamegon National Forest was created in 1933. The Ojibwa name "Chequamegon" has several translations, the most often used is "place of shallow water," referring to the shallow waters of Chequamegon Bay. 1933 also saw the start of the Civilian Conservation Corps, or CCC, which was designed to put men back to work during the hard days of the Great Depression. These men fought fires, cleared trails, built campgrounds, and improved public recreational facilities in the Chequamegon and surrounding regions. Their work boosted conservation efforts and helped the economic recovery of the nation. In addition to the CCC were the Federal Emergency Conservation Work (ECW) and the Work Progress Administration (WPA) programs.

CCC enrollees were paid $30 a month to work six-hour days, five days a week. Many left because of the harsh conditions and strenuous work, but the improvements made by enrollees are still noticeable today. Although the program ended in 1942, it is remembered through the NACCCA (National Association of CCC Alumni).

Thanks to the all the men and women who shaped northern Wisconsin, the pull of these tranquil forests and lakes continues today for the enjoyment of all.

CHAPTER 2

A WORKING FOREST

W hen people visit America's National Parks and Forests, there is an expectation of pristine wilderness and total preservation of resources. However, National Forests differ from the National Parks. While National Forests do preserve unique features and environments, they are primarily working forests. One of their goals is to produce and harvest forest products. To better understand the National Forests, let's briefly look at each of the Forest programs.

WATER AND SOIL PROGRAMS

Water and soil programs protect the two media necessary for a healthy forest. Water is needed for wetlands, vegetation growth (trees), fisheries, and recreational opportunities. Water resources in the Chequamegon are plentiful, with more than 800 lakes and 600 miles of streams and rivers throughout the nearly 857,000 acres. To protect and enhance this resource, the Forest Service ensures rules and regulations are followed on timber management, sewage treatment, and erosion control, among others.

Soil management goals are to maintain productivity and minimize the compaction, disturbance, and erosion of soils. The effects of timber harvesting, road construction, and recreational activities on soils must all be considered.

VEGETATION RESOURCE PROGRAMS

Vegetation resource programs manage the abundance of trees and other vegetation on the Forest.

Yes...There still are BIG trees on the Chequamegon National Forest!

There are many competing—and sometimes conflicting—demands placed on vegetation. These include maintaining raw resources for the logging and bough-cutting industries, recreation, biodiversity, watershed protection, and wildlife management, just to name a few. The absence of trees or new growth is just as important as mature stands of trees when managing wildlife such as sharptail grouse and deer. The key is to maintain a balance to meet all resource needs.

WILDLIFE AND FISH RESOURCE PROGRAMS

Wildlife and fish resource programs are an integral part of vegetation management. With hundreds of species of birds, mammals, reptiles, and fish, it is very important to ensure any forest activity complements overall goals. Timber harvesting, along with prescribed burns and mowing, allow forest openings needed for nesting sites, browse, and cover. In other areas, mature stands are left to meet the needs of different species.

For aquatic settings, habitat improvement is also conducted. Besides maintaining water quality and preventing erosion, in-stream and lake structures add habitat and protective cover. Work on stream banks, such as brushing and stabilization, help maintain or improve habitat. Damming of certain waterways creates impoundments that also enhance habitat.

RECREATION PROGRAMS

Recreation programs are designed for a variety of recreational experiences and settings. Demands for recreation change over time and occasionally conflict with one another. Detailed Forest Plans attempt to meet many of these needs, as you will see in the individual Ranger District chapters.

Overall goals are to:
◆ provide a range of activities for all seasons.
◆ create opportunities for both motorized and non-motorized recreation.
◆ enhance wild and scenic experiences along selected lakes and rivers.
◆ preserve unique, natural characteristics in designated wilderness areas.
◆ provide facilities, such as boat landings, picnic areas, campgrounds, and trails.

An ongoing goal is to make these recreational opportunities available to people who are physically challenged.

CULTURAL RESOURCE PROGRAMS

With these vast lands and their associated history, one would expect signs of historic and prehistoric habitation. The effort to find and preserve these sites is part of the **Heritage Resource Program**. To date, over 450 cultural sites have been found. Over sixty sites are prehistoric in nature, and one dates back 5,000 years.

A Forest program called **Passport in Time** is a unique recreational and learning experience for volunteers who gain hands-on experience in historic preservation and archaeological digs. For more information on this program, call the Forest Headquarters.

BIODIVERSITY

Biodiversity is now *the* major issue in managing any forest. The goal of biodiversity is to provide habitat for a wide variety of flora and fauna to prosper. The greater the diversity of species, the better chance the ecological system has of survival.

For example, it is difficult to support waterfowl in an area of mature pine forests. Ducks especially are not receptive to that type of cover. Variety in vegetation and ages permits more species of birds, mammals, and reptiles to survive.

FOREST MASTER PLAN

How can you participate in developing the Forest Management Plan for the Chequamegon National Forest? Every ten years, the National Forest Service develops a plan of how to meet the goals of each Forest. The process looks at both the public issues and Forest management concerns. Based on the issues identified, a number of alternative management plans are developed to balance competing needs. Comments are solicited and public hearings are held. Public input is critical. You are invited by the Forest Service to share your thoughts and ideas. Contact local Ranger District offices or the Forest Headquarters in Park Falls for details.

CHAPTER 3

FOR YOUR INFORMATION

The aim of this book is to acquaint you with the recreational opportunities throughout the Chequamegon National Forest. To enjoy its beauty fully, without endangering the fragile forest environment, we offer a number of hints, suggestions, and a few important rules.

While much of the land within the Forest boundary is federally-owned, there are other properties—especially lake properties—owned by private parties. Please respect the rights of these property owners by not trespassing. Forest maps from Ranger District offices highlight federally-owned property.

"Tread lightly" is not only a catchy phrase, but your way of protecting the environment. The Forest ecosystem faces many harsh elements, such as rain, wind, and freezing conditions, that threaten its delicate balance. When further mistreated by visitors, adverse impacts can, and do, occur. Erosion, vegetation loss, and destruction of unique features may take an eternity to heal.

And, *when* you are treading lightly, it is important to know *where* you are going. The Forest has a road numbering system that we mention throughout this book. **FR is the abbreviation for Forest Road.** It will be followed by a number (for example, FR 144). These roads are identified by brown signs with yellow numbers. Roads may have a town or county name, or a number as well.

Following a few simple rules will help maintain precious resources for generations to come.

◆ Obtain Ranger District maps and rules for the areas you wish to visit.
◆ Drive only on roads. Avoid running over young trees, brush, and grasses.

◆ Stay off roads and trails that are wet and soft. They can be easily rutted or torn up.
◆ Avoid traveling across meadows, steep hillsides, stream banks, and other sensitive areas, as they can be easily scarred.
◆ Stay away from wildlife, especially when they are birthing or tending their young. They have difficulty enough surviving without interference from visitors.
◆ Obey trail, gate, and regulation signs for your own safety and enjoyment, and the safety and enjoyment of others. Fines can be costly.
◆ Respect the rights of private landowners. Get permission to cross private land.

Brown signs with yellow numbers pinpoint the location of Forest Roads (FR).

Special Areas within the Forest Boundary

Wilderness and Semi-Primitive Areas

There are a number of designated wilderness and semi-primitive non-motorized areas throughout the Forest. Each area was established to provide a particular type of experience for the explorer. To obtain the desired experience, it is important to come prepared and follow the specific rules.

While these areas are not as vast as those in the Western United States, they are large enough to get lost in! Northern Wisconsin weather can turn rainy, snowy, and cold with little warning.

A compass, detailed map, and proper clothing, such as rain gear or layered winter clothing, **are a must**. Other needed supplies include **safe** drinking water, extra socks, and first-aid kit with bandages, sunscreen and insect repellant. Specific activities may require additional equipment. Follow the old scouting motto, *"Be prepared."* And as always, let someone know where you are going and when you will return.

Mechanical devices such as bicycles, carts, and motorized vehicles are not allowed in wilderness areas. Violators will be ticketed and fined. In semi-primitive non-motorized areas, regulations allow bicycles and carts, but no motorized vehicles. Semi-primitive areas also receive some timber management, while wilderness areas are left in their natural state.

Research Natural Areas

We describe a number of research natural areas (RNAs) throughout this book. They are used primarily for research and education, rather than public use. Although access to these areas may not be restricted, it is very important not to upset the delicate ecological balance. Again, tread lightly.

Forest Service rules state, *"Research Natural Areas are a part of a national network of ecological areas designated in perpetuity for research and education and/or to maintain biological diversity...Research natural areas are for non-manipulative research, observation, and study. They preserve a wide spectrum of pristine representative areas that typify important forest... situations that have special or unique characteristics of scientific interest...and maintenance of biological diversity."*

If you would like to know more about RNAs, contact the Forest ecologist at the Forest Headquarters in Park Falls.

Watchable Wildlife Areas

A visit to a watchable wildlife area is a unique opportunity to see and hear many species of woodland birds and other animals.

Please do not feed the animals nor try to pick them up, especially the babies. These are wild creatures and they can bite! We also do not want them to lose their fear of people.

A number of impoundments have been developed or improved to enhance wildlife habitat. These areas are used by waterfowl, furbearing animals, and other wetland species. The advantage impoundments have over natural areas is the ability to maintain the desired type and amount of habitat by controlling water levels. These areas are great for observing different types of wildlife and wetland vegetation. They offer a more wilderness-like experience, so come prepared with appropriate equipment.

Normally, animals are most active at sunrise and sunset. Use the surrounding vegetation as natural viewing blinds. You can also see signs of wildlife anytime by the tracks, scats, and nests they leave behind. Field guides, binoculars, and audio tapes will help you identify resident or visiting creatures.

Health and Safety Considerations

Drinking Water

Safe drinking water is a must. While Forest wells and other drinking water supplies are tested to ensure safety, the same cannot be said of lakes and streams. Although natural bodies of water may look clean and their water temperature is cold, this does not mean the water is safe to drink. Bacteria and giardia parasites live in these waters as part of the natural ecology. When ingested, such microorganisms can cause serious health problems. They are more prevalent where warm-blooded mammals, such as beaver, are in the vicinity.

Bring along a supply of **safe** drinking water, water treatment chemicals, or special filters. If these are not available, be sure to boil the water for a minimum of fifteen minutes.

Insects

Bugs can be a real problem during the summer. Black flies and mosquitoes may be particularly obnoxious. Make sure you carry an effective insect repellent or wear clothing that will protect you from bites and stings.

The deer tick can carry Lyme Disease and pass it on to humans and animals. This disease causes *flu-like conditions, along with aching joints, rash, etc.*, in both humans and animals, especially dogs. Ticks are found on grasses, where they can attach themselves to a passerby. Wear light-colored clothing so ticks can be easily found. Tuck pant legs into boots or socks, and shirts into pants. Apply an insect repellant with at least 30 percent DEET or permethrin to all outer clothing and exposed skin. An excellent pamphlet on Lyme Disease is available from the Wisconsin Department of Natural Resources (DNR) and Forest offices.

Recreational Opportunities

Recreational Waters

Fishing and boating activities require compliance with state and local regulations. A current Wisconsin fishing license and appropriate stamps (e.g. trout stamps) are needed by anyone sixteen or older. It is important to get a copy of the current fishing regulations, which also give size limits, health advisories, and other important information.

Naturally occurring metals found in some lakes can be absorbed by fish, thereby contaminating the food chain. The amount of fish that can be safely eaten varies accordingly. Check fishing regulations for details.

Contour maps of the lakes can be obtained from the DNR or private vendors. DNR offices are listed at the end of chapters 4-7.

The Forest is located in what is called "Ceded Territories" where Native Americans harvest fish using traditional methods. Depending on the amount of fish they take, the daily limit of fish varies from year to year on each lake.

Boat registration and life vests are required for all boaters. Observe posted conditions related to outboard motors and speed limits. Gasoline motors are not permitted on some lakes.

Points of Interest

The Forest is full of interesting natural and man-made things to see and do. There are many picnic areas, some with shelters that can be reserved. Call Ranger District offices for information.

Camping

For an enjoyable camping experience, observe Forest camping regulations, including the ones listed below:

◆ Pets are permitted, but need to be leashed so as not to disturb other campers.
◆ Quiet hours are 10 P.M. to 6 A.M.
◆ Leave your campsite as you would like to find it.
◆ Pay your camping fee within 30 minutes of picking a site.

Reservations may be made for selected sites. Call the National Campground Reservation System at 1-800-280-2267 (TTY 1-800-879-4496).

For sites that accommodate mobility-impaired campers, call the local Ranger District office.

Dispersed Camping and Hunting Camps

Certain rules apply when camping outside the established campgrounds:
◆ A 21-day camping permit is needed for dispersed camping outside designated Forest campgrounds. After 21 days, you must move at least one mile from your original camping site.
◆ Keep campsites at least 50 feet from any water or trail.
◆ Bury all human waste and wash water at least 100 feet from any water source. Do not bury food scraps, as forest animals will simply dig them up after you leave.
◆ Pack out what you packed in.
◆ Do not wash yourself or your pets with soap in the lakes or streams. This causes pollution and is illegal.

When camping, and particularly when backpacking, it is important to store food properly at all times, especially after dark. Forest animals such as skunk, raccoon, chipmunk, squirrel, and black bear enter campsites looking for food and are noted for damaging equipment in their quest. Red squirrels and chipmunks love to chew into packs, looking for cookies. Store food in your car—not in your tent. In the back country, suspend food from a branch, 10 to 15 feet off the ground, but well below the branch as well.

Hunting

Hunting is permitted throughout the Forest, except in established campgrounds and special designated areas. A current Wisconsin hunting license and applicable stamps are needed. State rules and bag limits are enforced on the Forest. Check with the Ranger District office before baiting for current rules.

Portable tree stands and ground blinds made of natural materials are permitted if removed at the end of the season. Please note that according to CFR 261.10A, you cannot build or maintain permanent blinds or tree stands; cut or trim brush or trees to create a shooting lane; or use nails, wire, screws, or other metal objects to fasten blinds to trees. If a tree is harvested, these metal objects could cause serious injuries to loggers or sawmill operators.

Trails

There are over 800 miles of trails throughout the Forest. Many are set aside for multiple use, such as biking, horseback riding, cross-country skiing, and snowmobile-ATV-motorcycle riding. Please observe signs that explain the type of use and restrictions. If you are not sure what activities are permitted on a trail segment, call the local Ranger District office. Tread lightly on these trail systems. Don't cause damamge that will take time and money to repair.

Gathering of Forest Products

Woodland environments with forest openings are ideal for the growth of wild berries and of the natural items for gathering. Wild rice is found in many locations. A state permit is required for its harvest. Permits may not be required for gathering of Forest products such as berries, mushrooms, nuts, and pine cones for personal use. Permits are needed for cutting Christmas trees, boughs, and firewood in quantity. A fee may be charged for these permits. Contact the Ranger District office for details.

CHAPTER 4

GLIDDEN/ HAYWARD

Ranger Districts

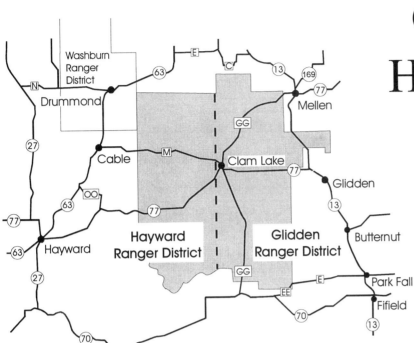

Together, the **Glidden and Hayward Ranger Districts** cover more than 460,800 acres of land and water, of which 372,239 acres are federally owned. Because of their common borders and features, we have combined these two districts into one chapter.

Old mountain ranges, rolling glacial terrain, wetlands, and lakes offer clues to the past. The topography was shaped by the ancient bedrock, which forms the base of this landscape, and by the glaciers that passed this way over the last million years. Forest vegetation is a mix of northern hardwoods (oak, sugar and red maples, aspen, and white birch) and scattered pine plantations (conifers). The wet lowlands have a rich, aromatic cover of balsam, cedar, and tamarack.

Notable points of interest are the Great Divide National Scenic Byway, Chippewa Flowage, Porcupine Lake Wilderness, Morgan Falls, St. Peter's Dome, Chequamegon Area Mountain Bike Association (CAMBA) Trail System, and several semi-primitive areas.

Area communities can provide needed supplies and services. Park Falls, Glidden, and Mellen lie to the east on Hwy 13; Clam Lake is in the middle, at the junction of the two districts on Hwy 77; Hayward and Cable are to the west on Hwy 63; Drummond and Grand View are just north of the Hayward District on Hwy 63.

FOR MORE INFORMATION ABOUT THESE AREAS, CONTACT:

Hayward Ranger District
604 Nyman Ave.
Rt 10, Box 508
Hayward, WI 54843
(715) 634-4821   TTY (715) 634-4821
or
Glidden Ranger District
Hwy 13 North
P.O. Box 126
Glidden, WI 54527
(715) 264-2511   TTY (715) 264-2511

Special Forest Management Areas
Hayward Ranger District

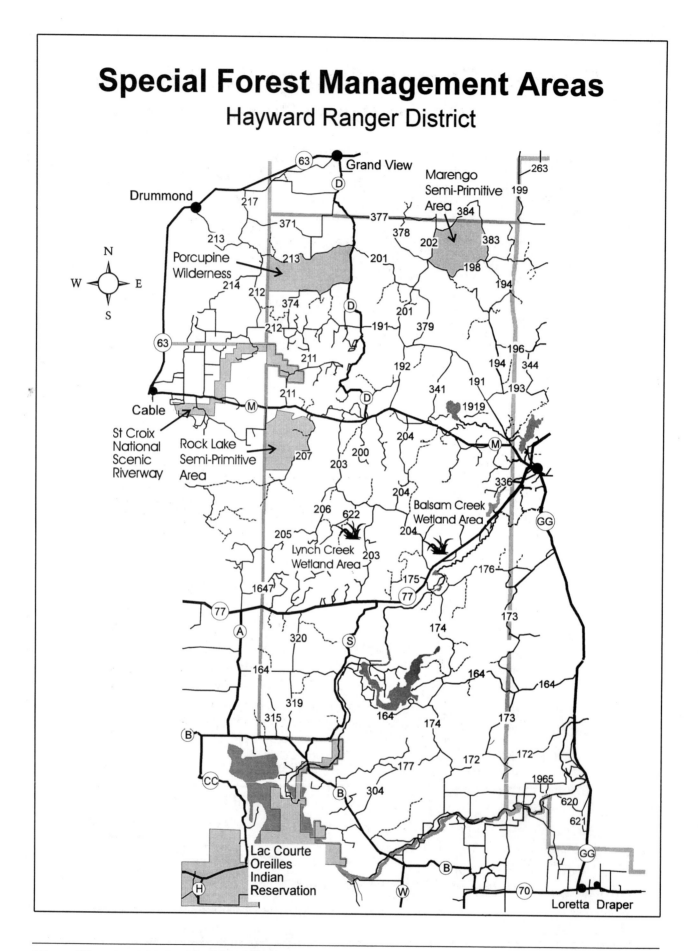

Special Forest Management Areas
Glidden Ranger District

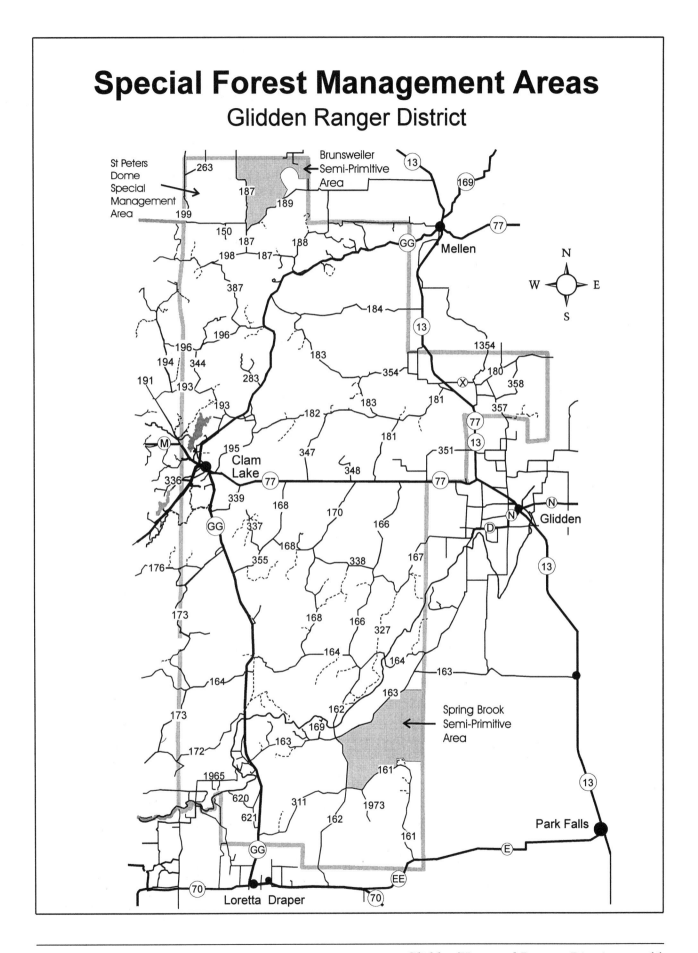

St Peters Dome Special Management Area

263

Brunsweiler Semi-Primltive Area

187

189

13

169

199

150

187

188

77

198

187

187

GG

Mellen

387

184

13

196

196

1354

183

354

180

358

194

344

283

X

191

193

181

357

193

183

77

182

181

13

M

195

347

351

336

Clam Lake

348

77

N

339

77

77

N

Glidden

GG

337

168

170

166

D

168

355

338

167

176

168

166

327

173

168

166

164

164

163

164

163

173

162

169

Spring Brook Semi-Primitive Area

172

163

1965

161

620

311

1973

13

621

162

161

GG

70

EE

Park Falls

Loretta Draper

70

E

N

W

E

S

THE FOREST

The **Hayward and Glidden Ranger Districts** are located in the heart of the Northern Highlands of Wisconsin. In fact, St. Peter's Dome is more than 1,600 feet high. This elevation is a result of two very important geological features—a large dome of igneous rock that covers the northern area of Wisconsin and much of central and eastern Canada, and the remnants of the Penokee Range. Based on geological evidence, the Penokee Range once stood as tall and majestic as the Rocky Mountains. Four major continental glaciers and the natural erosion of wind and rain, have reduced the mountains down to their present form. Still, they are a majestic sight.

The final glacier created the rolling hills and highlands of the terminal moraine in the northern part of the region. By contrast, the southern topography is flat, with many areas of wetland—the result of ground moraines and pitted outwash. West of Clam Lake, the soil becomes more sandy.

Forest cover also varies with soil type. The southern and east central regions are a mix of aspen and maple. These give way to an oak forest in the southwest, near the Chippewa Flowage. The west central region is mainly forested with red pines. Uplands feature stands of maple, except west of Clam Lake, where oak predominates. In the north, hardwoods, such as sugar and red maples, ash, and yellow birch, dominate the landscape. Throughout the two districts, you will find a scattering of red-pine plantations. In the lowlands are forests of cedar, tamarack, and balsam.

The majority of lakes and flowages are found west of Clam Lake and along the Chippewa and Namekagon river systems. Many of these lakes were formed when large chunks of ice were washed away from the glaciers' leading edge and covered with soil and rock. As the ice melted, depressions were formed that filled with water.

Semi-Primitive Non-Motorized Areas

◆ **Brunsweiler Semi-Primitive Non-Motorized Area**, 3,490 acres, is located about eight miles west of Mellen on Cty GG, then north (right) four miles on FR 187 to the southern boundary of this triangular-shaped area. FR 189 makes up the southeastern boundary of this semi-primitive area and FR 187 the western boundary. The northern end is the district border.

Brunsweiler is located in the Penokee Range. The topography is one of rolling hills, valleys, and scenic overviews. The Brunsweiler River and Spring Brook—a Class I trout stream—flow through the area. Since it is not heavily used, Brunsweiler offers an experience of solitude. As such, you need to come prepared. Gated or bermed trails provide access points for visitors on Mineral Lake Road and FR 187.

◆ **Marengo Semi-Primitive Non-Motorized Area**, 2,809 acres, is located northwest of Clam Lake. Take Cty M west about seven miles, then head three miles north (right) on FR 192 to the intersection with FR 191. Turn west (left) on FR 191 and travel one mile. Continue north on FR 201 for two miles, then north on FR 202 for two miles to the North Country Trail parking lot, on the east side of the road.

The Marengo Semi-Primitive Area is located on the northern end of the Hayward District. FR 202 makes up the western boundary, FR 384 the northern, FR 383 the eastern, and FR 198 the southern boundary.

The Marengo River Valley is an area of rolling hills, high points, and steeply-sloped valleys. This is one of the few places on the Hayward District where you can see for miles. The North Country National

Scenic Trail (NCT) crosses the area and accesses three overlooks. Juniper Rock Overlook is located about one mile east of FR 202 on the NCT. You can look west to the Long Mile Lookout Tower (about 3.5 miles away) or east into the Marengo River Valley. Just east of the Marengo River, about 200 feet south of the NCT, is an adirondack shelter.

Also east of the river is an old Swedish settlement. What remains of the foundations of a house, barn, spring house, and the Green Mountain School are just off the NCT. People lived in the Marengo Valley from the 1880s to 1930. Beyond the Swedish settlement are two additional overlooks along the trail, affording views both west and north. The scenery in the Marengo area is good any time of the year, but it is particularly striking in the autumn.

◆ **Rock Lake Semi-Primitive Non-Motorized Area**, 2,960 acres, is located about seven miles west of Clam Lake on Cty M, and just south of Cty M. The area is bordered by FR 207 on the east and FR 628 on the northwest corner. Rock Lake Semi-Primitive Area varies from flat terrain and enormous swamps in the northwest corner to a glaciated terrain of deep kettle holes and small lakes. In the south and east, the terrain is rolling and rocky. This is also a prime area for fall color viewing. The eastern half of the semi-primitive area contains an old road system for hiking and mountain biking (part of CAMBA). The trails range from good roadbeds to mere paths, overgrown with saplings. There are a number of small lakes scattered throughout, offering interesting areas to explore.

◆ **Springbrook Semi-Primitive Non-Motorized Area**, 7,600 acres, is located nine miles west of Butternut (Hwy 13) on Bear Lake Road (which turns into FR 163). FR 163 makes up the northern boundary, FR 162 the western, and FR 161 the southern boundary. The District border forms the eastern boundary.

This area is relatively flat with several scenic creeks, wetlands, and swamps. The eastern terri-tory boasts a number of older trees, while in the west, an old network of logging roads is slowly being reclaimed by the forest. Covered with northern hardwoods, the Springbrook Semi-Primitive Area offers a more primitive experience. Because of its primitive nature, the area is great for people interested in orienteering. Parking can be found along FR 163. Gated or bermed logging roads are the main access points into the area.

Special Management Areas

◆ **St. Peter's Dome Special Management Area**, 4,810 acres, is located west of Mellen (Hwy 13) on Cty GG eight miles, then north (right) on FR 187 for five miles to FR 199. FR 187 and FR 199 will take you to the southern, western, and eastern boundaries of this special management area.

A series of ridges and steep valleys run east and west, parallel to the Penokee Range. The terrain is very steep, with 60- to 80-foot drops into the creek valley below.

Two points of interest, Morgan Falls and St. Peter's Dome, are to the east of FR 199. The dome is a red-granite summit, with an elevation of more than 1,600 feet. On a clear day, you should be able to see Lake Superior, twenty miles to the north. Just before you reach the dome, there is an old red-granite quarry.

Morgan Falls is just off the trail to the dome .5 miles from the parking lot. The sound of water falling 70 feet to the valley floor echoes throughout the valley. In the winter, the sight of the frozen falls is worth the snowshoe walk in.

Located on FR 199 is a large parking area and trail access to St. Peter's Dome and Morgan Falls. There area no other facilities. The trail is steep and does take some effort. The three-mile round trip to the dome takes about two hours.

While the main attractions here are Morgan Falls and St. Peter's Dome, the special management area is also popular with hunters and cross-country skiers.

Summertime at Morgan Falls, in St. Peter's Dome Special Management Area

Wetland Habitat Areas

◆ **Balsam Creek Wetland Habitat Impoundment** is located about eight miles southwest of Clam Lake on Hwy 77, then west (right) one mile on FR 175. It has the look of a beaver pond, with wetlands on the east shore and a forest fringe of white spruce. Formed by a dam at FR 175, this shallow pond is home to ducks, great blue herons, and furbearers.

Wilderness Areas

◆ **Porcupine Lake Wilderness**, 4,446 acres, is located in the northwest corner of the Hayward District. From Clam Lake, travel about 10 miles west on Cty M, then north (right) on Cty D about eight miles. The southwest corner of the wilderness area is located where Cty D and FR 374 meet. The boundaries include Cty D on the east, FR 374 on the south, FR 214 and FR 212 on the west, and FR 213 on the north. Access points can be found along any of these roads or from Two Lakes Campground, located just to the west of the wilderness area.

The landscape varies from rolling hills in the west to flat uplands and swamps in the east. Forest cover is mainly sugar maple, red maple, and white birch, although some stands of aspen, red oak, pine, balsam, cedar, spruce, and tamarack are also found.

The Porcupine Lake Wilderness contains six lakes larger than five acres and numerous ponds. Lake Sixteen is privately owned. The most popular lake is Porcupine Lake. There is a one-half mile trail from FR 213 that leads to the north end of the lake. There are a number of nice camping areas along the lake.

Another interesting feature is the North Country National Scenic Trail, which winds from west to east through the wilderness. In keeping with the wilderness experience, the trail is not marked. If you plan on hiking the North Country Trail, you will need a map and compass. No motorized or mechanical equipment or vehicles are permitted.

Wildlife

Waterfowl and other birdlife are plentiful throughout the Forest. Ducks, bald eagles, ospreys, song birds and other migratory birds can frequently be seen, depending on the season.

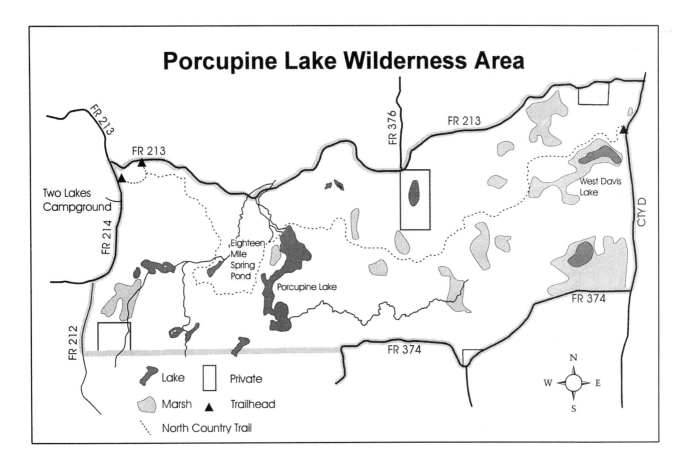

Porcupine Lake Wilderness Area

Two Lakes Campground

Eighteen Mile Spring Pond

Porcupine Lake

West Davis Lake

FR 213
FR 376
FR 213
FR 214
FR 212
FR 374
FR 374
CTY D

Lake
Marsh
North Country Trail
Private
Trailhead

N
W E
S

The two districts have a good population of black bear and large white-tailed deer. There are also plans to reintroduce elk in the Clam Lake area in the spring of 1995. Elk *would* be a sight to see.

Another mammal that was reintroduced is the fisher. Because of this successful effort, fisher range and population have both expanded. Bobcats are also present, although they are very elusive. Beavers can be seen on many lakes and rivers. The best viewing time is in the early morning or evening.

Watchable Wildlife Areas

◆ **Day Lake Picnic Area and Campground** is located .5 miles northwest of Clam Lake on Cty M, then north (right) .6 miles on FR 1294 to the day use area. The campground is to the north. A nature trail connects the day use area

to the campground. Wildlife, such as bald eagles, great blue herons, white-tailed deer, loons, raccoons, grouse, small mammals, large predatory birds, and songbirds, can occasionally be seen along the trail. A portion of this trail has been paved to provide access to all users.

◆ **Lynch Creek Wetland Habitat Impoundment Trail** is located 10 miles east of Cable on Cty M, then south (right) 4.5 miles on FR 203, and south (right) .3 miles on FR 622 to the trailhead. The impoundment is to the east. The western half of the area is covered with red pine, while the eastern half contains an open field and scattered spruce and tag alder. This open area is ideal for duck nesting habitat and blueberries. The impoundment is shallow, and is drawn down every several years to imitate the area's natural drought cycle. Wood duck nesting boxes have been added.

There are two trails. The northern trail is .2 miles long and features a viewing platform overlooking Lynch Creek. The trail is firm, fairly smooth, and covered with pine needles and grass. It poses a moderate degree of difficulty for people with disabilities because of the hilly terrain. The southern trail is .45 miles long and goes to a clearing across the flowage from the viewing platform.

Unofficial Wildlife Viewing Areas

◆ **FR 211 Osprey Nest** is located about six miles east of Cable on Cty M, then .5 miles north on FR 211. The nest is visible from the road. An interpretive sign explains this wildlife setting. This is also a good place for viewing other types of birds.

◆ **Gates Lake** is located west of Glidden on Cty N, then south and west on Cty D. Continue west on Mertig Road, which turns into FR 167. The lake is about 1.5 miles inside the Forest. Geese were brought to the lake to establish a resident flock.

Lynch Creek Wetland Habitat Impoundment viewed from FR 622. Note wildlife observation platform on the left.

◆ **Mineral Lake Boat Landing** is located west of Mellen (Hwy 13) on Cty GG eight miles, then north (right) .4 miles on FR 187, then west (left) .4 miles on FR 1411 to the boat landing. A bald eagle nest is visible across the lake from the landing. It is a little left of center, in the middle of three trees.

Hunting

Hunting is allowed throughout the Forest, except in campgrounds and special-use areas. It is important to keep in mind that you will encounter others who will be using the Forest for hiking, nature watching, and other recreational pursuits.

These two districts are noted for black bear and large white-tailed deer. The northeast portion of the Glidden Ranger District is especially noted for these type of game. The region has a heavy forest cover with many swamps, is not easily accessible, and receives little hunting pressure. If elk are reintroduced, special precautions will be needed when deer hunting. These animals would have protected status for some time.

Hunter Walking Trails

There are four maintained hunter walking trails in the Hayward District and nine in the Glidden District. The trails are mainly in cutover aspen stands. Contact the local Ranger District office for current maps.

◆ **Black Creek Hunter Walking Trail**, 4.7 miles long, is located just west of Cty GG on FR 163, about thirteen miles south of Clam Lake.

◆ **Day Lake Hunter Walking Trail**, 2.5 miles long, is located just northwest of Clam Lake on Cty M. One trail is on Trail Segment 721, the others are on FR 343 to the north.

◆ **Diamond Lake Hunter Walking Trail**, 3.5 miles long, is located 6.5 miles east of Cable on Cty M, then north (left) four miles on FR 211, then west (left) one mile on FR 212, and finally north (right) .75 miles on FR 374.

◆ **Dingdong Creek Hunter Walking Trail**, eight miles long, is located five miles east of Clam Lake on Hwy 77, then north (left) three miles on FR 347, then just east on FR 182.

◆ **Foster Junction Hunter Walking Trail**, 2.5 miles long, is located 3.5 miles west of Mellen on Cty GG. Parking is available on Cty GG and FR 604.

◆ **Ghost Creek Hunter Walking Trail**, 2.25 miles long, is located seven miles southwest of Clam Lake on Hwy 77, then three miles north (right) on FR 204.

◆ **Little Moose River Hunter Walking Trail**, 6.25 miles long, is located 7.5 miles southwest of Clam Lake on Hwy 77, then south (left) one mile on FR 174, and then east (left) 1.5 miles on FR 176.

◆ **McCarthy Lake Hunter Walking Trail**, 1.25 miles long, is located west of Mellen on Cty GG, then southeast on FR 184, then southeast on FR 183, and is across from FR 353.

◆ **No Name Lake Hunter Walking Trail**, five miles long, is located south of Cty GG on FR 163 east and south of Clam Lake.

◆ **Sanguine Hunter Walking Trail**, 3.5 miles long, is located .75 miles west of Cty GG on FR 176, about four miles south of Clam Lake.

◆ **Twin Lake Hunter Walking Trail**, one mile long, is located on FR 195 just west of Woodtick Lake, which is two miles north of Hwy 77 at Clam Lake.

◆ **Two Axe Hunter Walking Trail**, 4.9 miles long, is located 23 miles east of Hayward on Cty B, then south (right) one mile on FR 1604.

Gathering of Forest Products

A woodland environment with forest openings is ideal for the growth of wild berries and other natural items for gathering.

Blackberries and raspberries can be found along forest roads where small wildlife openings create sunny places for berries to flourish. Blueberries can be found in the sandy soils around Day Lake Campground and along the interpretive trail that links the Day Lake Day Use Area to the campground.

Wild rice can be found along the west side of Bear Lake, as well as on the Chippewa River above Moose Lake. A state permit is required to harvest wild rice. Berries and wild rice are harvested in the latter part of the summer.

The gathering of other forest products such as boughs and firewood, may also require a permit. Contact the local Ranger District office about possible permits.

Recreational Waters

Lakes

Within the borders of the Glidden and Hayward Ranger Districts are more than 190 lakes ranging from two acres to 15,300 acres. Most lakes are in the Hayward Ranger District west of Clam Lake. Listed below are lakes that have public boat landings.

◆ Atkins Lake

Surface Area: 190 acres
Depth: Maximum 81 feet, mean 29 feet
Fishery: Northern pike, walleye, smallmouth bass, panfish, and trout
Location: Travel west of Clam Lake on Cty M about 8.5 miles, then north (right) about six miles on FR 192, continuing on FR 201 to the northeast end of lake.
Lake Conditions: The bottom is mainly sand. Water is clear, with visibility down to 19 feet.
Shoreline: It is mostly mixed hardwoods with scattered conifers. The lake has a well developed shoreline.
Facilities: An unimproved boat landing is on county land.
Contour Map Available: Yes

◆ Beaver Lake

Surface Area: 35 acres
Depth: Maximum 12 feet, mean 5 feet
Fishery: Brook trout, brown trout, channel catfish, and yellow perch
Location: Travel eight miles west of Mellen on Cty GG, then north (right) three miles on FR 187, then west (left) on FR 198 two miles, and finally north (right) .1 mile on FR 1372 to the boat landing.
Lake Conditions: Water is light brown, with visibility down to five feet. Aquatic vegetation is sparse; lake bottom is mostly sand.

Shoreline: The eastern shore is a mix of paper birch and red pine. The northern end of the lake has a tag alder swamp, while the rest of the shore contains white spruce, jack pine, and hardwoods.
Facilities: There is a campground on the east end of the lake on FR 1800 and an unimproved boat landing on the south side, north of FR 198.
Contour Map Available: Yes

◆ Black Lake

Surface Area: 130 acres
Depth: Maximum 15 feet, mean 8 feet
Fishery: Musky, northern pike, largemouth bass, and panfish
Location: Located on the southern fringe of the District. From Clam Lake, take Cty GG south for about 12 miles, then west (right) 4.5 miles on FR 172, then north (right) on FR 178 for .5 miles.
Lake Conditions: Water is dark brown, with visibility down to three feet. Tree drops have been added to improve fish habitat.
Shoreline: The majority of the shoreline is mix of hardwoods, balsam fir, and pines, with a small wetland at the inlet.
Facilities: A boat landing is on southwest side and a campground is farther north.
Contour Map Available: Yes

◆ Chippewa Flowage (Lake Chippewa)

Surface Area: 15,273 acres
Depth: Maximum 92 feet, mean 15 feet
Fishery: Musky, northern pike, walleye, largemouth bass, smallmouth bass, and panfish
Location: Located on the southwest corner of the Hayward Ranger District. The Chippewa Flowage is a valuable resource now owned by the Wisconsin DNR. From Hayward, head east on Cty B about

Lakes
Glidden/Hayward Ranger Districts

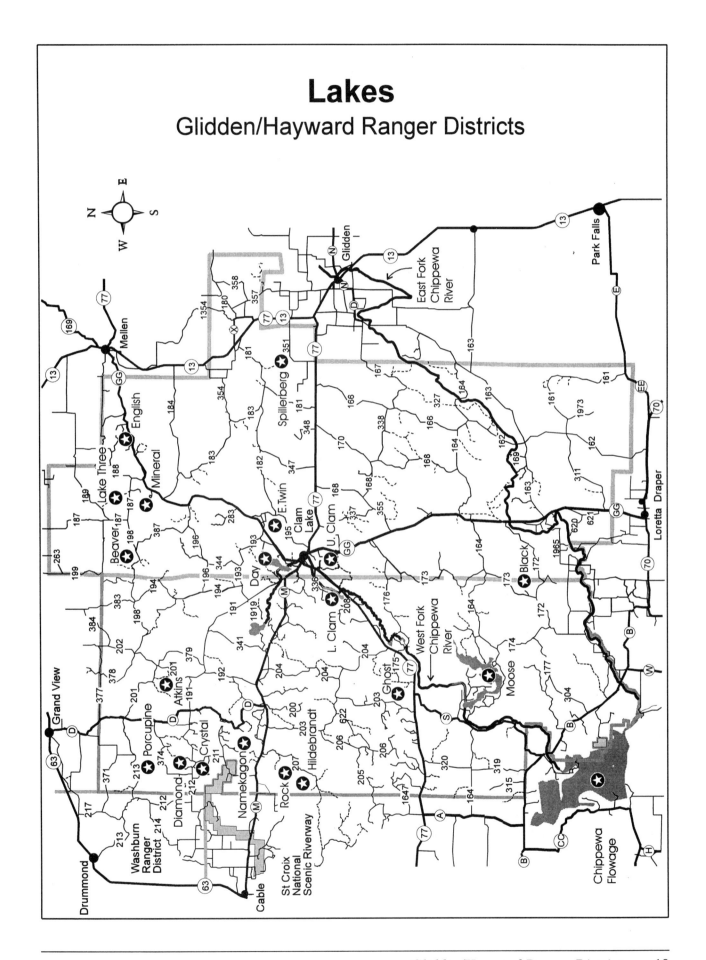

thirteen miles, then south (right) two miles on Cty CC to the flowage.

Lake Conditions: The flowage flooded ten named lakes and several unnamed lakes when created. Water level in the lake can fluctuate several feet throughout the year due to draw-down and refilling. This will change the characteristics of the flowage, both for fishing and boating. A number of fish cribs have been added to the flowage. Water is medium brown.

Shoreline: A large amount of the shoreline is in public ownership, with a scattering of cottages and resorts. The shoreline is irregularly shaped with many bays and 140 islands. Seventy percent of the shore is wetland, with the rest mixed hardwoods.

Facilities: There are no Forest-owned lands on the flowage. However, private facilities are located throughout the area. Two public boat landings can be found on Cty CC about three miles north of New Post.

Contour Map Available: Yes

◆ Crystal Lake

Surface Area: 122 acres

Depth: Maximum 29 feet, mean 17 feet

Fishery: Walleye, northern pike, largemouth bass, smallmouth bass, and panfish

Location: From Cable, travel about seven miles east on Cty M, or from Clam Lake, travel west about thirteen miles on Cty M. At FR 211, turn north and travel four miles. The road to the landing is west of FR 211 and about .8 miles north of Junek Point Road. The landing is on the south end of the lake.

Lake Conditions: The lake bottom is sandy with areas of gravel. There is little vegetation. Water is clear, with visibility down to four feet.

Shoreline: The shoreline is upland hardwoods and scattered pines, and is well developed.

Facilities: The landing is classed as undeveloped.

Contour Map Available: Yes

◆ Day Lake

Surface Area: 650 acres

Depth: Maximum 20 feet, mean 7 feet

Fishery: Musky, crappie, panfish, and largemouth bass

Location: From Clam Lake, travel west on Cty M for .5 miles to FR 1294, then north (right) .2 miles to FR 1292, and then west (left) to the boat landing.

Lake Conditions: Being a relatively new flowage, there are numerous stumps and floating bogs. Five fish cribs have been added to improve fish habitat.

Shoreline: The shore has a forest cover of pine and birch. Islands dot the lake, while floating bogs move to different areas of the lake depending on water level and wind direction.

Facilities: There are a campground and a picnic area with associated facilities near the boat landing and three handicap accessible fishing piers.

Contour Map Available: Yes

◆ East Twin Lake

Surface Area: 110 acres

Depth: Maximum 15 feet, mean 7 feet

Fishery: Musky, panfish, and largemouth bass

Location: From Clam Lake, travel north three miles on Cty GG, then south (right) .7 miles on FR 190, then continue south (right) .1 mile on FR 250 to the boat landing.

Lake Conditions: Water is medium brown with visibility down to four feet. Three fish cribs have been added in front of the fishing pier.

Shoreline: The shoreline is minimally developed, and is edged with hardwoods, birch, and tag alder.

Facilities: Near the boat landing are a campground and a picnic area with associated facilities.

Contour Map Available: Yes

◆ Ghost Lake

Surface Area: 142 acres

Depth: Maximum 27 feet, mean 10 feet

Fishery: Musky, largemouth bass, and panfish

Location: Travel southwest from Clam Lake, seven miles on Hwy 77, then west (right) on FR 175.

Lake Conditions: The bottom is mainly muck, with scattered areas of sand and gravel. Aquatic vegetation is scarce in the clear water.

Shoreline: The shore has a cedar, balsam, and hemlock fringe and several small resorts. Most of the shore is owned by the Forest.

Facilities: There is an improved boat landing on east side of the lake.

Contour Map Available: Yes

◆ Lake Three

Surface Area: 72 acres

Depth: Maximum 13 feet, mean 6 feet

Fishery: Largemouth bass and panfish

Location: From Mellen, travel west on Cty GG eight miles, then north (right) 3.7 miles on FR 187 to the entrance of Lake Three Campground.

Lake Conditions: Water is light brown, with visibility down to ten feet. The bottom is mostly muck with some sand and gravel. Aquatic vegetation is moderately dense.

Shoreline: The shoreline is a mix of aspen, birch, white spruce, and balsam, and is minimally developed.

Facilities: A gravel boat landing and a campground are located on the lake. A solar-powered aerator has been added to help prevent winter kill conditions. It is the only one of this type this far north. The North Country Trail runs beside the lake.

Contour Map Available: Yes

◆ Lost Land Lake

Surface Area: 1,303 acres

Depth: Maximum 21 feet, mean 12 feet

Fishery: Musky, northern pike, walleye, largemouth bass, smallmouth bass, and panfish

Location: Travel east from Hayward or west from Clam Lake on Hwy 77. At Cty A, turn north on Upper A Road and travel three miles north, then east (right) until the road turns into FR 205. The boat landing is on the right.

Lake Conditions: There is abundant aquatic vegetation. Water is clear, with visibility down to nine feet.

Shoreline: The west shore is bog and scrub swamps, with northern hardwoods covering about 60 percent of the shoreline. There are a number of resorts and homes along the shore.

Facilities: Unimproved public landing is on the west shore off FR 205.

Contour Map Available: Yes

◆ Lower Clam Lake

Surface Area: 229 acres

Depth: Maximum 22 feet

Fishery: Musky, walleye, largemouth bass, smallmouth bass, and panfish

Location: Travel one mile south of Cty M on Hwy 77, then west (right) on FR 336.

Lake Conditions: Water is a light brown with visibility down to five feet.

Shoreline: Most of the shore is hardwood bottoms set against a forest of hardwoods and pine and areas of sedge meadow. There are homes and resorts on the lake. At the mouth of the outlet is a five-foot high logging dam, a remnant of the logging era.

Facilities: A boat landing is on the north shore off FR 336.

Contour Map Available: Yes

◆ Mineral Lake

Surface Area: 225 acres

Depth: Maximum 29 feet, mean 12 feet

Fishery: Most noted for musky, along with walleye, smallmouth bass, and panfish

Location: From Mellen (Hwy 13), travel west on Cty GG eight miles, then north (right) .4 miles on FR 187, then west (left) .4 miles on FR 1411 to the boat landing.

Lake Conditions: The bottom is a mix of muck, sand, gravel, and rock. The water is light brown, with visibility down to five feet.

Shoreline: The shore is a mix of aspen, birch, large Norway pine, and tag alder. There is minimal development.

Facilities: A campground, picnic area, and boat landing can be found on the south shore.

Contour Map Available: Yes

◆ Moose Lake

Surface Area: 1,601 acres

Depth: Maximum 18 feet, mean 8 feet

Fishery: Musky, walleye, largemouth bass, smallmouth bass, and panfish

Location: Travel about 25 miles east of Hayward on Hwy 77, then south (right) six miles on FR 174, then west (right) on FR 1643 to the east side of the lake.

Lake Conditions: Water is dark brown, with visibility down to four feet. The lake contains a number of stumps and wood debris, because it was an impoundment used for driving logs. Fish cribs have been added to provide fish habitat.

Shoreline: Eighty-nine percent of the shoreline is a mix of hardwoods, big white pines, and balsam firs. The rest is swamp. The area is well developed with many homes and resorts.

Facilities: There are a boat landing and a rustic campground on the east shore on FR 1643.

Contour Map Available: Yes

◆ Namekagon Lake

Surface Area: 3,208 acres

Depth: Maximum 50 feet, mean 16 feet

Fishery: Musky, northern pike, walleye, largemouth bass, smallmouth bass, and panfish

Location: It is about midway between Cable and Clam Lake on Cty M, then north on Cty D. The boat landing is about five miles north, on the west side of the road.

Lake Conditions: There is an abundance of aquatic vegetation, especially in the bays. Water is light brown. Fish cribs have been placed near the fishing pier at the campground.

Shoreline: The shoreline is irregularly shaped, with many small bays. Northern hardwoods can be found along the shore, which is well developed.

Facilities: There is a boat landing at the picnic area with beach, accessible toilets, and an open shelter at the north end of the lake, west of Cty D. An outlet, which is on the west shore off FR 211, is the beginning of the St. Croix/Namekagon National

Scenic River. The outlet is an old logging dam that also serves as a canoe landing.

Contour Map Available: Yes

◆ Potter Lake

Surface Area: 29 acres

Depth: Maximum 11 feet, mean 8 feet

Fishery: Largemouth bass, musky, and panfish

Location: From Mellen (Hwy 13), travel west on Cty GG 7.5 miles, then north (right) .4 miles on FR 185 to the boat landing.

Lake Conditions: Water is light brown, with visibility down to five feet. Aquatic vegetation is present. Several tree drops have been added for fish habitat.

Shoreline: The shoreline has aspen and ash trees with a dense tag-alder fringe. As the lake is entirely federally-owned, there is minimal development.

Facilities: There are a picnic area and a gravel boat landing just north of Cty GG.

Contour Map Available: Yes

◆ Spillerberg Lake

Surface Area: 74 acres

Depth: Maximum 24 feet, mean 9 feet

Fishery: Musky, largemouth bass, walleye, and panfish

Location: From Glidden (Hwy 13), travel north on Hwy 13 seven miles, then west (left) .5 miles on FR 355, then south (left) two miles on FR 181 to a spur road to the boat landing.

Lake Conditions: Water is light brown with visibility down to eight feet. Aquatic vegetation is present. The bottom is sandy with some gravel and boulders.

Shoreline: Although only ten percent of the lake is federally-owned, there is minimal development. The shoreline cover is white spruce, cedar, and tag alder.

Facilities: There are a picnic area and a gravel boat landing.

Contour Map Available: Yes

Walk-In Lakes

Listed below are several lakes in the District that only have walk-in access.

◆ Hildebrand Lake

Surface Area: 16 acres
Depth: Maximum 42 feet, mean 12 feet
Fishery: Largemouth bass, northern pike, and panfish
Location: From Cable, travel east about eight miles on Cty M, then south (right) 3.4 miles on FR 207, then west (right) one mile on West Rock Trail to the Rock Lake Semi-Primitive Area.
Lake Conditions: The bottom is rocky, with scattered areas of sand, gravel, and muck. Water is clear, with visibility down to 17 feet.
Shoreline: The shore is upland hardwoods and conifers, and a small shrub swamp on the north end. The northeast side is steep but accessible.
Facilities: None. It is over a .5-mile walk into the lake.
Contour Map Available: Yes

◆ Pole Lake

Surface Area: 12.5 acres
Depth: Maximum 21 feet
Fishery: Planted trout, largemouth bass, perch, and panfish
Location: From Clam Lake, take Cty GG south of Hwy 77 two miles, then west (right) on FR 1275 1.5 miles, continue north about .5 miles. The lake is to the east one-fourth mile.
Lake Conditions: Aquatic vegetation is sparse and water is clear.
Shoreline: The southeast and southwest shores are a spruce bog, with the remaining shoreline aspen, birch, and Norway pine. There is no development on the lake, as it is entirely owned by the Forest Service.
Facilities: No facilities on the lake. From the parking lot, it is a quarter-mile walk in.
Contour Map Available: Yes

◆ Porcupine Lake

Surface Area: 75 acres
Depth: Maximum 33 feet
Fishery: Largemouth bass, northern pike, and panfish
Location: From Clam Lake, travel west about ten miles on Cty M to Cty D, then north (right) on Cty D about ten miles, then west (left) 3.5 miles on FR 213 to the trailhead just west of Porcupine Creek.
Lake Conditions: Water is medium brown, with visibility down to four feet.
Shoreline: The shoreline is a mix of upland hardwoods and conifers, with a bog wetland on the south shore and several small wetlands along the west shore. There is no development, as it is part of the wilderness area.
Facilities: None
Contour Map Available: Yes

◆ Rock Lake

Surface Area: 33 acres
Depth: Maximum 25 feet
Fishery: Smallmouth bass, largemouth bass, and panfish
Location: From Cable, travel east about eight miles on Cty M, then south (right) 2.6 miles on FR 207. The trail to the lake will be to the west (right) in the Rock Lake Semi-Primitive Area.
Lake Conditions: There is an abundance of vegetation. Water is clear.
Shoreline: There are birch, aspen, white spruce, and pine along the shore. There is no development, as it is part of the semi-primitive area.
Facilities: None
Contour Map Available: Yes

Rivers

◆ East Fork of the Chippewa River

Length: Sixty-four miles
Gradient, Average: Four-foot drop per mile
Fishery: Suckers in springtime, brown trout in the

upper reaches. Walleye, musky, smallmouth bass, panfish, and channel cats nearer to the flowage.

Description: The East Fork of the Chippewa River has its beginning in Iron County, to the east. As a small trout stream, it flows southwest through Glidden to the District boundary. Below FR 1285 are stretches of Class II rapids. It is about 4.5 miles through Pelican Lake to the landing off FR 164. The next landing is at Stock Farm Bridge Campground. There are also Class II rapids downstream from this canoe landing. The next landing, downstream about five miles, has one road crossing (FR 162). The stream continues its southwesterly path after crossing FR 164 and FR 162 before entering Bear Lake. Just above Bear Lake is Butternut Landing on FR 169. This is the most southwesterly boat landing on Forest lands. Below this point are some Class II rapids before you enter Bear Lake.

From this point down to the flowage, most of the shore is privately-owned. From Bear Lake, the stream begins to widen as it meanders about seven miles to Blaisdell Lake. There is a boat landing on the north shore. From here it's about ten miles through Hunter Lake and Barker Lake to the Chippewa Flowage and Winter Dam.

The shoreline throughout the river varies from pasture lands to forest to wetlands and bogs. About forty percent of the shore is wetlands. A landing can be found on the south shore just before the dam. From here, you can proceed into the flowage or portage to the lower reaches of the Chippewa River. Both branches combine in the flowage and flow south after leaving Winter Dam, which forms the Chippewa Flowage. The river below the dam is mostly shallow and meandering, with only riffle areas.

Access Points: FR 1285 Canoe Landing is located four miles south of Glidden on Cty D, then west (right) on FR 167 for four miles to FR 1285. Turn east (left) and travel two miles to the canoe landing. This is the most easterly access point for the East Fork of the Chippewa River.

Stock Farm Bridge Canoe Landing is located west of Butternut on FR 163 nine miles, then north (right) on FR 164 four miles to the spur leading to the canoe landing.

Butternut Canoe Landing is located six miles north of Loretta (Hwy 70) on Cty GG, then four miles east (right) on FR 163, and then one mile north on FR 169 to the canoe landing.

Other landings can be found on Blaisdell Lake and near the dam.

◆ Namekagon River

Length: Thirty-four miles
Gradient, Average: Six-foot drop per mile
Fishery: Panfish, walleye, and northern pike
Description: Namekagon River has its start at Namekagon Lake and flows south and west 98 miles, where it joins the St. Croix River. This is the start of the National Scenic Riverway, which is administered by the National Park Service. Only a small section of the river lies within the Forest boundary. The upper section of the river varies from an intimate, cold-water trout stream closed in by forest, to a wide, slow-moving stream, flowing through marshy areas. There are numerous rapids along the river and at least one very low bridge.
Access Points: In the Forest, the main canoe access point is at the dam, which is on the west side of the lake, about a mile north of Cty M on FR 211.

◆ West Fork of the Chippewa River

Length: Twenty-seven miles
Gradient, Average: Upper reaches, 15-foot drop per mile; river near flowage, 4-foot drop per mile.
Fishery: Suckers in spring time. Walleye, smallmouth bass, panfish, and excellent musky in the lower reaches.
Description: The West Fork of the Chippewa River has its beginning in Chippewa Lake just north of Cty M about four miles northwest of Clam Lake. It flows southeasterly into Day Lake, then south into Upper Clam Lake, just south of Cty M and Hwy 77. In this upper reach, the river is mainly minnow habitat, with a shoreline of willow and tag alder.

An impoundment of the West Fork of the Chippewa River, just north of Hwy 77 at Clam Lake.

From Upper Clam Lake, the river flows southwest towards the Chippewa Flowage, passing first through Lower Clam Lake, then over a rock dam. It continues its way for about nine miles, passing through Cattail Lake and Meadow Lake before reaching Partridge Crop Lake. Along the way there are a number of rapids and rock dams that were used during the logging era. It is a pleasant, six-hour trip from Hwy 77 near Lower Clam Lake to the bridge on FR 174. The water flows slowly except in several small rapids. Travel is difficult in low-water conditions.

In these sections, the river widens and has a shoreline of forest cover with many marsh and wetland fringes. Fishing also improves, with many warm-water species present.

After passing under Belsky Bridge on FR 174, the river meanders southward, where it joins Ghost Creek. The river begins to widen as it enters Moose Lake. Keep to the north shore as you travel west to the dam. From here, the river follows Cty S to Cty B, just above the flowage. This section has at least ten sections of Class I and II rapids. During high water, the rating increases, as does the danger.

In October, Moose Lake is drawn down and the stretch of river from Moose Lake to Cty B is at its best for canoeing. However, the increased water flow also increases the hazard class of the rapids in this section. **It can become very treacherous during high water conditions.**

From the bridge on FR 174 to the bridge on Cty B is another good day trip. This fifteen-mile, seven hour trip takes you through Moose Lake (portage at the dam) to the backwaters of the flowage. This section offers excellent musky fishing, lots of scenic natural shoreline, and many interesting rapids. Water flow is slow in spots, except for the area below Moose Lake, where water flow increases. The trip is best taken in moderate water levels.

Access Points: Lower Clam Lake has two access points. The better put-in point is on private land where Hwy 77 crosses the river, about three miles west of Clam Lake. The public landing is on Lower Clam Lake, on the west shore off FR 336.

FR 174 access is about seven miles southwest of Clam Lake on Hwy 77, then .5 miles east on FR 174.

Trout Streams

The Hayward/Glidden Ranger Districts have thirty-nine trout streams within their boundary. The majority are Class II trout waters. Several of the more noted streams include the **Brunsweiler River, Spring Brook, Marengo River, Twenty Mile Creek, and Eighteen Mile Creek.**

POINTS OF INTEREST

Auto Tours

◆ **Fall Color Tour 1** starts in Cable at Hwy 63 and Cty M. Travel east on Cty M into the Forest and between Twin Lakes. At Lake Namekagon, you turn north (left) on Garmisch Road, traveling several miles through an area of overhanging trees. At Cty D, turn south (right), then left back onto Cty M. After about one mile, turn north (left) on FR 192 through an area of hardwood forest with a scattering of pine plantations. From FR 192, continue north on FR 201, then FR 202 and finally 7 Mile Road.

At Holmes Road, turn west (left) to Hwy 63. Continue into Grand View, where you will take a left turn on to Cty D. Continue south on Cty D past the North Country National Scenic Trail and Porcupine Lake Wilderness. At the southern edge of this area, turn west (right) on Diamond Lake Road FR 374. Follow it around the north end of Diamond Lake, then turn west (right) on to FR 372. Continue west on Lake Owen Drive, past Lake Tahkodah, turning south (left) on Jalowitz Road, continuing to Cty M. At Cty M, turn west (right), traveling back to Cable.

QUICK REFERENCE
Auto Tour Highlights Within the Glidden/Hayward Ranger Districts

Fall Color Tour 1
Length: 52 miles
Highlights
  Fall Colors in the National Forest
  Twin Lakes
  Lake Namekagon
  North Country National Scenic Trail
  Porcupine Lake Wilderness
  Diamond and Tahkodah Lakes

Great Divide Scenic Byway
Length: 29 miles
Highlights
  The Great Divide
  Clam Lake CCC Camp
  Dead Horse Slough Trailhead
  Clam Lake

  Ghost Creek CCC Camp
  Balsam Creek Wetland Habitat Area

Penokee Highlands Route
Length: 47 miles
Highlights
  Scenic Penokee Range
  Penokee Overlook
  Potter & Mineral Lake Campgrounds
  Day Lake Day Use Area
  Clam Lake
  Great Divide Scenic Byway
  Clam Lake CCC Camp
  Dead Horse Slough Trailhead

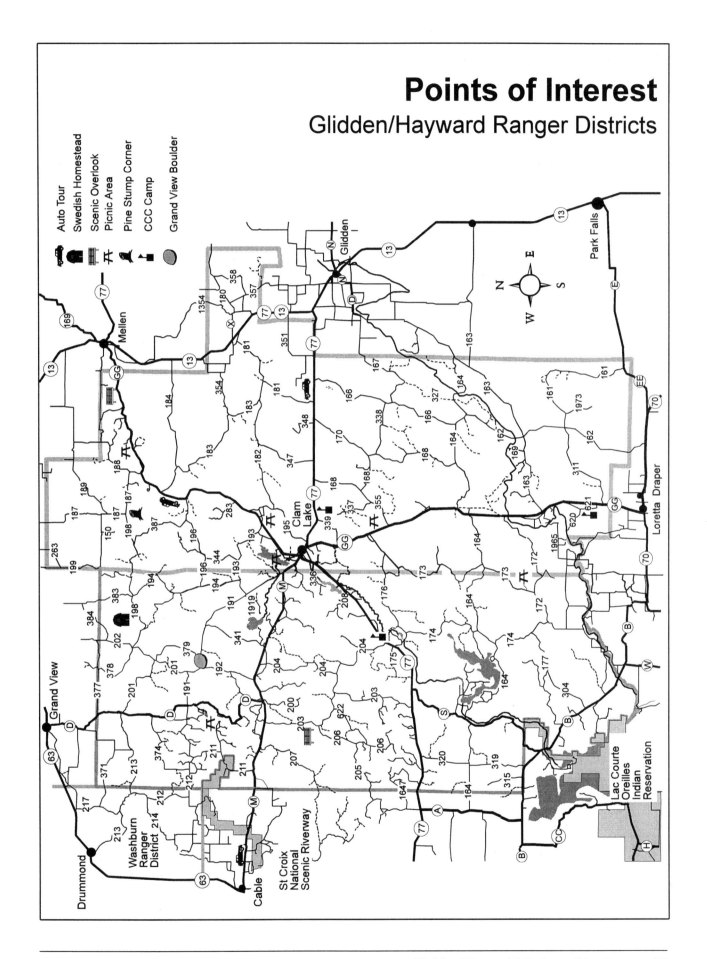

Points of Interest
Glidden/Hayward Ranger Districts

Auto Tour
Swedish Homestead
Scenic Overlook
Picnic Area
Pine Stump Corner
CCC Camp
Grand View Boulder

A Venerable Piece of U.S. History

1933. The Great Depression rages on and morale is at an all-time low. Setting about to bring immediate economic relief and sweeping reform to the battered U.S. economy, newly elected Democratic president Franklin D. Roosevelt promises a "New Deal" for the "forgotten man."

The administration's first objective was to bring relief to America's vast number of unemployed workers. The Civilian Conservation Corps (CCC) was established to provide America's youth with temporary jobs working in the national forests. On March 21, 1933, President Roosevelt addressed Congress saying, *"I propose to create a Civilian Conservation Corps to be used in simple work, not interfering with normal employment, and confining itself to forestry, the prevention of soil erosion, and similar projects."*

America Goes To Work

In truth the work was hard, and the pay was low. These young men, averaging in age from 18-25, planted trees, built bridges, dams and firetowers, improved wildlife habitat, fought forest fires, and improved access to woodlands across the United States. They also made lake and stream improvements, performed roadside cleanups, constructed trails and roads, installed telephone lines, and planted fish in lakes and streams.

It took some doing to teach these young men to work as a team. R.U. Harmon, Forest Supervisor out of Park Falls writes in 1933,

"We were exceedingly disappointed with the first efforts of the CCC Camps. To teach these men the way of the woods seemed like a stupendous task. After a month or so of worry, work and unsettled conditions, the men are gradually developing into well organized productive camps...They will be a smooth running, well organized machine at the end of the enrolled period."

Bittersweet Memories

Indeed, they did become a well organized machine. Along the way, the camaraderie often turned into friendships that lasted a lifetime. As Bill Emmerson, a one-time camp superintendent at the Jump River Camp, stood among the now tall trees at the site of his former camp, he remarked,

"It is entirely planted to red pine and you'd never know there had been all that structure and all that activity on that couple of acres. I stood there a long time and, in reverence, solemnly brought back those fine people, the crises, the sadness, the joys, the drudgery, the games, the fun—individual conversations and meals that had lodged somewhere in my memory, and came forth as I stood there. Individual enrollees—some brilliant, some faceless humans with a serial number. The brilliant ones were there in my memory, the faceless Joes were in my heart. If I ever make it to heaven, I know they'll be there. As I forced myself to turn and walk through the pines to my car, I wasn't sure whether the spot on my cheek was from the wind, or because I felt sorta like I was standing at the grave of a loved one. No one would ever understand that, except those who had been there."

A President's Legacy Lives On

This was to be the most powerful of President Roosevelt's Depression Era programs. By the time it ended in 1943, the CCC had employed close to three million men.

Much of what we take for granted today in the Forest can be traced back to the tireless efforts of these young men. Huge tracks of forested land, richly restored wildlife habitat, and a top-notch network of roads and trails providing access to the Forest, are all the result of efforts by the CCC, making the National Forests one of America's most treasured heirlooms.

♦ **Great Divide Scenic Byway**, 29 miles, was designated in 1989 for its outstanding scenic qualities. Old-growth hardwoods and majestic white pines frame this corridor. It extends the width of the two districts, covering 29 miles of Hwy 77. The scenic byway is so named because the water from the area runs either north to Lake Superior and on to the North Atlantic or south to the Mississippi and on to the Gulf of Mexico.

Besides the scenic beauty of the route, there are a number of stops along the way. From Glidden westward, these include the Clam Lake CCC Camp and the Dead Horse Slough Trailhead, one mile west of FR 335. The historic Clam Lake was a hub of activity during the logging era. Ghost Creek CCC Camp is just before FR 204. Balsam Creek Wetland Habitat Area is on FR 175. Other interpretive signs and stops are planned.

♦ **Penokee Highlands Route** takes you through the scenic Penokee Range, which offers both spectacular scenery and historic areas. From Mellen, travel southwest on Cty GG. You will pass the Penokee Overlook. This will give visitors a bird's-eye view of the surrounding Penokee Range. Next there will be Potter and Mineral Lake Campgrounds. Just before Clam Lake, you can stop at the Day Lake Day Use Area for a picnic or to enjoy watching the area wildlife.

At Clam Lake, turn east (left) on Hwy 77, which is a section of the Great Divide Scenic Byway. Just east of Clam Lake is the former Clam Lake CCC Camp. This historic camp has an interpretive walking trail where visitors can learn about camp life during the Great Depression era. Across the highway is the trailhead for Dead Horse Slough. Continue east to Hwy 13 just north of Glidden. Turn north (left) on Hwy 13 to travel back to Mellen. The Great Divide Wayside is located on Hwy 13, for visitors who wish to learn about the Great Divide watershed.

Civilian Conservation Corps Camps

There were a number of CCC camps established throughout the District. Many were started in 1933, with all camps being phased out in 1942. Camps did not always stay in one place; they were moved to other local sites or other parts of the state depending upon need. Close to three million young men were enrolled. Below is a listing of camps. The letter "F" represents a federal camp.

♦ **Camp Beaver F-11**, Clam Lake

♦ **Camp Cable F-43, Company V-1676**, Cable

♦ **Camp Chippewa River F-10**, Loretta

♦ **Camp Clam Lake F-15, Company 653**, is located just east of Clam Lake on Hwy 77. There are interpretive displays explaining the CCC days.

♦ **Camp Ghost Creek F-14, Company 652**, is located about seven miles southwest of Clam Lake on Hwy 77, just before FR 204, on the south side of the highway. There is an interpretive display that describes the camp's history.

♦ **Camp Loretta F-24, Company 648**, is located three miles north of Loretta on Cty GG, then west (left) on FR 621 for .4 miles to a trailhead.

♦ **Camp Mineral Lake F-12, Company 638**, Marengo

♦ **Camp Moose River F-13, Company 3606**, Glidden

♦ **Camp Morse F-23, Company 640**, Morse

◆ **Camp Sawyer F-31 Company 2617,** Winter

◆ **Camp Taylor Lake F-36, Company V-1676,** Grand View

Picnic Areas

◆ **Beautiful Pine Walk Picnic Area**
Location: About 2.5 miles south of Hwy 77 (Clam Lake) on Cty GG.
Description: This picnic area is part of an ongoing effort by the Wisconsin Federation of Business and Professional Women's Clubs. They have been involved with this 40-acre red-pine plantation since 1933. The area is named after the "Beautiful Pine Walk" interpretive trail through the pines.
Facilities: There are grills, vault toilets, picnic tables, and an interpretive trail.

◆ **Black Lake Picnic Area**
Location: Travel 26 miles east of Hayward on Cty B, then at the intersection with Cty W, turn north (left) on Fishtrap Road and travel for five miles. Continue straight north on FR 172 for 3.3 miles, then to FR 173 for .4 miles to the campground entrance road.
Description: This picnic area, located at the Black Lake Campground, is lightly used most of the season. Fishing on Black Lake and hiking the Black Lake Trail are the main attractions.
Facilities: There are two boat landings, marked swimming area, sandy beach, drinking water, picnic area, campground, and vault toilets. One of the toilets is accessible to the mobility impaired.

Day Lake beach and picnic area, west of Clam Lake.

◆ **Day Lake Day Use Area**
Location: From Clam Lake, travel .5 miles west on Cty M to FR 1294, then north .6 miles to the day use area.
Description: This is a "new" lake formed in 1968 by a dam on the Chippewa River. It offers exceptional views of bald eagles, loons, and other wildlife. There are many things to do at the picnic area and adjacent campground to the north.
Facilities: The picnic area includes a marked swimming beach, fishing pier, vault toilets, drinking water, access to an interpretive trail, Day Lake Dam, West Fork of the Chippewa River, and a quaint bridge to an island where you can fish or take a break on the bench and enjoy the view! There is an access ramp into the day use area shelter and down to the beach.

◆ **East Twin Lake Day Use Area**
Location: Travel west from Clam Lake on Cty M .2 miles, turn north (right) on Cty GG three miles. Turn south (right) on FR 190 veering to the east .6 miles to FR 250, which leads into the picnic area.

Day Lake Recreation Area

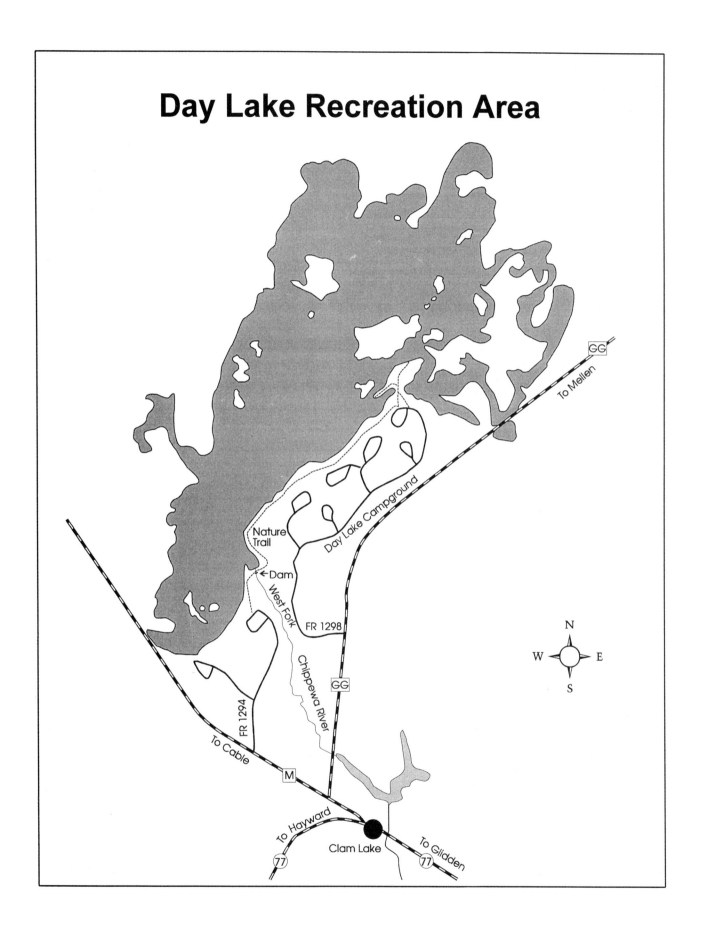

To Mellen

GG

Nature Trail

Day Lake Campground

←Dam

West Fork

FR 1298

Chippewa River

GG

FR 1294

N
W E
S

To Cable

M

To Hayward

To Glidden

Clam Lake

77   77

The Penokee Overlook west of Mellen provides one of the best views of the Penokee Range and the Great Divide.

Description: Visitors will be treated with a scenic view of this lake area from the picnic grounds. The lake offers good fishing for a variety of species.
Facilities: There are vault toilets, picnic tables, grills, drinking water, and a parking area.

◆ Namekagon Picnic Area
Location: Located 11 miles east from Cable on Cty M, then north (left) on Cty D 5.5 miles to FR 209. Turn west (left) on FR 209; travel .3 miles to the picnic area.
Description: The big attractions are the fishing on Lake Namekagon and the campground. Mountain bike and hiking trails are nearby. It is about four miles from the Porcupine Lake Wilderness and the North Country National Scenic Trail.

Facilities: There is an improved boat landing, picnic area, accessible fishing pier, marked swimming area, sandy beach, drinking water, and a semi-enclosed shelter with fireplace and pay phone. Two vault toilets are accessible to the mobility impaired. An access ramp takes you into the day use area, shelter, and down to the beach.

◆ Potter Lake Picnic Area
Location: From Mellen (Hwy 13), travel west on Cty GG 7.5 miles, turn north (right) on FR 185 and travel .4 miles to the picnic area.
Description: Picnic area is on the southeast shore of Potter Lake in a remote, undeveloped setting.
Facilities: There are picnic tables, vault toilets, grills, and a boat landing.

◆ Spillerberg Lake Picnic Area
Location: From Glidden (Hwy 13), travel north on Hwy 13 seven miles, then west (left) .5 miles on FR 355, then turn south (left) on FR 181 and travel two miles to a spur road to the picnic area.
Description: This picnic area is on the northwest shore of Spillerberg Lake in a setting of hardwoods and sentinel white pines.
Facilities: There are picnic tables, grill, vault toilets, and an unmarked swimming area.

Structures and Landmarks

◆ **Crystal Springs Overlook**, one of the nicest vistas that can be reached by car, is located 9.5 miles east of Cable on Cty M, then south (right) on FR 203 for 1.5 miles to the overlook. There is no parking area here, but the road is wide enough to pull off safely. The view overlooks a boggy area with small ponds scattered through it. It is a beautiful spot when the blue sky is reflected in the ponds or during the fall when the area is framed by the brilliant colors of birch and maple forests.

◆ **Grand View Boulder** is located eight miles west of Clam Lake on FR 191. This is a large erratic boulder that was wrenched from the bedrock of the Penokee Range about three miles to the north by the last continental glacier. It is over a billion years old, formed from limy mud of an ancient sea floor. The muds were solidified into dolomite, then changed into marble by the heat and pressure of mountain building. We know the rock's age and origin because it contains small fossils of algae and by using radiometric methods.

◆ **Penokee Overlook** is located four miles west of Mellen on Cty GG. This viewing platform built atop a tall bluff, offers one of the best views of the Penokee Range and the Great Divide. The geology of the area dates back billions of years. The range was once as tall as today's Rocky Mountains, but four major continental glaciers reduced to what you see today.

Facilities include an overlook, picnic tables, grills, and vault toilets.

◆ **Pine Stump Corner** is located eight miles west of Mellen on Cty GG, then north and west on FR 187 to the corner of FR 198 and FR 187. A large pine stood in the intersection of these three roads—that was a local gathering point for many years. All that remains today is its stump.

◆ **Swedish Homesteads** are located about six miles northwest of Clam Lake in the Marengo Valley. They can be reached by walking on the North Country National Scenic Trail, either east of FR 202 or west of FR 383. Immigrants began settling in the valley in the 1880s. The rolling hills were similar to their homeland. Remains of several of the homesteads and a school can still be seen. The Forest Service has an excellent brochure that leads you on a self-guided trip through the area. It takes about three hours to complete the 4.5-mile tour. The trail may be difficult in some areas due to steep terrain.

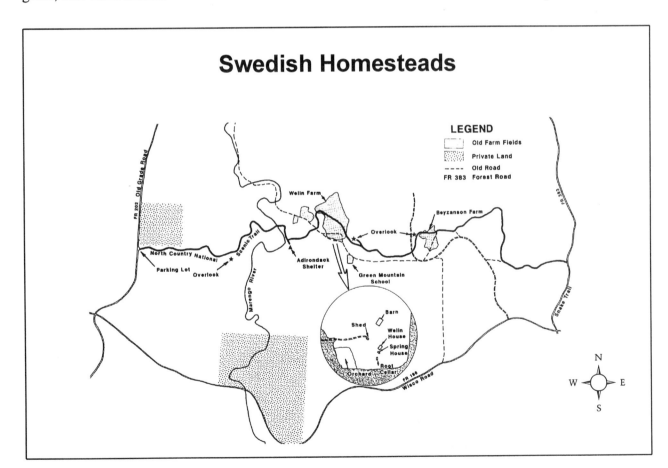

Swedish Homesteads

LEGEND
Old Farm Fields
Private Land
Old Road
FR 383 Forest Road

CAMPGROUNDS

Established Campgrounds

There are nine campgrounds in the Glidden/Hayward Ranger Districts. Campground hosts are present at some campgrounds during summer months to welcome you and answer questions.

◆ Beaver Lake Campground

Location: Travel eight miles west of Mellen on Cty GG, then three miles north (right) on FR 187. Continue on FR 198 two miles to the campground.

Number of Sites: Ten rustic sites that accommodate RVs up to 30 feet long. Half the sites are close to the lake.

Facilities: Each site has a fire grill, parking spur, picnic table, and tent pad. There are vault toilets and drinking water. The boat landing is .5 miles from the campground. There is also a spur trail to the North Country National Scenic Trail.

Description: The sites are in an open area of birch and scattered red pines with a nice view of the lake. Family-oriented camping in a pleasant setting.

Reservations and Fee: Sites are on a first-come, first-serve basis. Fee is $6. Open from late May to early September.

◆ Black Lake Campground

Location: Travel 26 miles east of Hayward on Cty B, then at the intersection with Cty W turn north (left) on Fishtrap Road and travel five miles. Continue straight north on FR 172 for 3.3 miles, then on to FR 173 for .4 miles to the campground.

Number of Sites: Twenty-nine moderate sites that accommodate RVs 35 to 45 feet long. Three sites on the north end are accessible to the mobility impaired. Three walk-in sites are available.

Facilities: Each developed site has a fire grill, parking spur, picnic table, and tent pad. There are two boat landings, marked swimming area, sandy beach, drinking water, picnic area, and vault toilets. One of the toilets is accessible to the mobility impaired.

Description: This campground is lightly used most of the season. Fishing on Black Lake and hiking the Black Lake Trail are the main attractions.

Reservations and Fee: Twelve sites can be reserved by calling 1-800-280-2267, TTY 1-800-879-4496. Other sites are on a first-come, first-serve basis. Fee is $6. Open from May 1 to November 30.

◆ Day Lake Campground

Location: Take Cty GG north from Clam Lake .5 miles to FR 1298, which leads to the campground.

Number of Sites: Sixty-six moderate sites and two walk-in sites. Moderate sites can accommodate RVs up to 45 feet long. There are six barrier-free sites with paved access to a fishing pier.

Facilities: Each developed site has a fire grill, parking spur, picnic table, and tent pad. The day use area and campground have fishing piers, an interpretive trail, vault toilets, marked swimming area, beaches, drinking water, and a watchable wildlife area.

Description: This is a family-orientated camping area with playground, swings, scenic views, and access to an excellent fishing lake.

Reservations and Fee: Sixteen sites can be reserved by calling 1-800-280-2267, TTY 1-800-879-4496. Other sites are on a first-come, first-serve basis. The barrier-free sites can be reserved by calling 1-715-264-2511. Fee is $7. Open from late May to early December.

Campgrounds
Glidden/Hayward Ranger Districts

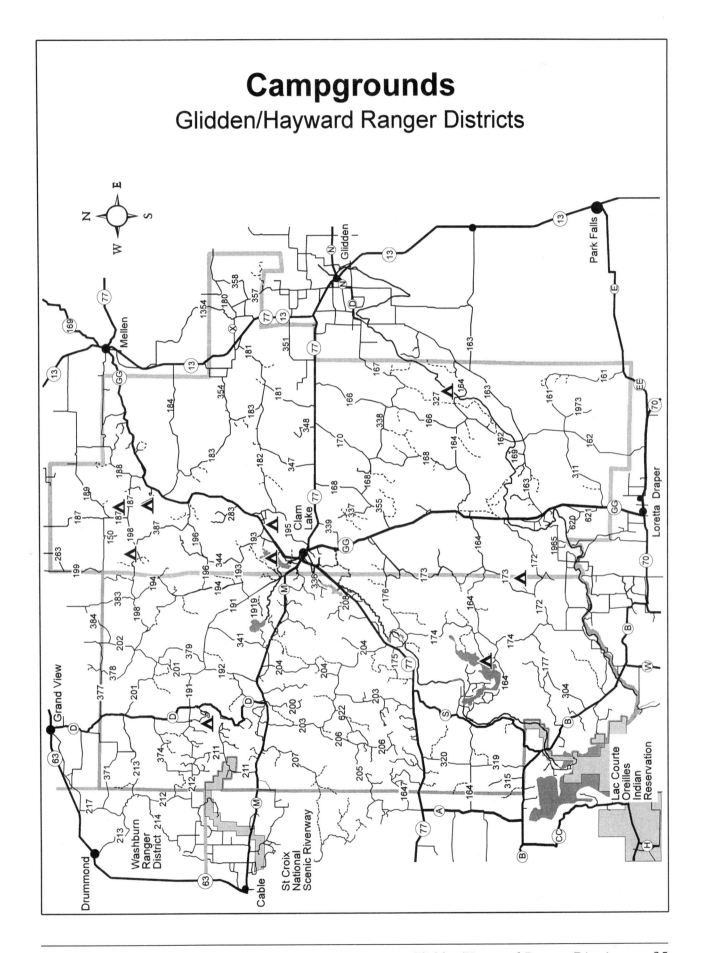

◆ East Twin Lake Campground

Location: From Clam Lake, travel four miles north on Cty GG, then east (right) on FR 190 for one mile.

Number of Sites: Twelve rustic sites, mainly for tent camping or RVs up to 30 feet long. Only one or two sites can handle larger RVs.

Facilities: Each site has a fire grill, parking spur, picnic table, and tent pad. There is also an accessible fishing pier, drinking water, and vault toilets.

Description: The campground is in an area of open aspen and birch. It has a high use, especially with families.

Reservations and Fee: Sites are on a first-come, first-serve basis. Fee is $7. Open from late May to early September.

◆ Lake Three Campground

Location: Located twelve miles west of Mellen on Cty GG, then north (right) on FR 187 four miles to the campground.

Number of Sites: Eight rustic sites for tent or small trailers up to 30 feet long.

Facilities: Each site has a fire grill, parking spur, picnic table, and tent pad. There are vault toilets, drinking water, and a boat landing. The North Country National Scenic Trail is adjacent to the campground.

Description: This is a quiet setting among young hardwoods. Several sites have a nice view of the lake. Especially pretty in fall.

Reservations and Fee: Sites are on a first-come, first-serve basis. Fee is $6. Open from late May to early December.

◆ Mineral Lake Campground

Location: The campground is located about twelve miles west of Mellen on Cty GG on the west (right) side of the road.

Number of Sites: Twelve rustic sites, located away from the lake, for tent camping and small trailers up to 30 feet.

Facilities: Each site has a fire grill, parking spur, picnic table, and tent pad. Facilities include vault toilets and drinking water. A picnic area and boat landing are located one mile north on FR 187.

Description: This campground is in a quiet hardwoods setting. Eagles feed on the lake regularly.

Reservations and Fee: Sites are on a first-come, first-serve basis. Fee is $6. Open from late May to early September.

◆ Moose Lake Campground

Location: Located about 25 miles east of Hayward on Hwy 77, then south (right) on FR 174 six miles to FR 1643. Turn west (right) on FR 1643 and travel 1.5 miles to the campground.

Number of Sites: Fifteen rustic sites, of which four are tent-only. Other sites can accommodate RVs 25 to 40 feet long. Sites are not accessible to the mobility impaired. There is one walk-in site.

Facilities: Each site has a fire grill, parking spur, picnic table, and tent pad. There is a boat landing, marked swimming area, sandy beach, drinking water, and vault toilets.

Description: Located in a setting of maple and birch trees, the campground is not heavily used except during major holidays and during the Moose Lake Festival.

Reservations and Fee: Six sites can be reserved by calling 1-800-280-2267, TTY 1-800-879-4496. Others site are on a first-come, first-serve basis. Fee is $6. Open from May 1 to November 30.

◆ Namekagon Lake Campground

Location: Located eleven miles east from Cable on Cty M, then north (left) on Cty D for 5.5 miles to FR 209. Turn west (left) on FR 209 and travel .3 miles to the campground.

Number of Sites: Thirty-four moderate sites suitable for RVs up to 45 feet. Four sites are on the water. Seven sites have a view of the lake. Sites are generally larger than at other campgrounds.

Facilities: Each site has a fire grill, parking spur,

picnic table, and tent pad. There is an improved boat landing, picnic area, accessible fishing pier, marked swimming area, sandy beach, drinking water, and a semi-enclosed shelter with fireplace and pay phone. Two of the vault toilets are accessible to the mobility impaired. There is a access ramp into the day use area shelter and down to the beach.

Description: The campground fills up several weekends each summer (30 to 60 percent full on most weekdays from Memorial Day to Labor Day). A big attraction is the fishing on Lake Namekagon. The campground is close to mountain bike trails and hiking trails, and is about four miles from the Porcupine Lake Wilderness and the North Country National Scenic Trail.

Reservations and Fee: Seventeen sites can be reserved by calling 1-800-280-2267, TTY 1-800-879-4496. Other sites are on a first-come, first-serve basis. Fees are $6 for most sites and $7 per night for sites 12-20. Open from May 1 to November 30.

◆ Stock Farm Bridge Campground

Location: Located eleven miles southwest of Glidden on Cty D, then west on FR 167, then south (left) on FR 166 five miles, and finally east on FR 164 about two miles.

Number of Sites: Seven rustic sites

Facilities: Each site has a fire grill, parking spur, picnic table, and tent pad. Vault toilets and drinking water are available. There is no garbage pickup—you need to pack it out.

Description: Located in a large pine plantation and on the East Fork of the Chippewa River, this campground is not used much in the summer time. It is popular with fishermen and hunters during the fall hunting season.

Reservations and Fee: No fee

Dispersed Camping

If you are looking for an ideal out-of-the-way site, all Forest lands are open for camping. Several of the more popular areas for dispersed camping include: **Brunsweiler Semi-Primitive Area, Rock Lake Semi-Primitive Area, and Porcupine Lake Wilderness**. In general, look around lakes for the best sites.

TRAILS

◆ Black Lake Trail

Length: 4 miles
Type: Hiking
Degree of Difficulty: Easy
Trailhead: From Hayward, travel 26 miles east on Cty B, then north (left) on Fishtrap Road 4.8 miles to the intersection of FR 172. Continue straight (north) 3.3 miles on FR 172, then north (left) .5 miles on FR 173, and then east (right) on the campground road .5 miles to the trailhead on the west side of the road.
Description: This is a four mile loop trail around Black Lake. It is a narrow path through the Forest, with Black Lake visible for about three-quarters of the trail. A trail brochure provides an interpretation of the logging history of the Black Lake area. Points of interest are marked along the trail.
Points of Interest: There are many interesting points concerning the logging era. Among those are the remains of an old CCC camp.
Type of Landscape: Flat, forested shoreline and wooded paths.

◆ Day Lake Campground Interpretive Trail

Length: .5 miles
Type: Hiking and interpretive
Degree of Difficulty: Easy
Trailhead: From Clam Lake, travel north .5 miles on Cty M to FR 1294. Turn north (right) and travel .6 miles to the Day Lake Picnic Area parking lot. Cross the Day Lake Dam and follow the shoreline to the beginning of the trail.
Description: This site was selected as a watchable wildlife area. Ecological processes and vegetation types are interpreted.
Points of Interest: Visitors will be treated with exceptional views of bald eagles, loons, great blue herons, and ospreys.
Type of Landscape: Lake views on flat to gently rolling terrain can be expected along this trail. The trail ends north of the Day Lake Campground on a peninsula overlooking the lake.

◆ Dead Horse Run Snowmobile and ATV Trail

Length: 53 miles
Type: Multiple-use (ATV, snowmobile, off-road motorcycle)
Degree of Difficulty: Moderate
Trailheads: On the southern end, start at Loretta (Hwy 70), travel north on Cty GG three miles, then west (left) .4 miles on FR 621 to the trailhead. This is a former CCC camp.

On the northern end, travel 2.5 miles on Hwy 77, east of Clam Lake to the Dead Horse Slough parking area on the north side of the highway.
Description: This trail system has one loop on the north end and connects to the Tuscobia State Trail System on the south end. From the Loretta parking lot, the trail extends to the northeast, crossing FR 164 twice before heading north near FR 166. The trail heads west, then north along FR 168, then crosses Hwy 77 at FR 347. It extends three miles farther north before looping back to the west and south to the second parking area. From this lot, the trail extends south near FR 333 and FR 337 before completing the loop at FR 168. Visitors will be rewarded with dramatic views of scenic wetlands like the Dead Horse Slough and the Chippewa River.
Points of Interest: The Loretta parking area is a former CCC camp operated during the 1930s. The Dead Horse Slough trailhead and parking area is on the Great Divide National Forest Scenic Byway (Hwy 77). On the south side of this parking area is the former Clam Lake CCC camp, which is

Trails
Glidden/Hayward Ranger Districts

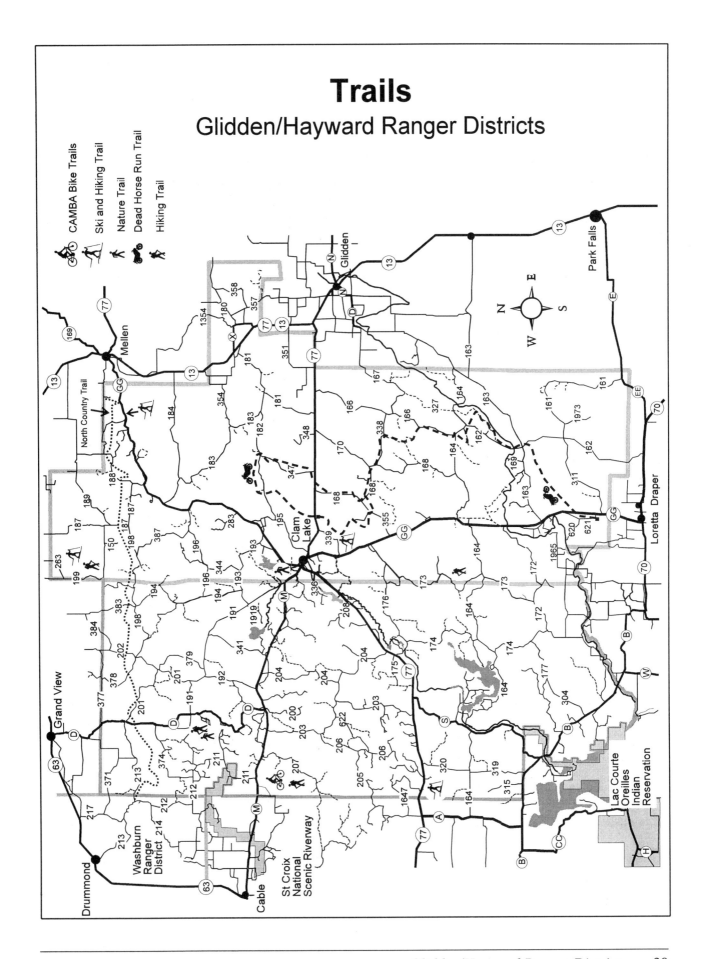

now interpreted. Visitors are given an insight into the life of the CCC camp residents.

Type of Landscape: Flat to gently rolling terrain accented with hardwoods, conifers, pines, and lowland swamps and bogs.

◆ Morgan Falls/St. Peter's Dome

Length: 1.5 miles
Type: Hiking
Degree of Difficulty: Difficult
Trailhead: From Mellen, travel west on Cty GG 10 miles, then north (right) 4.5 miles on FR 187, and west (left) .5 miles on FR 199 to the trailhead on the east side of road.
Description: From the parking lot, it's a .5-mile hike to Morgan Falls, then an additional one-mile hike to the top of St. Peter's Dome. The way is steep and can be stressful. Just before you reach the dome, there is an old granite quarry that can be explored. Visitors should allow two hours to make the round trip.
Points of Interest: Morgan Falls makes its downward 70-foot plunge into the creek below. Caution should be taken, as there are many rocky segments on steep terrain. Once atop St. Peter's Dome, visitors will be rewarded with a view of two states (Wisconsin and Minnesota) and Lake Superior that is breathtaking in the fall months, with a kaleidoscope of color from forests and farmlands.

Type of Landscape: Steep valleys, rolling hills, and forest cover.

◆ Mukwonago Ski Trail

Length: 5 miles
Type: Cross-country skiing
Degree of Difficulty: Easy to difficult
Trailhead: Travel eighteen miles east of Hayward on Hwy 77. The parking lot is on the south side of the highway, just past the Chequamegon National Forest entrance sign.
Description: This is a new trail designed for skating as well as classic cross-country skiing. Currently, there are three loops open on the trail system, a 2.5-km loop, a 4.5-km loop, and a 7-km loop with plans to add a 13 km loop to the trail system. The trail begins at Mukwonago Lake, a pretty bog lake next to Hwy 77, and winds through oak and white pine

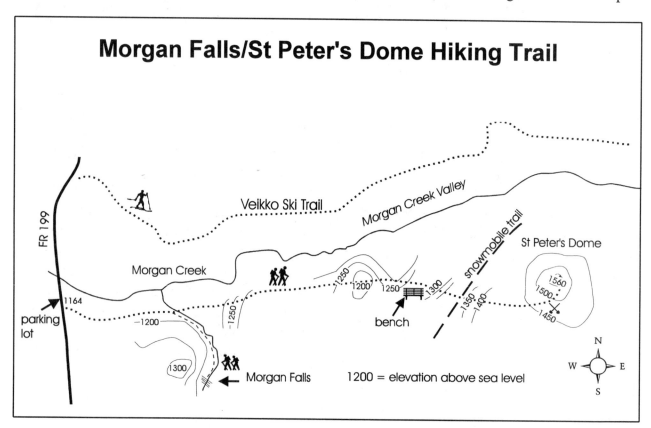

Morgan Falls/St Peter's Dome Hiking Trail

FR 199 · Veikko Ski Trail · Morgan Creek Valley · snowmobile trail · St Peter's Dome · 1560 · 1500 · 1450 · Morgan Creek · 1164 · 1250 · 1200 · 1250 · 1300 · 1350 · 1400 · parking lot · 1200 · 1300 · Morgan Falls · bench · 1200 = elevation above sea level · N W E S

forests in rolling to hilly terrain.

Points of Interest: Because of the oak forest, there are many deer in the area. This is an enjoyable route for mountain bikers.

Type of Landscape: Rolling hills of oak and white pine with several marshes and two small lakes.

◆ Namekagon Cluster, CAMBA Trail System

Length: 45 miles

Type: Mountain biking

Degree of Difficulty: Easy to difficult

Trailheads: The trail system has two trailheads— one at the Rock Lake Trail parking lot and one at the Namekagon Town Hall on Cty M. To reach the Namekagon Town Hall trailhead, drive ten miles east of Cable on Cty M, or fifteen miles west of Clam Lake on Cty M. The trailhead is on the south side behind the town hall. There is a parking area and a pay phone.

Description: The Chequamegon Area Mountain Bike Association (CAMBA) has marked, mapped, and described a series of loop trails in the Rock Lake area for off-road biking. These trails use part of the Rock Lake trail system. Each of the four loops is well marked with bright blue reassurance markers and directional signs. The Namekagon and Glacier loops, each ten miles in length, are of moderate difficulty. The Patsy Lake loop is 12.5 miles in length and is easy to moderate. The Rock Lake loop is 12.5 miles in length and is moderate to difficult. All loops have sections of single track and are fun riding. For people who cannot read maps, narratives on CAMBA maps give detailed descriptions.

Type of Landscape: Trail loops pass mainly through oak and maple forest, with some areas of pine plantation and cut-over aspen. The lakes and open swamps along the trail add interesting features.

Namekagon Trail

◆ Namekagon Nature Trail

Length: 1 mile

Type: Hiking and nature walk

Degree of Difficulty: Easy

Trailhead: From Cable, travel eleven miles east on Cty M, then north (left) 5.5 miles on Cty D to FR 209. Turn west (left) on FR 209 and proceed .3 miles to the parking lot on the north side of road.

Description: The Namekagon Nature Trail is a short loop of the Namekagon Hiking and Ski Trail. There are 26 stations along the trail as it passes through wildlife openings, hemlock and white cedar groves, and over boardwalks. It takes about 45 minutes to complete this self-guided tour.

Points of Interest: The trail traverses many types of wildlife habitat. It is easy to see the biodiversity of animals and vegetation in the area.

Type of Landscape: Relatively flat with a view of Taylor Creek.

◆ Namekagon Trail

Length: 3 miles

Type: Hiking and cross-country skiing

Degree of Difficulty: Easy

Trailhead: From Cable, travel eleven miles east on Cty M, then north (left) on Cty D for 5.5 miles to FR 209. Turn west (left) on FR 209 and proceed .3 miles to the parking lot on the north side of the road (parking in the winter is across from the summer lot).

Description: The Namekagon Trail has three interconnecting loops. The east loop serves as a one-mile interpretive and hiking trail in the summer, with toilets and water available at Namekagon Campground on the south side of FR 209. In the winter, all three miles of trail are groomed.

Points of Interest: The trail traverses maple stands, wildlife openings, and an island of 150-year-old hemlock.

Type of Landscape: Relatively flat with mature hardwood and conifer forest and wildlife openings. Nesting boxes for bluebirds and tree swallows have been added.

◆ North Country National Scenic Trail

Length: 31.6 miles

Type: Hiking, cross-country skiing, and limited mountain biking

Degree of Difficulty: Moderate to difficult

Trailheads: There are a number of trailheads along this route. Any one of the road crossings can provide access.

From Cable, travel east eleven miles on Cty M, then north (left) on Cty D. The trail will cross Cty D about 1.5 miles north of FR 374. You can continue north and turn west (left) on FR 213 and proceed to the Two Lakes Campground, where there is a second trailhead.

From Mellen (Hwy 13), travel west on Cty GG for four miles to the Penokee Overlook parking area. The Penokee Trail System connects with the North Country National Scenic Trail. Or you can continue west on Cty GG two miles to FR 604, then turn north (right) and travel .7 miles to the parking area on the west (left) side of the road. There is also a trailhead at Lake Three Campground, which is ten miles west of Mellen on Cty GG, then turn north (right) on FR 187 three miles, then north (right) on FR 187 for .6 miles to the parking area on the west (left) side of road.

Description: From the Two Lakes Campground on Lake Owen, the trail enters the Porcupine Lake Wilderness. The trail is not well marked in the wilderness, so it is important to have a current map and compass. It extends eastward for 6.6 miles around lakes and crosses several wet areas. Depending on beaver activity and related flooding, the eastern portion of the trail, in the wilderness area, may vary slightly. This trail passes north of East Davis Lake, where it crosses Cty D and leaves the wilderness area.

The trail continues eastward for six miles, paralleling FR 201 for several miles, passing a fire tower before crossing FR 378 to reach FR 202. This is the beginning of the Marengo Semi-Primitive Area. The trail continues eastward 3.4 miles through a very scenic stretch along the trail to FR 383. There are overviews, adirondack shelters, deep valleys, and the historic Swedish Settlement along the Marengo River.

Passing along the Penokee Range, you will travel 5.1 miles, from FR 383 to Beaver Lake Campground. As you reach Beaver Lake, use caution when crossing the bridge on the north boundary of the lake. Beaver activity causes flooding in this area. Rubber boots and a hiking staff may be necessary. From here to FR 187 and Lake Three Campground is 4.7 miles. An adirondack shelter is located west of the Lake Three trailhead.

From Lake Three, the trail meanders eastward three miles, crossing Brunsweiler River to reach FR 188. Then the trail dips south to John Frank Lake, then back north, crossing FR 188 twice to cover three more miles. From FR 188, it is 3.3 miles to FR 604, crossing a small creek north of English Lake. The last stretch is 2.2 miles from FR 604 to FR 390. About halfway, a side spur leads up to the Penokee Overlook.

North Country National Scenic Trail

60.5 = Total miles of North
Country National Scenic Trail
from the western edge of
the Washburn Ranger District.

⊥ = Trail Shelter

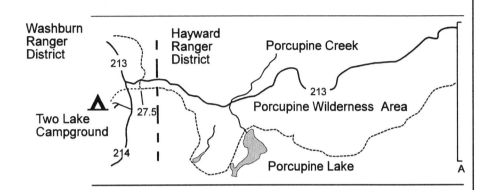

Washburn
Ranger
District

Hayward
Ranger
District

Porcupine Creek

213

213

Porcupine Wilderness Area

27.5

Two Lake
Campground

214

Porcupine Lake

A

A

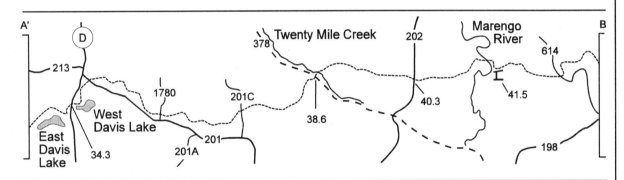

A'

D

Twenty Mile Creek

202

Marengo
River

B

378

614

213

1780

201C

40.3

41.5

West
Davis Lake

38.6

East
Davis
Lake

34.3

201A

201

198

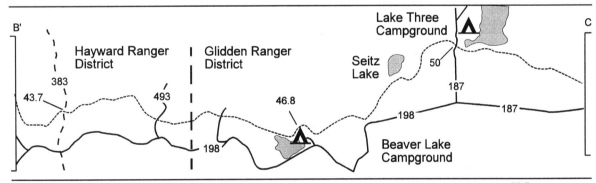

B'

Lake Three
Campground

C

Hayward Ranger
District

Glidden Ranger
District

Seitz
Lake

50

383

43.7

493

46.8

187

187

198

187

198

Beaver Lake
Campground

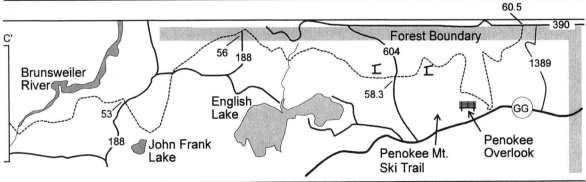

60.5

390

C'

Forest Boundary

56 188

604

1389

Brunsweiler
River

58.3

53

GG

English
Lake

Penokee
Overlook

188

John Frank
Lake

Penokee Mt.
Ski Trail

Points of Interest: This segment of the North Country National Scenic Trail is punctuated by the Penokee Range, with elevations up to 1,700 feet. Campgrounds at Three Lake and Beaver Lake provide resting points and seasonal drinking water. The Penokee Overlook has a dramatic view from platforms overlooking the Penokee Range.

Type of Landscape: Rolling hills with steep valleys and wetlands, with a forest cover of maple, yellow birch, aspen, red and white pines, hemlock, and balsam.

◆ Penokee Ski and Hiking Trail

Length: 7.6 miles

Type: Hiking and cross-country skiing

Degree of Difficulty: Moderate

Trailhead: From Mellen (Hwy 13), travel west on Cty GG four miles to the Penokee Overlook parking area on the north (right) side of the highway.

Description: Hikers and skiers have three interconnected loops from two to six miles in length from which to choose. This trail connects with the North Country National Scenic Trail system. There is an adirondack shelter with fire grills on the west-ern loop open for visitors to use.

Points of Interest: Visitors will enjoy the views from the Penokee Overlook platforms.

Type of Landscape: Rolling glacial terrain with steep valleys.

◆ Pole Lake Hiking Trail

Length: .3 miles

Type: Hiking

Degree of Difficulty: Moderate

Trailhead: From Clam Lake, travel west on Hwy 77 one mile, then east (left) on FR 1266 and travel .4 miles, then turn south, continuing on FR 1266 for .5 miles to the trailhead on the east (left) side of road.

Description: This trail accesses Pole Lake.

Points of Interest: Visitors will be treated with some of the best rainbow trout fishing in the area.

Type of Landscape: Hardwood forests and rolling hills.

◆ Rock Lake National Recreation Trail

Length: 12.5 miles (21 km) long in six interconnecting loops (2, 4, 7.1, 11.5, and 16 km long), with a short loop around Rock Lake that adds 1.8

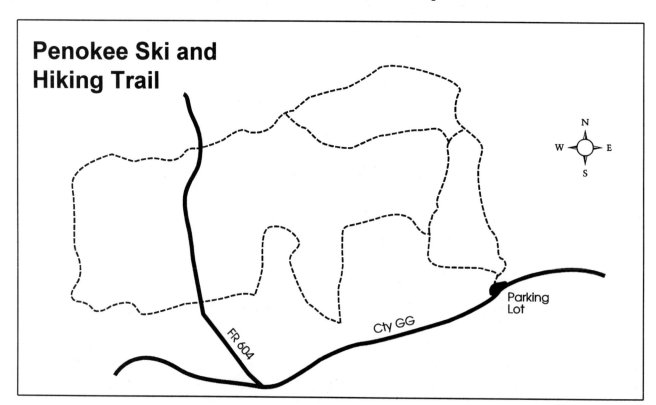

Penokee Ski and Hiking Trail

Rock Lake National Recreation Trail

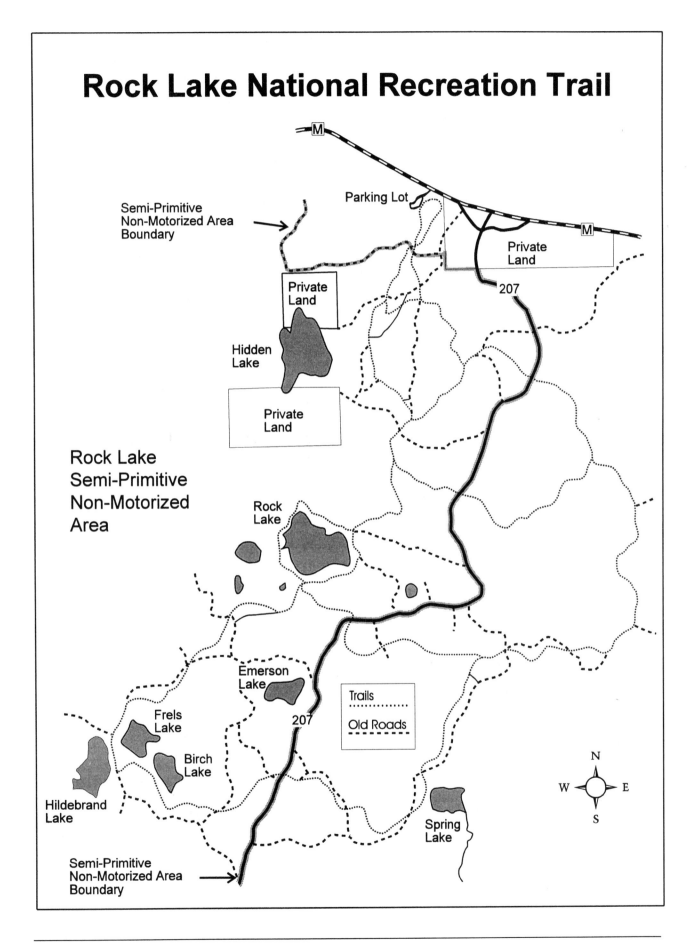

km to either the 11.5 or 16 km loop.

Type: Cross-country skiing, hiking, and mountain biking

Degree of Difficulty: Moderate to difficult

Trailhead: From Cable, travel east on Cty M for seven miles to the trailhead and a large parking lot on the south side of Cty M. Glacier Pines, a ski and bike shop next to the trailhead, has water and a pay phone.

Description: This trail is groomed in the winter for classic cross-country skiing. In the spring, summer, and fall, it offers great mountain biking opportunities—this is part of the CAMBA trail system. It is best ridden by intermediate to advanced riders.

Points of Interest: Short hikes off FR 207 offer quick access to lakes along the trail. Rock Lake and Hildebrandt Lake are well worth hiking into during the fall color season, and are great places to have a picnic. We recommend either the north shore of Rock Lake or Hildebrand Lake.

Type of Landscape: Terrain is rolling hills with several scenic areas. The most notable are Rock Lake and the Frels-Hildebrand-Birch Lake area.

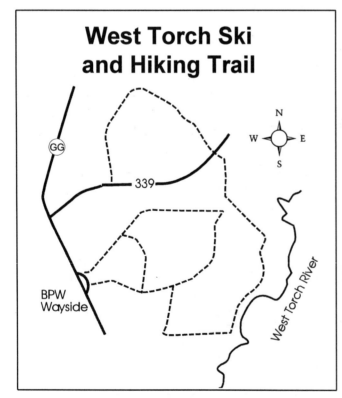

West Torch Ski and Hiking Trail

◆ Veikko Ski Trail

Length: 3.3 miles

Type: Hiking and cross-country skiing

Degree of Difficulty: Difficult, a more experienced level of hiking and skiing is suggested. This trail is not tracked, but it is dragged. Skiers need to track as they go. This is also a two-way trail, so skiers have to backtrack to the parking area.

Trailhead: From Mellen (Hwy 13), travel ten miles west on Cty GG, then 5.5 miles north (right) on FR 187 to the trailhead on the west (left) side of the road.

Description: This is a lineal trail from FR 187 to FR 199 that offers dramatic views of valleys and horizons in the Penokee Range. The Morgan Creek sheer cliffs provide an eery but fantastic view of St. Peter's Dome. Caution needs to be taken, as there are many rocky segments on steep terrain. When viewing scenery from the edge of cliffs, be aware of where the cliff drops off to the valley below.

Points of Interest: Visitors will be treated with great views of St. Peter's Dome, Morgan Creek, and sheer cliffs with glacial rock outcroppings.

Type of Landscape: Rolling hills, steep-sided valleys, and forest cover with magnificent panoramic views of hardwood forests, especially in the fall.

◆ West Torch Ski and Hiking Trail

Length: 6.5 miles

Type: Hiking and cross-country skiing

Degree of Difficulty: Easy to moderate

Trailhead: From Clam Lake (Hwy 77), travel south on Cty GG three miles to the trailhead on the east (left) side of the highway.

Description: There are four interconnecting loops ranging in length from 1.2 to 5.6 miles. The area is a red-pine plantation planted in 1933.

Points of Interest: Large red and white pine plantations and small wetlands offer a scenic diversity to this upland trail system. A sign dedicated to the Wisconsin Federation of Business and Professional Women's Clubs is located near the trailhead. A short interpretive trail loop winds

through the forest for .3 miles. This trail focuses on vegetation identification and ecological processes.
Type of Landscape: Flat to gently rolling hills with forests of pine and aspen.

Snowmobile Trails

The Hayward and Glidden Ranger Districts have a number of developed snowmobile trails. The Forest Service provides the land for the trails, but the maintenance and grooming are done by area clubs. Routes may change from year to year. It is best to get a current trail map from area chambers of commerce or snowmobile clubs.

In the Hayward Ranger District, there are 114 miles of groomed snowmobile trails which are part of a greater snowmobile trail network that links area villages and towns. Many trails are concentrated around Namekagon Lake. One important trail is listed below.

◆ **State Trail 5** extends from the Cable/Hayward area southeast, passing between Lost Land Lake and the Chippewa Flowage before connecting with the Tuscobia State Trail and on to Park Falls.

In the Glidden Ranger District there are several trails that follow the Dead Horse Run Trail System, which connects the Tuscobia State Trail with the Great Divide Trail.

◆ County Line Snowmobile Trail
Length: 14.5 miles
Type: Snowmobiling
Degree of Difficulty: Moderate
Trailhead: This trail connects Clam Lake with Sanborn. It does not have any specific trailhead and parking area but does offer the long-distance snowmobiler an opportunity to connect to a variety of trails.

Description: This trail transects the Penokee Range and offers snowmobilers an invigorating trail ride. Riders will cross Morgan Creek over a quaint wooden bridge as they travel north of the range. Beaver dam crossings also offer a unique experience and a close view of beaver activity.
Points of Interest: Creek and beaver crossings are interesting sights along the trail.
Type of Landscape: Gently rolling glacial terrain and dramatic inclines in the Penokee Range area.

◆ Great Divide Snowmobile Trail
Length: 22 miles
Type: Snowmobiling
Degree of Difficulty: Moderate to difficult
Trailhead: This trail connects with State Trail 13 by Cayuga and State Trail 9 near Clam Lake. It does not have any specific trailhead and parking area but does offer the long-distance snowmobiler an opportunity to connect to a variety of trails.
Description: Narrow, winding trails are provided for the intermediate to advanced snowmobiler. The trail connects Cayuga and Clam Lake communities with gently rolling terrain, perfect for snowmobilers who want to test their skills on the winding trail. **Extra time should be allowed to travel this trail.**
Points of Interest: Snowmobilers will be treated to a panoramic view of scenic wetlands and tall forests of pine, aspen, and hardwoods. Visitors may catch glimpses of white-tailed deer and a beaver pond with a lodge and dam.
Type of Landscape: Gently rolling terrain with wet lowland areas.

SURROUNDING AREA FACILITIES

Private Campgrounds

CABLE

◆ **Holz's Island View Campground:** located east of Cable on Cty Hwy D; on Lake Namekagon; Rt 2, Box 460, Cable, WI 54821; (715) 794-2461.

HAYWARD

◆ **Black Bear Lodge Resort & Campground:** 25 campsites; on the Chippewa Flowage; Rt 5, Box 5393, Hayward, WI 54843; (715) 945-2676.

◆ **Boulder Lodge Campground & Resort:** located 22 miles east of Hayward on Hwy 77 East, on Ghost Lake in the Chequamegon National Forest; Rt 7, Hayward, WI 54843; (715) 462-3002.

◆ **East Fork Resort & Campground:** Rt 1, Box 292, Winter, WI; (715) 266-5723.

◆ **Lake Chippewa Campground:** 100 campsites; on the Chippewa Flowage; Rt 9, Box 9345, Hayward, WI 54843; (715) 462-3672.

◆ **Musky Tale Resort:** on the West Fork of the Chippewa Flowage; Rt 4, Box 4259, Hayward, WI 54843; (715) 462-3838.

◆ **Reel Livin' Resort:** on Lost Land Lake; Rt 7, Box 7395, Hayward, WI 54843; (715) 462-3822.

MELLEN

◆ **Riverside Campground:** located just past Copper Falls State Park on Hwy 169; Rt 1, Box 35, Mellen, WI 54546; (715) 682-3379.

State Campgrounds

◆ **Copper Falls State Park**, 2,252 acres, is located just north of Mellen on Hwy 13, then about two miles east on Hwy 169, then north on a town road. Facilities include campsites, picnic area, shelters, swimming, and hiking. A system of trails takes you to overviews of the various falls.

◆ **Flambeau State Forest**, 88,000 acres, is located between Park Falls and Winter on Hwy 70. Cty M and W pass through the forest. The main feature is the sixty miles of river. The North and South Branches of the Flambeau River combine within the forest, providing a great recreational resource. Other recreational opportunities include two hiking and ski trail systems; campgrounds on Connor Lake and Lake of the Pines; canoe camping along the river; a picnic area on Connor Lake; and many scenic areas.

Attractions

◆ **Chippewa Queen:** located on the Chippewa Flowage near Hayward; 1.5 hour cruises daily in summer through Aug 31; dinner, cocktail, and fall color cruises; (715) 462-3874.

◆ **Scheer's Lumberjack Shows:** located one mile south of Hayward on Hwy B at the Lumberjack Bowl Pancake House; world class lumberjacks compete in a variety of events; refreshments, dinner shows; Hayward, WI.

Bike Rentals

◆ **Bay City Cycles:** mountain bike rentals; 412 2nd St. West, Ashland, WI 54806; (715) 682-2091.
◆ **Glacier Pines:** located seven miles east of Cable on Cty M; (715) 794-2055.
◆ **New Moon Ski and Bike:** located in Hayward (715) 634-8685 and Telemark (715) 798-3811.
◆ **Seely Hills Ski and Bike:** located on Hwy 63 in Seely; (715) 634-3539.

Boat Rentals

◆ **Big Bear Enterprises:** located in the Flambeau River State Forest, HCR Box 50, Winter, WI 54896; (715) 332-5261.
◆ **Chippewa Flowage Boat Rentals:** P.O. Box 4288, Hayward, WI 54843; (715) 462-3874.

Horseback Riding

◆ **Appa Lolly Riding Stables**, Hayward & Telemark Lodge in Cable; (715) 634-5059.
◆ **Mrotek's Riding Stable**, Hayward; (715) 462-3674.

Museums

◆ **Cable Natural History Museum:** located on Cty M in Cable; exhibits focus on the natural history of Northern Wisconsin with animal mounts on display. Interpretive program and activities are provided; P.O. Box 416, Cable, WI 54821; (715) 798-3890.
◆ **Clam Lake Wood Carvers Museum:** located on Hwy 77 in Clam Lake.
◆ **Fishing Hall of Fame:** located three blocks south on Hwy 27 in Hayward; museum in the shape of a 500-ton musky; antique outboard motors, fish-ing equipment, 400 fish mounts of freshwater fish, refreshments, gift shop; Box 33, Hall of Fame Drive, Hayward, WI 54843; (715) 634-4440.
◆ **Historyland:** located one mile east of Hayward on Cty Trunk B; Chippewa village and logging camp, cook shanty restaurant, guided tours, boat trips; Hayward, WI 54843; (715) 634-2579 or (800) 255-5937.

Emergency Numbers

◆ **Sheriff**
Ashland County (715) 682-7023
Bayfield County (715) 373-5607
Sawyer County (715) 634-4858

◆ **Hospitals**
Ashland Memorial Center, 1615 Maple Lane, Ashland, WI 54806; (715) 682-4563
Hayward Area Memorial Hospital, Hwy 27/77, Hayward, WI; (715) 634-8911
Flambeau Medical Center, 98 Sherry Avenue, Park Falls, WI; (715) 762-2484

Other Information Contacts

◆ **County**
Ashland County Forestry Department, P.O. Box 165, Glidden, WI 54527; (715) 264-3000
Bayfield County Forestry Department, Courthouse, P.O. Box 445, Washburn, WI 54891; (715) 373-2191
Sawyer County Forestry Department, Courthouse, P.O. Box 351, Hayward, WI 54843; (715) 634-4839

◆ **State**
WI DNR Brule Area Headquarters, Hwy 2, P.O. Box 125, Brule, WI 54820; (715) 372-4866
WI DNR Flambeau State Forest, HCR Box 51, Winter, WI 54896; (715) 332-5271

WI DNR Mellen Ranger Station, Mellen, WI 54546; (715) 274-5123

WI DNR Hayward Ranger Station, Hwy 27S, Rt 2, P.O. Box 2003, Hayward, WI 54843; (715) 634-2688

◆ Federal: National Forest Service

Glidden Ranger District, Hwy 13 North, P.O. Box 126, Glidden, WI 54527; (715) 264-2511, Fax: (715) 264-3307, TTY: (715) 264-2511

Hayward Ranger District, 604 Nyman Ave., Rt. 10, P.O. Box 508, Hayward, WI 54843; (715) 634-4821, TTY (715) 634-4821, Fax: (715) 634-3769

◆ Federal: National Park Service

St. Croix National Riverway, P.O. Box 100, Trego, WI 54888; (715) 635-8346

◆ Chambers of Commerce

Ashland Area Chamber of Commerce, 340 W. 4th St., Ashland, WI 54806-0746; (715) 682-2500, (800) 284-9484

Bayfield County Tourism and Recreation, P.O. Box 832, Washburn, WI 54891; (715) 373-6125, (800) 777-7558

Cable Area Chamber of Commerce, P.O. Box 217, Cable, WI 54821-0217; (715) 798-3833, 800-533-7454

Mellen Area Chamber of Commerce, P.O. Box 793 Mellen, WI 54546; (715) 274-2330

Hayward Chamber of Commerce 125 W. 1st St., Hwy 27/63, P.O. Box 726, Hayward, WI 54843-0726; (715) 634-8662, (800) 826-3474

Sawyer County Snowmobile Recreation Association, P.O. Box 351 Hayward, WI 54843; (715) 634-4893, (800) 826-3474

CHAPTER 5

MEDFORD

Ranger District

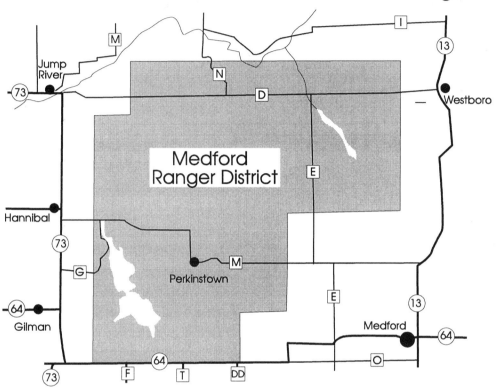

The **Medford Ranger District** covers more than 167,680 acres of land and water, of which 123,864 acres are federally-owned. This is an area of rolling hills, wetlands, kettle lakes, and river bottoms formed by receding glaciers some 10,000 years ago. Today, it is heavily forested with northern hardwoods and scattered lowlands of cedar, larch, black spruce, and hemlock.

Notable points of interest are Bear Creek and Ice Age Semi-Primitive Non-Motorized Areas, Chequamegon Waters Flowage, Mondeaux Flowage, Perkinstown Motorized Trail, and Ice Age National Scenic Trail.

Area communities include Medford and Westboro on Hwy 13 east of the District; Gilman, Hannibal, and Jump River on Hwy 73 west of the District; and Perkinstown in the south-central part of the District.

FOR MORE INFORMATION ABOUT THIS AREA, CONTACT:
Medford Ranger District
850 N. 8th, Hwy 13
Medford, WI 54451
(715) 748-4875
TTY (715) 748-4875

THE FOREST

The **Medford Ranger District**, which is part of the Northern Highlands of Wisconsin, began billions of years ago when the Earth's bedrock rose to form a dome. This is also the southern extent of what is called the Precambrian Canadian Shield. With land elevations more than 1,400 feet above sea level, this is one of the highest areas in the state. The highest point in the state, Timm's Hill, is located only eight miles to the northeast. Fifty to two-hundred feet of glacial till, brought to the area by the glacier, rest on top of the ancient bedrock. The last advance of the continental glacier stopped about halfway through the District, forming an irregular landscape of rugged hills and ridges of the terminal moraine. Farther to the north are the gently rolling hills of the ground moraine.

Many lakes and wetlands in the southern half of the District were formed when ice, combined with soil and rock, was left in place by the receding glacier. As these great chunks of ice melted, they left depressions surrounded by sand and gravel. Shallow areas filled with water to form wetlands, while deeper ones formed lakes.

The Medford Ranger District is just north of the vegetation "tension" zone, where the warmer, southern hardwoods zone gives way to the cooler, northern conifers zone. This District is also just north of the transition from the Central Lowlands to the Northern Highlands. A bulge formed in the hard igneous bedrock billions of years ago created a dome. The bedrock slops southward and downward. South of the terminal moraine you will find an area of old glaciated material. This gives way to the Central Lowlands, an area of sand and ancient sea bottom.

The forest in this District is primarily hardwoods, with more than 23,000 acres in aspen.

There are also scatterings of pine, spruce and other conifers. The red-pine plantations seen throughout the District were planted by the Civilian Conservation Corps (CCC) workers in the 1930s. This wide mix of forest vegetation makes it ideal for nature and wildlife observation.

Nature/Natural Areas

◆ **Kidrick Swamp** is not an identified Research Natural Area. However, it is a unique wetland environment. The swamp covers more than four square miles in the northwest corner of the District. It extends from Bear Creek Semi-Primitive Non-Motorized Area northeast to Upper Steve Creek Wetland Habitat Area. It can be reached by FR 114, which runs along the southeast edge, or FR 113 on the western edge. This area is shallow bedrock and rubble covered by sphagnum moss and other wetland plants. Trees include black spruce and tag alder with hardwood islands. Birdlife is abundant, including several species of special interest.

◆ **Twin Lake Bog Research Natural Area** is located just north of South Twin Lake. From the intersection of Cty D and Cty E, travel south four miles on Cty E, then east (left) on FR 102, then south (right) .25 miles on FR 566 to FR 1504 at North Twin Lake Campground. This area is an acid bog with wooded fringe. Plants such as ladyslipper and pitcher plant are present. The only access to the area is cross-country on foot. There are no trails or signs.

Special Forest Management Areas
Medford Ranger District

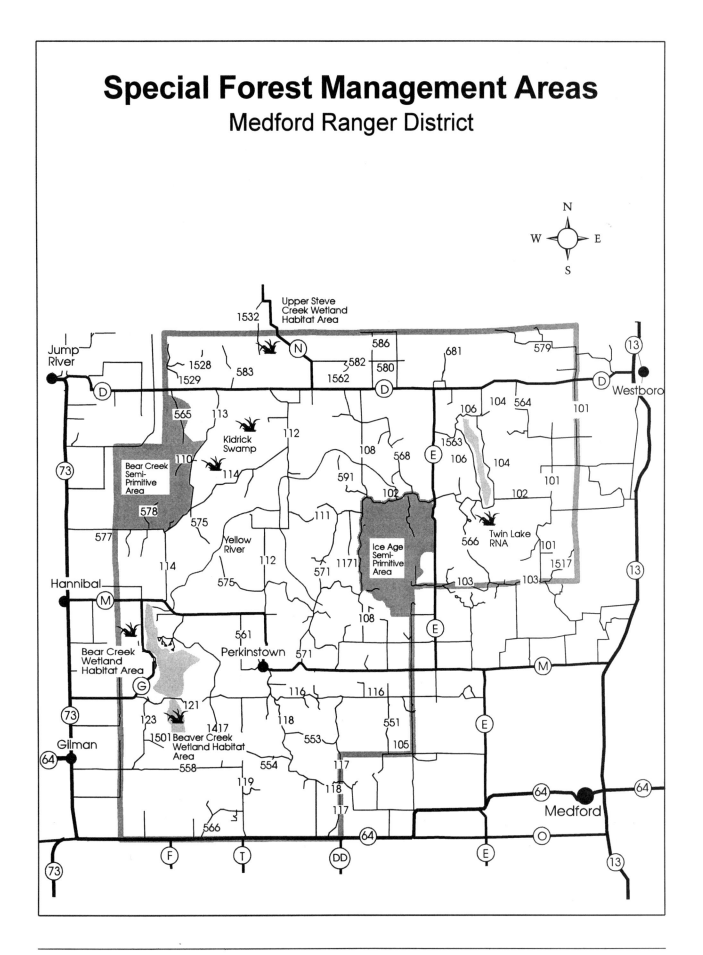

Semi-Primitive Non-Motorized Areas

◆ **Bear Creek Semi-Primitive Non-Motorized Area**, 5,420 acres, is located on the far west side of the District. From Hannibal, take Hwy 73 north 1.5 miles, then east (right) on Konsella Road (FR 577) two miles, which will bring you to the southwest corner of the property. The Bear Creek Area is bordered by FR 577 on the south, FR 114 and FR 113 on the east, a branch of Levitt Creek on the north, and the District boundary on the west.

This area, named for the creek passing it, is flat with low ridges. During spring and rainy times of the year, it is hard to walk here without getting wet feet. Mosquitoes are in abundance. The lowland ridges that rise above the surrounding wetlands have a mix of mature hardwood trees, including red oak, butternut, hickory, and sugar maple.

Several gated roads provide foot access into the area. These include FR 1521 on the west, FR 578 on the south, and FR 110 on the east. FR 565 provides foot access to a number of old logging trails on the north. The property, because of its wet lowland nature, is the least known and used semi-primitive area in the District. It also provides a more challenging primitive experience.

◆ **Ice Age Semi-Primitive Non-Motorized Area**, 5,520 acres, is located in the central part of the District. From Medford, travel north on Hwy 13 about four miles, then west on Cty M seven miles. At Cty E, turn north (right) and continue on Cty E to FR 102. This places you at the northeast corner of the area. The North Fork of the Yellow River and Cty E make up the eastern boundary, with FR 102 on the north and FR 108 on the west. The southern boundary is formed by FR 1508 and a northwest flowing creek from Kleutch Lake.

Located on the terminal moraine, the terrain is a mix of rolling hills and gravelly ridges with kettle and pothole lakes. Forest cover includes aspens in the north with paper birch on the ridges, and tamarack and spruce in the lowlands. Several gated trails provide access into the area.

An eight-mile section of the Ice Age Trail traverses the northern third of the area. A seven-mile loop was added to the central portion of the area, which is accessed off the Ice Age Trail. A trail for the mobility impaired that can accommodate wheelchairs, is located west of Cty E on FR 102.

This area has been actively managed, it does not offer as challenging a primitive experience as the Bear Creek Semi-Primitive Area.

Wetland Habitat Areas

◆ **Bear Creek Wetland Habitat Area** is located just west of Chequamegon Waters Flowage. From Gilman, travel two miles north on Hwy 73, then east (right) on Cty G about 5.5 miles. The property will be to the west after you pass FR 1502. It is part of the Chequamegon Waters Flowage and the outlet of Bear Creek. The area can be entered by small boats by passing under the bridge on Cty G. Its open water, wild rice, forest, and wetland fringe offer habitat for many species of birds, reptiles, and mammals. Eagles, ospreys, and cormorants frequent the area.

◆ **Beaver Creek Wetland Habitat Area** is located two miles north of Gilman on Hwy 73, then east (right) on Cty G 2.5 miles. Continue east on FR 121 to Chequamegon Waters Flowage. This waterfowl and wetland area is the southern portion of the flowage. Its shallow, open water with wooded marsh fringes, nesting boxes, and upland hardwoods, is a haven for waterfowl, eagles, osprey, cormorants, other birds, and aquatic mammals. Small boats can enter the area by passing under the FR 121 bridge. The water is very shallow, most of it under five feet in depth.

◆ **Upper Steve Creek Waterfowl Management Area**, 1.75 acres, is located on the northern border of the District. Take Cty D, either east of Hwy 73 or west of Hwy 13, to Cty N. Travel north on Cty N about two miles into Price County, then west (left) and south on Steve Creek Road near Steve Creek Flowage. You have gone too far north if you cross the Jump River. At Steve Creek Flowage, you will need to travel south on FR 1532 to the impoundment dam. The road may not be accessible during wet weather.

Habitat improvements to the flowage include nesting boxes, planting of wild rice, and about twenty 10 x10-foot nesting islands for waterfowl. Located away from shore, these islands help keep away shoreline predators. The shoreline is covered with hardwoods and shrubs. The western shore is a hilly glacial esker. It is an ideal, out-of-the way spot for both wildlife watching and picnicking. It offers a more primitive experience.

heron from local rookeries, and waterfowl during migration. Tundra swans also make a stop during their migratory flights.

◆ **Mammals and Reptiles**
Mammals include the muskrat, beaver, white-tailed deer, mink, otter, black bear, skunk, porcupine, raccoon, and much more. There is also a group of amphibians that make the flowage and rivers their home. They include the mink, green, leopard, and wood frogs, painted turtles, and spotted salamanders. Spring peepers welcome each spring with their lively chorus.

Wildlife

Upper Steve Creek Waterfowl Area is ideal for wildlife viewing or a quiet picnic spot.

◆ **Birds**
In Kidrick Swamp, a variety of birds can be found, including the northern waterthrush, yellow-bellied flycatcher, Nashville warbler, alder flycatcher, Lincoln sparrow, and common yellow-throated warbler.

In wetland management areas, you may also see bald eagle, osprey, belted kingfisher, common loon, marsh hawk, double-crested cormorant, blue

Hunting

The Medford Ranger District offers ideal habitat for snowshoe rabbits, gray squirrels, waterfowl including mallards and wood ducks, common woodcock, white-tailed deer, and black bear. Geese can be found at the Pershing State Wildlife Area to the west of the District.

Birdwatch:
Chequamegon's Permanent Residents

Listed below is a partial list of bird species that permanently inhabit the Chequamegon National Forest.

Northern Goshawk
Spruce Grouse
Ruffed Grouse
Sharp-tailed Grouse
Rock Dove
Eastern Screech-Owl

Great Horned Owl
Barred Owl
Northern Saw-Whet Owl
Red-bellied Woodpecker
Downy Woodpecker
Hairy Woodpecker
Black-backed Woodpecker
Pileated Woodpecker
Gray Jay
Blue Jay
American Crow

Common Raven
Black-capped Chickadee
Boreal Chickadee
Red-breasted Nuthatch
White-breasted Nuthatch
European Starling
Northern Cardinal
Red Crossbill
American Goldfinch
Evening Grosbeak
House Sparrow

Hunter Walking Trails

The Medford Ranger District maintains several walking trails for hunters. All hunters are encouraged to write, phone, or visit the Ranger District office to obtain up-to-date trail maps.

◆ **Trail FR 102**, in the central part of the District, is located between FR 108 and FR 568. There are three trails, one on the north side and two on the south side.

◆ **Trail FR 108**, in the central part of the District, is located off FR 108 between FR 102 and FR 568, and FR 102 and FR 111. There are six trails, three on each side of the road.

◆ **Trail FR 1501**, in the southwest corner of the District, is located east of FR 123. It leads to a trail to the southern end of the Chequamegon Waters Flowage. Waterfowl hunting can be found in the area as well as deer and grouse.

◆ **White Birch Hunter Walking Trail**, in the central part of the District, is accessible to those in wheelchairs. It is located west of Cty E on FR 102 in the Ice Age Semi-Primitive Area. This trail has a slight grade, acceptable for motorized wheelchairs.

Gathering of Forest Products

A woodland environment with forest openings is ideal for the growth and harvesting of numerous edible forest products. These include wild raspberries, blackberries, choke cherries, elderberries, blueberries, strawberries, beaked hazelnuts, and morel mushrooms. Wild berries and other pioneering plants are frequently found along old logging roads, recent timber-harvested areas, abandoned gravel pits, and other areas open to sunshine. With a limited amount of conifers in the District, pine cones are not as plentiful as elsewhere.

RECREATIONAL WATERS

Lakes

The Medford Ranger District has over forty lakes and flowages, ranging in size from 1 to 2,714 acres. Many lakes are in the southern half of the District. Cty M passes through the middle of this region. Two of the largest lakes are Chequamegon Waters Flowage and Mondeaux Flowage, which are located at opposite ends of the District. Many lakes were formed when blocks of ice, left in the terminal moraine, melted, leaving water-filled depressions. This is why many smaller lakes are deeper than expected for their size. Most of these lakes do not produce large numbers of fish.

◆ Anderson Lake

Surface Area: 43 acres
Depth: Maximum 32 feet, mean 12 feet
Fishery: Northern pike, walleye, largemouth bass, crappie, perch, panfish, and bullhead
Location: The lake is one mile east of Perkinstown and just south of the intersection of Cty M and FR 571.
Lake Conditions: The bottom is 85% muck with the remainder sand, gravel, and boulder. Water is turbid, with visibility down to three feet. Aquatic vegetation is present.
Shoreline: Upland forest covers 50% of the shore, with hardwood swamp and tag alder covering the rest.
Facilities: An undeveloped boat landing is located south of the intersection of Cty M and FR 571. You need to carry in your boat. Parking is along the road.
Contour Map Available: Yes

◆ Chequamegon Waters Flowage

Surface Area: 2,730 acres
Depth: Maximum 22 feet, mean 5 feet, with the deepest hole a flooded gravel pit 100-foot in diameter.
Fishery: Northern pike, largemouth bass, crappie, perch, and panfish. One of the top largemouth bass fisheries in the State.
Location: Located on the western edge of the District, take either Cty M three miles east of Hwy 73 or about 22 miles west of Hwy 13.
Lake Conditions: The bottom is 80% muck, 20% sand and gravel, and a lot of wood debris. Water is dark brown, with visibility down to two feet. Aquatic vegetation is present throughout the flowage. An aerator is maintained by the Bass Anglers Sportsmen Club to help prevent winter kill conditions.
Shoreline: The shoreline is 80% upland forest with 20% shrub swamp.
Facilities: There are a number of boat landings. These include Cty G just south of Cty M on the northwest corner of the flowage; Miller Dam, east of Cty G; FR 121 on the southwest corner of the flowage; Chippewa Campground west of FR 1417; and on Cty M at the north end of the flowage. The Miller Dam boat landing is considered the best landing overall. Chippewa Campground is the largest and most modern campground in the District.
Contour Map Available: yes

◆ Chub Lake

Surface Area: 6 acres
Depth: Maximum 25 feet
Fishery: Black crappie and panfish
Location: From Hwy 64 and Cty T intersection, take FR 119 north four miles. The lake will be on the right side of road.
Lake Conditions: The bottom is muck. Water is

Lakes
Medford Ranger District

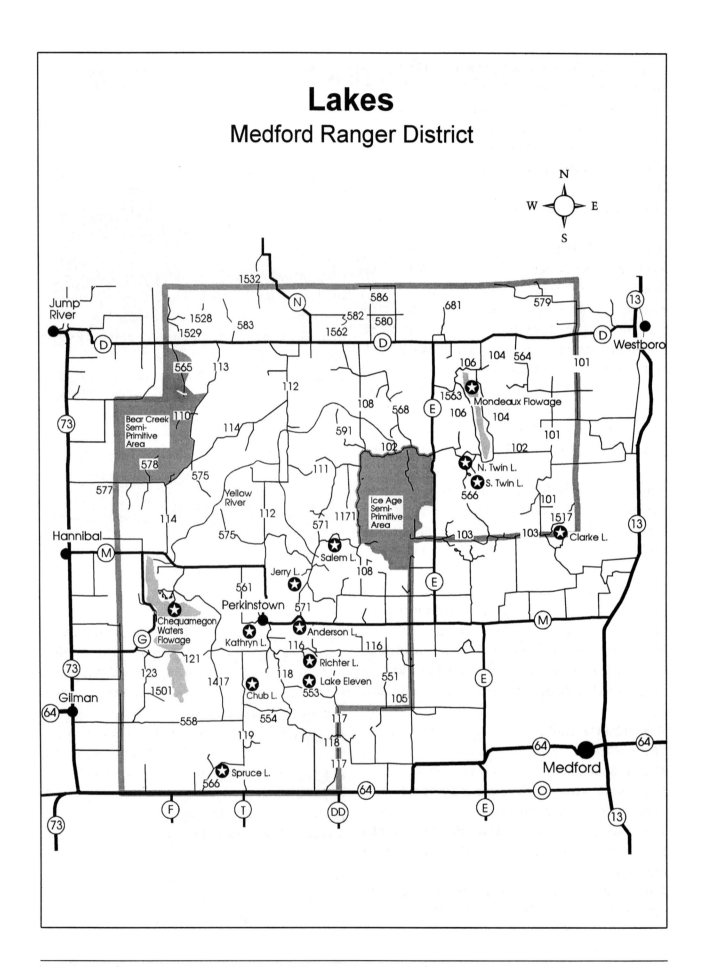

dark brown, with visibility down to two feet. There is a mix of aquatic vegetation.

Shoreline: The northwest shoreline is a tamarack-spruce swamp with the remaining shore a mix of hardwoods and conifers.

Facilities: None, walk-in access to lake is through the swamp.

Contour Map Available: No

◆ Clarke Lake

Surface Area: 12 acres

Depth: Maximum 19 feet, mean 9 feet

Fishery: Northern pike, largemouth bass, crappie, perch, and panfish

Location: Located at the east central corner of the District, travel three miles north of Cty M on Cty E, then east (right) on FR 103 about five miles. Continue east on FR 1517 about .5 miles. The landing will be on Horseshoe Lake.

Lake Conditions: The bottom is 70% muck, 20% sand, and 10% rock. Water is medium brown, with visibility down to four feet. A variety of aquatic vegetation is present.

Shoreline: The shoreline is predominantly leatherleaf and tamarack with two patches of upland hardwood.

Facilities: Boat landing is on Horseshoe Lake. Take FR 103 east of Cty E five miles, then continue east on FR 1517 about .5 miles. There is a 300-foot long, 6-foot wide channel from the east shore of Horseshoe Lake into Clarke Lake.

Contour Map Available: Yes

◆ Kathryn Lake

Surface Area: 62 acres

Depth: Maximum 58 feet, mean 15 feet

Fishery: Walleye, northern pike, largemouth bass, yellow perch, and panfish

Location: Located just southwest of Perkinstown, take FR 121 south for .5 miles, then west into the campground.

Lake Conditions: The bottom is mostly muck with scattered gravel, rubble, and boulders. Water is

This scenic view of the Mondeaux Flowage is typical of many Northern Wisconsin lakes.

clear, with visibility down to eight feet. Aquatic vegetation is abundant. An aerator was installed by the lake association to help prevent winter kill conditions. Several fish cribs have been added to improve fish habitat.

Shoreline: Seventy-five percent of the shore is upland hardwoods with the remaining area wetland. The shoreline is moderately developed.

Facilities: Boat landing is west of FR 121 at Kathryn Lake Campground.

Contour Map Available: Yes

◆ Mondeaux Flowage

Surface Area: 416 acres

Depth: Maximum 10 feet, mean 5 feet

Fishery: Musky, northern pike, largemouth bass, crappie, perch, and panfish

Location: This long and narrow flowage is located in the northeast section of the District. From Westboro (Hwy 13), take Cty D west for about seven miles, then south on FR 104 for one mile, then west (right) one mile on FR 106 to the north end of the flowage.

Lake Conditions: The bottom is 60% muck, 30% sand, and 10% gravel. Water is clear, with visibility down to five feet. Aquatic vegetation is abundant in the summer. Wild rice and stumps are found throughout the flowage. An aerator was installed by the Westboro Conservation Club to help prevent winter kill conditions. Fish cribs have also been added to enhance fish habitat.

Shoreline: Most of the shoreline is upland hardwoods and conifers with scattered areas of tag-alder swamps. The western shore with its hills and ridges, is an esker.

Facilities: Three boat landings can be found off FR 106. They are located at Picnic Point Campground, Spearhead Point Campground, and Lakeview Picnic Area.

Contour Map Available: Yes

◆ North Twin Lake

Surface Area: 33 acres

Depth: Maximum 62 feet, mean 18 feet

Fishery: Northern pike, largemouth bass, black crappie, perch, and panfish

Location: Located in the northeast portion of the District, this lake is just southwest of Mondeaux Flowage. Take FR 102 1.2 miles east of Cty E, then south on FR 566 about .75 miles. The lake will be to the east.

Lake Conditions: The bottom is 60% muck, 30% sand, and 10% gravel. Water is clear, with visibility down to six feet. Aquatic vegetation is relatively sparse.

Shoreline: Upland hardwoods make up 80% of the shoreline, with tamarack and black spruce covering the remaining 20%. The eastern shore is well developed with private cottages.

Facilities: Boat landing is east of FR 566. Outboard motors over ten horsepower are not permitted.

Contour Map Available: Yes

◆ Richter Lake

Surface Area: 45 acres

Depth: Maximum 53 feet, mean 19 feet

Fishery: Northern pike, walleye, largemouth bass, crappie, perch, and panfish

Location: From Perkinstown, travel south one mile on FR 121, then east (left) on FR 116 about two miles. Richter Lake will be to the right.

Lake Conditions: The bottom is 60% gravel, 20% sand, and 20% muck. Water is clear. Aquatic vegetation is present.

Shoreline: The shoreline is entirely northern hardwoods and is well developed.

Facilities: An undeveloped boat landing can be found on the northwest shore off FR 116. Parking is along the road.

Contour Map Available: Yes

◆ Salem Lake

Surface Area: 13 acres

Depth: Maximum 50 feet, mean 20 feet

Fishery: Northern pike, largemouth bass, and panfish

Location: Travel 1.5 miles east of Perkinstown on Cty M, then three miles north on FR 571, and then east (right) one mile on Salem Lake Road. The lake is to the south.

Lake Conditions: The bottom is 50% muck, 40% gravel, and 10% sand. Water is medium brown.

Shoreline: Conifer-shrub swamps make up 90% of the shoreline with the remainder hardwood-grass uplands.

Facilities: There is a carry-in landing on the east shore. Parking is along the road.

Contour Map Available: Yes

◆ South Twin Lake

Surface Area: 26 acres

Depth: Maximum 48 feet, mean 19 feet

Fishery: Largemouth bass and panfish with special regulations on bass limit and size

Location: Located in the northeast portion of the District, this lake is southwest of the Mondeaux Flowage. Take FR 102 east of Cty E, then south on FR 566 for about one mile, just past North Twin Lake, then east (left) on FR 1504.

Lake Conditions: The bottom is 70% gravel and 30% muck. Water is clear with a visibility down to eleven feet. Aquatic vegetation is present. Tree drops and cribs have been added to improve fish habitat.

Shoreline: The shore is upland forest.

Facilities: There is a carry-in landing on the north shore, off FR 1504.

Contour Map Available: Yes

◆ Spruce Lake

Surface Area: 22 acres

Depth: Maximum 63 feet, mean 23 feet

Fishery: Brown, rainbow, and brook trout

Location: Located about two miles west of Cty T on Hwy 64, then north on FR 556 for a little over one mile. The lake and landing will be to the east (right) of the road.

Lake Conditions: The bottom is muck. Water is light brown with visibility down to eight feet. Aquatic vegetation is minimal.

Shoreline: Conifer bog accounts for 95% of the shore with 5% grass uplands.

Facilities: Boat landing is a carry-in, down a bank on the north end of the lake, off FR 556. Parking is along the road.

Contour Map Available: Yes

Walk-In Lakes

The following walk-in lakes on Forest property have no motorized access. You need to carry in equipment and watercraft at least 100 feet.

◆ Jerry Lake

Surface Area: 10 acres

Depth: Maximum 33 feet

Fishery: Largemouth bass, crappie, and panfish

Location: Travel just east of Perkinstown on Cty M, then north on FR 571 for .75 miles to the parking lot. The lake is 500 feet to the west along an access trail.

Lake Conditions: The bottom is muck. Water is dark brown, with visibility down to two feet. Aquatic vegetation is sparse.

Shoreline: The lake is surrounded by a tag-alder swamp.

Facilities: Carry-in access is off FR 571.

Contour Map Available: Yes

◆ Lake Eleven

Surface Area: 8 acres

Depth: Maximum 35 feet

Fishery: Largemouth bass, crappie, and panfish

Location: Travel 2.5 miles east of Perkinstown on Cty M, then south on FR 115, then west (right) a short distance on FR 116, then south (left) on 597, and west on FR 597A to the north end of lake.

Lake Conditions: The bottom is mostly muck with scattered spots of gravel. Water is light brown. Aquatic vegetation is sparse. Tree drops have been added along the shore to improve fish habitat.

Shoreline: The shoreline is a mix of upland hardwoods and conifers with tamarack-spruce swamps.

Facilities: Carry-in access is off FR 597A.

Contour Map Available: Yes

Rivers

There are 121 miles of streams and rivers within the District's boundary. The Black River and Jump River just touch the border of the District. Many waterways have enough water to canoe during the spring or rainy times. Other times of the year, water levels are low, resulting in exposed rocks and boulder fields. During high water, some of the rivers can be very dangerous due to rapids and fast-moving water. For detailed information, contact the Ranger District office.

◆ Yellow River

Length: Fifteen miles
Gradient, Average: Seven-foot drop per mile
Fishery: Northern pike, smallmouth bass, and panfish
Description: Both the North Fork and South Fork are found in the central area of the District. Each branch flows west, crossing FR 112 before they join. From this point to the dam is about twelve miles. The stream flows through a forest setting with minimal swamp-tag alder edge. Boulder fields, shallow ripple areas, and Class I rapids can be found along the way. You may have to portage around beaver dams. Water levels are normally good for canoeing until midsummer. The North Fork is best for canoeing when the water is high in the spring or after a heavy summer thunderstorm. The river south from FR 575 has many shallow riffle areas. Please note, the South Fork is not suitable for canoeing.

Access Points: Canoes can be put in on the north branch at FR 112, about one mile north of FR 111. From this point to Cty M, near the flowage, there are no other road crossings or easy identified takeout points. Vehicle access to the river is available off Sheep Ranch Road (FR 575). The bridge was washed out in 1926.

Trout Streams

The Medford Ranger District has only two trout streams within its boundaries, **Mink Creek** and **Camp Eleven**. Both are on the east side of the District off the Mondeaux Flowage.

Points of Interest

Auto Tours

◆ **Chequamegon Waters Flowage/ Perkinstown Tour** is about 32 miles long and travels through the southern portion of the District. You will see a variety of forest vegetation. The change of color can be very pretty in fall. This tour starts at Perkinstown, where you travel west on Cty M to Cty G. Turn left on to Cty G and travel south past the Chequamegon Waters Flowage on the left and Bear Creek Wetland Habitat on the right. Continuing south, you will pass Miller Dam, which forms the flowage. There are several places to stop to picnic. Continue south on Cty G, then east (left) on FR 121, then south on FR 123, and then east (left) on to FR 588.

Beginning on FR 558, you will take a number of different roads east and north for short distances. First, travel east on FR 558, then north on FR 119, then east on FR 554, then north on FR 118 and east on FR 553 to FR 117.

At FR 117, you can take a short side trip south 1.5 miles to the Old Iron Dam and water-powered sawmill located on Sawyer Avenue. Travel back north on FR 117, then west (left) on FR 116 one mile, and finally north (right) on FR 115 to Cty M. Here you can turn right and travel back to Hwy 13, or turn left to travel back to Perkinstown.

◆ **Mondeaux Flowage Fall Color Tour** is a 13-mile loop around Mondeaux Flowage and through the northeast corner of the District. Take Cty D west of Westboro (Hwy 13) to FR 104. At the corner of

---

QUICK REFERENCE
Auto Tour Highlights
Within the Medford Ranger District

Chequamegon Waters Flowage/ Perkinstown Tour
Length: 32 miles
Highlights
- Chequamegon Waters Flowage
- Bear Creek Wetland Habitat Area
- Miller Dam
- Old Iron Dam & Sawmill

Mondeaux Flowage Fall Color Tour
Length: 13 miles
Highlights
- Fall Colors in the National Forest
- Mondeaux Flowage
- Glacial Landforms

Points of Interest
Medford Ranger District

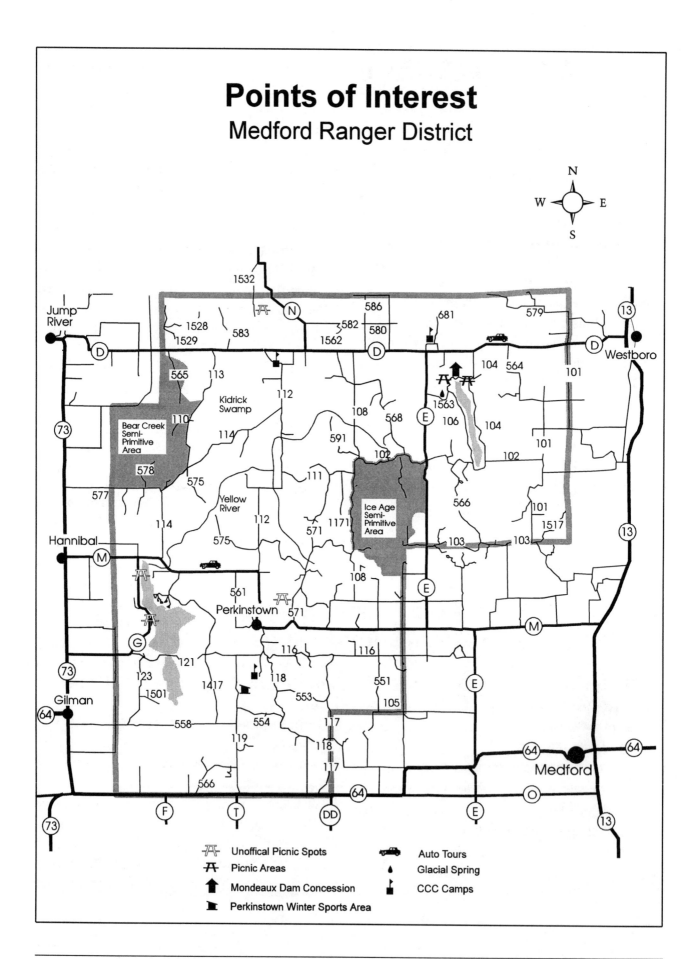

Unoffical Picnic Spots

Picnic Areas

Mondeaux Dam Concession

Perkinstown Winter Sports Area

Auto Tours

Glacial Spring

CCC Camps

Cty D and FR 104, proceed south on FR 104 along the eastern shore of the flowage. At FR 102, travel west (right) to FR 106, which takes you north along the western shore of the flowage. This part of the tour travels along an esker that is more scenic and rolling than the eastern shore. The west shore has a variety of trees that turn brilliant red, orange, and yellow colors in fall. At FR 1563, travel west (left) to Cty E, then north (right) and travel back to Cty D. Turn right to return to your starting point.

Civilian Conservation Corps Camps

There were three CCC camps in the Medford Ranger District. The degree of preservation of the camp sites varies greatly.

◆ **Camp Jump River F-17, Company 3651 and Fire Tower** are about sixteen miles west of Westboro or nine miles east of Jump River on Cty D, then south on FR 1972 about .25 miles, or west of the junction of FR 112 and FR 1972. This site is located a half-mile south of the fire tower. The site is now covered with a 30 year old white and red pine plantation. A number of cement foundations and the fire tower are all that remain of the camp. The opening in the pine plantation may hold locations of lath-tarpaper barracks used by the workers.

◆ **Camp Mondeaux River F-18, Company 1603** is located north of Mondeaux Flowage. From FR 104 travel west 1.5 miles on Cty D, then north on FR 581 about .5 miles. This forest road will turn to the left, then branch off to the north (right). About 100 feet after branching to the north, you will see an opening and a pine-spruce plantation. The camp was located on both sides of the road.

The fire tower is located a half-mile to the north of the camp. It was constructed in the 1930s and stands about 100 feet tall, with an observation platform at the top. It is one of three fire towers constructed in this District. At this time, it is not used by the Forest Service. Climbing the tower is strongly discouraged.

◆ **Camp Perkinstown F-16, Company 1692 and Fire Tower** are south of Perkinstown and Cty M on FR 121. Go .25 miles past FR 116, then turn south (left) on the town road. Continue another quarter-mile, then turn west (right) on a town road and continue .5 miles up a steep grade to the tower. Constructed in the 1930s, today the tower is a communication tower.

Picnic and Recreation Areas

◆ **Lake View Picnic Area**
Location: From Westboro (Hwy 13), take Cty D west about seven miles, then south on FR 104 one mile, then west on FR 106 to the picnic area.
Description: This is an open, wooded area, located on the northern shore of the Mondeaux Flowage.
Facilities: There is a developed boat landing, a picnic area with tables, fishing pier accessible to the physically challenged, and vault toilets. A swimming area can be found at the Pines Picnic Area. Take the footpath west, over the dam. A ramp over the dam provides access to the physically challenged. Parking is available at the landing and at the picnic area.

◆ **Perkinstown Winter Sports Area**
Location: Located southwest of Perkinstown. Take FR 121 south of Cty M, then FR 119, turn south (left). The parking lot is to the left.
Description: This facility is owned and operated by Taylor County. Cross-country ski trails can be found on the Forest property. There is one loop that heads east toward the fire tower and two loops west of FR 119. The trails are groomed by the

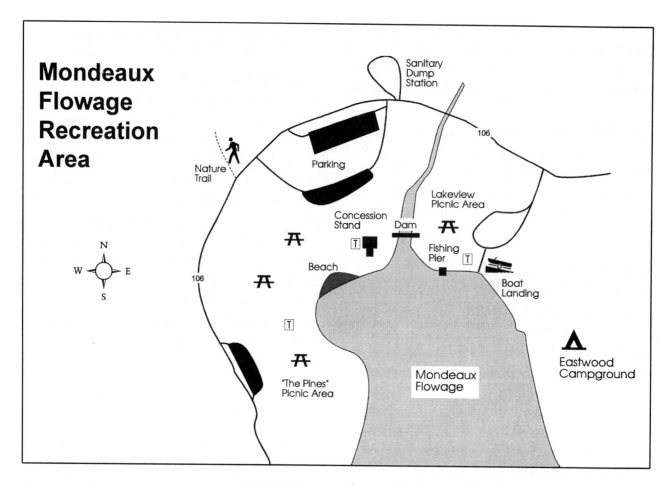

Mondeaux Flowage Recreation Area

Sanitary Dump Station

Parking

106

Nature Trail

Lakeview Picnic Area

Concession Stand

Dam

Fishing Pier

N

W   E

S

Beach

106

Boat Landing

"The Pines" Picnic Area

Mondeaux Flowage

Eastwood Campground

---

county. For information, contact the property manager (715) 748-1486, or the Taylor County Clerk (715) 748-3131.

Facilities: There is a warming chalet, telephone (715) 785-7722, with a snack bar and ski rental. A rope tow takes you to the top of the hill for snow tubing.

◆ Pines Picnic Area (Mondeaux Dam)

Location: Located at the northern end of Mondeaux Flowage. Take Cty D about seven miles west from Westboro (Hwy 13), then south on FR 104 one mile, then west on FR 106, just over the Mondeaux River.

Description: A concession building, built by the CCC and WPA, was renovated recently but retains its original charm. A large, outside stone patio gives a scenic overlook of the flowage.

Facilities: There is a marked swimming area, beach, playground, interpretive exhibits, horseshoe pits, paddleboat, and canoe rentals, flush toilets, showers, and grills. A trailer sanitary dump station is north of FR 106. There is a large parking lot next to FR 106 with limited parking at the concession. For information, contact the concession (715) 427-5746.

Spots off the Beaten Path

With more than a thousand square miles in the Chequamegon National Forest, there are countless places that make ideal spots for a quiet picnic outing. Here are just a few.

◆ Cty G Picnic Area is located one-half mile south of Cty M on Cty G and on the west shore of Chequamegon Waters Flowage. It is operated by the County and offers a picnic area with tables and shelter, vault toilets, and drinking water.

◆ **Jerry Lake** is located just east of Perkinstown on Cty M, then north .75 miles on FR 571. There is a small parking lot with a trail leading back to the lake, several scenic spots, and the Ice Age Trail.

◆ **Miller Dam** is located about three miles south of Cty M on Cty G and on the west shore of Chequamegon Waters Flowage. Memorial Drive takes you to the dam. There is an open area 100 feet north of the dam with open shelter, vault toilets, drinking water, and fishing supplies.

◆ **Steve Creek Flowage** can be reached by taking Cty D either east of Hwy 73 or west of Hwy 13 to Cty N. Travel north on Cty N about two miles into Price County, then west (left) and south on Steve Creek Road at Steve Creek Flowage. If you cross the Jump River, you have gone too far north. At Steve Creek Flowage, you will need to travel south on FR 1532 to the impoundment dam. This road may not be passible during wet weather. You will find a number of scenic spots along the west shore.

Structures and Landmarks

◆ **Glacial Springs Interpretive Site** is located west of Mondeaux Flowage on FR 1563. It can be reached by taking FR 1563 either east of Cty E or west of FR 106. The water, flowing freely from the hillside, comes from a glacial spring. Rainwater and snowmelt, on the hills above the spring, filter down through glacial soil, rock, and sand deposited by the receding glacier over 10,000 years ago.

When the groundwater reaches the impermeable layer of glacial material, it then travels horizontally until it leaves the open hillside. A nearly constant flow of about 4.5 gallons per minute gives visitors a cool drink of sparkling water. The site is continually monitored and the water tested to ensure its safety. A stairway to the spring was added for visitor convenience as well as an interpretive sign explaining how the spring was formed.

◆ **Mondeaux Flowage Dam and Concession Building**, located at the north end of Mondeaux Flowage on FR 106, is part of a National Register Historical District. These facilities were developed in the 1930s by the CCC and the Works Progress Administration (WPA). During the winter of 1936-7, the flowage basin was brushed out. In the summer of 1938, the dam was completed.

The concession building, located near the dam, was also completed in the summer of 1938. It was renovated recently and provides food service and boat rentals for visitors; phone (715) 427-5746.

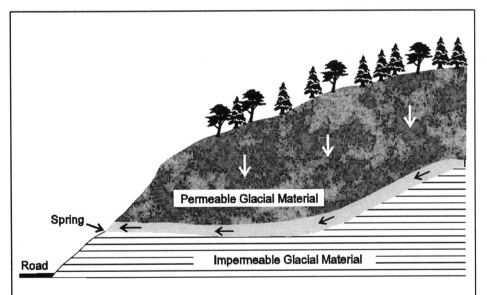

Permeable Glacial Material

Spring

Road

Impermeable Glacial Material

This cross-section shows how rainfall and snow melts pass through the permeable materials (soil, rock, and sand) to form a spring at the foot of a hill. The Glacial Springs, located west of Mondeaux Flowage, was formed in this manner. An interpretive display at the site provides additional information.

CAMPGROUNDS

Established Campgrounds

There are seven established campgrounds in the Medford Ranger District. They center around the three recreational areas, Chequamegon Waters Flowage, Mondeaux Flowage, and Perkinstown.

Campground hosts are available at some campgrounds during the summer months to welcome you and answer questions. The Taylor County Sportsmen's Club and Midway Telephone Company provide free firewood for all the campgrounds within this District. Campgrounds normally open one week before Memorial Day and close after Labor Day.

◆ Chippewa Campground
Location: Take Cty M east of Hwy 73 or west of Perkinstown, then one mile south on FR 1417 to the campground on the east shore of the Chequamegon Waters Flowage.
Number of Sites: Ninety modern sites in four paved loops, with many sites able to handle RVs up to 35 feet. Loop 1 has six sites by the water. Loop 2 has five sites near the water. Loop 3 has six sites close to the water, and Loop 4 has a path to the beach area. There are four sites for the physically challenged that can be reserved. Loop 4 is not suited for RVs. This loop is also open for winter camping, but there are no restrooms or drinking water available at the site.
Facilities: Each site has a fire grill, paved parking spur, picnic table, and tent pad plus free firewood. There are flush toilets, drinking water, and hot showers on three loops, with running water and vault toilets on the fourth. Other facilities include a boat landing, fish cleaning station, pay telephone (715) 668-5651, trailer sanitation station, two marked swimming areas, beaches, and play areas.

Description: This area is flat with mature hardwoods. Campers stay here when using the Perkinstown Motorized Trail, fishing, hunting, or just watching the wildlife.
Reservations and Fee: Sites may be reserved by calling 1-800-280-2267 or TTY 1-800-879-4496. Fees are $6, $8, and $12 depending on the site. Reservations for physically challenged sites can be made by calling the Ranger District office at (715) 748-4875, TTY (715) 748-4875. The main campground is open from mid-May to mid-September.

◆ Eastwood Campground
Location: Located in the Mondeaux Flowage Recreation Area. Take Cty D west of Westboro 6.5 miles, then two miles south on FR 104 to the campground entrance.
Number of Sites: Twenty-two moderate sites that handle RVs up to 30 feet. Four campsites are located near the lake. Winter camping is permitted.
Facilities: Sites are shady. Each site has a fire grill, parking spur, and picnic table. There are accessible vault toilets, drinking water, and a boat landing to the flowage. The Ice Age National Scenic Trail passes through the campground.
Description: These are nice, large sites in a setting of 60-year-old hardwood trees. A third of the sites overlook the flowage.
Reservations and Fee: Sites may be reserved by calling 1-800-280-2267, or TTY 1-800-879-4496. Other sites are on a first-come, first-serve basis. Fee is $6. Open from early May to the end of December.

◆ Kathryn Lake Campground
Location: Take FR121 south of Cty M .5 miles to the campground entrance.
Number of Sites: Ten rustic sites, also open for winter camping

Spearhead Point is the most popular campground on the Mondeaux Flowage, and offers campers a wide range of facilities, including modern vault toilets.

Facilities: Each site has a fire grill, parking spur, and picnic table. There are vault toilets, free firewood, drinking water, and a boat landing. There is also a small marked swimming area and beach.

Description: These sites are in a scenic hardwood setting. With its low usage, this campground is a nice way to get away from other campers.

Reservations and Fee: All sites are on a first-come, first-serve basis, and require a $6 fee. Open from early May to the end of December.

◆ North Twin Lake Campground

Location: Travel 8.5 miles west of Westboro (Hwy 13) on Hwy D, then four miles south on Cty E, then 1.5 miles east on FR 102, and finally south one mile on FR 566 to the campground.

Number of Sites: Six rustic sites

Facilities: Each site has a fire grill, parking spur, and picnic table. There are vault toilets, picnic area, free firewood, drinking water, 30-foot fishing dock, small beach, and a boat landing.

Description: This campground is located on a hill overlooking the lake. The sites are in an area of paper birch and fir. There are a number of private cottages on the lake.

Reservations and Fee: All sites are on a first come first serve basis with a $6 fee. Open from mid-May to mid-September.

◆ Picnic Point Campground

Location: Travel 6.5 miles west of Westboro (Hwy 13) on Hwy D, then south on FR 104, then west and south on FR 106, past West Point Campground to Picnic Point Campground.

Number of Sites: Three rustic sites

Facilities: Each site has a fire grill, parking spur, picnic table, and free firewood. There are vault toilets, drinking water, and a boat landing on Mondeaux Flowage.

Description: This small campground has an open area perfect for group camping. The Ice Age National Scenic Trail passes just north of the campground.

Reservations and Fee: All sites are on a first-come, first-serve basis with $6 fee. Open from early May to the end of December. During winter months, the entrance road may be too slippery to drive up the hill.

◆ Spearhead Point Campground

Location: Travel 6.5 miles west of Westboro (Hwy 13) on Hwy D, then south on FR 104, then west and south 1.5 miles on FR 106 to the entrance at the top of the hill.

Number of Sites: Twenty-seven moderate sites, with three modified sites for the physically challenged which can be reserved.

Chequamegon Waters Recreation Area

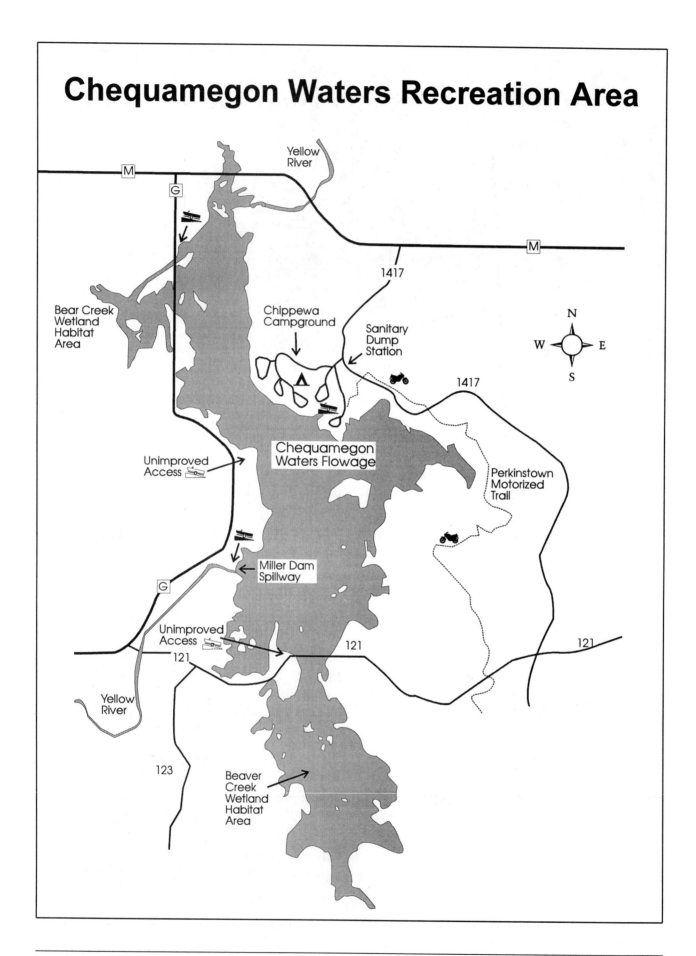

Yellow River

M

G

Bear Creek Wetland Habitat Area

Chippewa Campground

Sanitary Dump Station

1417

1417

N
W — E
S

Unimproved Access

Chequamegon Waters Flowage

Perkinstown Motorized Trail

Miller Dam Spillway

G

Unimproved Access

121

121

121

Yellow River

123

Beaver Creek Wetland Habitat Area

Mondeaux Flowage Recreation Area

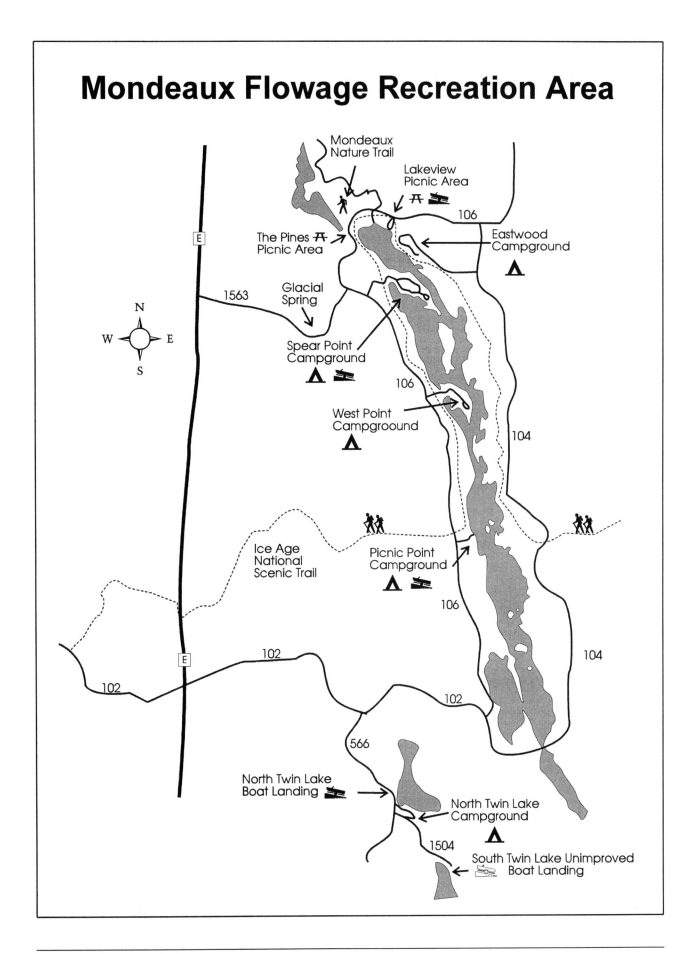

Mondeaux Nature Trail

Lakeview Picnic Area

The Pines Picnic Area

Eastwood Campground

106

1563

Glacial Spring

Spear Point Campground

West Point Campgroound

106

104

Picnic Point Campground

Ice Age National Scenic Trail

106

102

104

102

102

566

North Twin Lake Boat Landing

North Twin Lake Campground

1504

South Twin Lake Unimproved Boat Landing

N W E S

E

E

Facilities: Each site has a fire grill, parking spur, picnic table, and free firewood. There are vault toilets, open picnic shelter, drinking water, dump station, boat landing on west side of the flowage, and showers at the concession building by the dam.

Description: This campground is the most popular on the Mondeaux Flowage. Many sites have small docks that can be used for fishing or landing a boat. The Ice Age National Scenic Trail passes over the campground entrance road. Campground hosts may be present to welcome you.

Reservations and Fee: All sites are on a first-come, first-serve basis, with fees of $6 and $8. Three modified sites for the physically challenged can be reserved by calling (715) 748-4875. Open from mid-May to mid-September. Sites for Spearhead Point may be reserved through a campground reservation service by calling 1-800-280-2267 or TTY 1-800-879-4496.

◆ West Point Campground

Location: Travel 6.5 miles west of Westboro (Hwy 13) on Hwy D, then south on FR 104, then west and south on FR 106 about 2.5 miles to the campground entrance on the left.

Number of Sites: Fifteen moderate sites

Facilities: Each site has a fire grill, parking spur, and picnic table. There are vault toilets, free firewood, drinking water, and a boat landing on the Mondeaux Flowage.

Description: This campground is "enjoyed by those who prefer a smaller campground." It is family-oriented, with a setting of hardwood and hemlock. Swimming and other facilities are available at the Mondeaux Dam.

Reservations and Fee: All sites are on a first-come, first-serve basis with a $6 fee. Open from mid-May to mid-September.

Dispersed Camping

If you are looking to find an ideal out-of-the-way campsite for a wilderness experience, the Forest lands are open for camping. It is important to know where you are camping because 14 percent of the lands within the District border are privately-owned.

Several of the more popular areas for dispersed camping can be found at **Jerry Lake**, north of Perkinstown; **Lake Eleven**, south of Perkinstown; and along the **Chippewa Lobe Trail**, off the Ice Age Trail in the Ice Age Semi-Primitive Non-Motorized Area.

TRAILS

◆ Chippewa Lobe Interpretive Loop

Length: 7-mile loop, south of the main Ice Age National Scenic Trail

Type: Hiking and interpretive

Degree of Difficulty: Moderate

Trailhead: Located two miles west of Mondeaux Flowage in the Ice Age Semi-Primitive Non-Motorized Area, it can be reached by taking the Ice Age Trail either east of FR 108 for .5 miles or south of FR 102 about 1.5 miles. You can also take Birch Lake Trail south of FR 102 about one mile.

Description: This seven-mile loop has just been added to the Ice Age Trail System. Many unique glacial features, such as an esker, kettle, and erratic, are found along the trail. The trail is named after the glacial lobe that formed many local features. Interpretation of the glacial topography is planned. This trail segment offers solitude in a special place. There is one dispersed campsite on the southern end of the loop near a small lake.

Points of Interest: Unique glacial features

Type of Landscape: Northern hardwood forest with gently rolling hills.

◆ Ice Age National Scenic Trail

Length: 42 (approved) miles

Type: Hiking

Degree of Difficulty: Moderate

Trailhead: Trailheads and parking areas can be found at Hwy 64, Cty E, FR 563, and FR 571.

Description: This trail segment is part of a proposed 1,000-mile Ice Age National Scenic Trail through Wisconsin, traversing features of the last Ice Age. Starting on the eastern edge of the Forest, this trail segment extends west, then southwest across the District to Hwy 64. Scenic vistas of glacial wetlands and geological landforms, such as eskers, kames, and kettles, accent this section of

the trail. If you start at FR 101, the trail extends westward about 2.5 miles to the Mondeaux Flowage, then north about 2.5 miles along the flowage to the dam, where there are a picnic area, concession, and developed campground. The trail continues around the flowage, then south two miles, passing several campgrounds before it turns west. You will quickly reach Glacial Spring, just west of the Mondeaux Flowage on FR 1563. Glacial Spring Interpretive Point is a convenient spot to stop and drink from the clear spring.

The trail continues west, crossing Cty E and FR 102, and enters the northern end of the Ice Age Semi-Primitive Non-Motorized Area. Within this property, the trail extends about three miles to the southwest. There is a seven-mile loop trail to the south called the Chippewa Lobe Interpretive Loop.

After leaving the semi-primitive area, the trail crosses FR 108 and extends west one mile, then turns north a mile, then southwest about five miles, crossing FR 571, FR 576, and FR 572. Just before crossing FR 571 again, the trail passes Jerry Lake, where dispersed campsites are available. The trail swings east and south over Cty M and FR 116, then around Perkinstown, covering about four miles. It then turns west, passing Lake Eleven, where there is a dispersed camping area.

The trail continues southwest about 10 miles, crossing FR 118, FR 119, FR 1417, and FR 558 before it ends on Hwy 64, just west of Cty F.

The Forest Service has an excellent updated map for this section of the Ice Age Trail. ATVs and mountain bikes are not permitted on the trail. Horses are permitted on only part of the trail, from FR 116 to Hwy 64.

Points of Interest: You will find a number of unique land formations, remnants of our glacial past. Eskers are long, snake-like hills formed by

Trails
Medford Ranger District

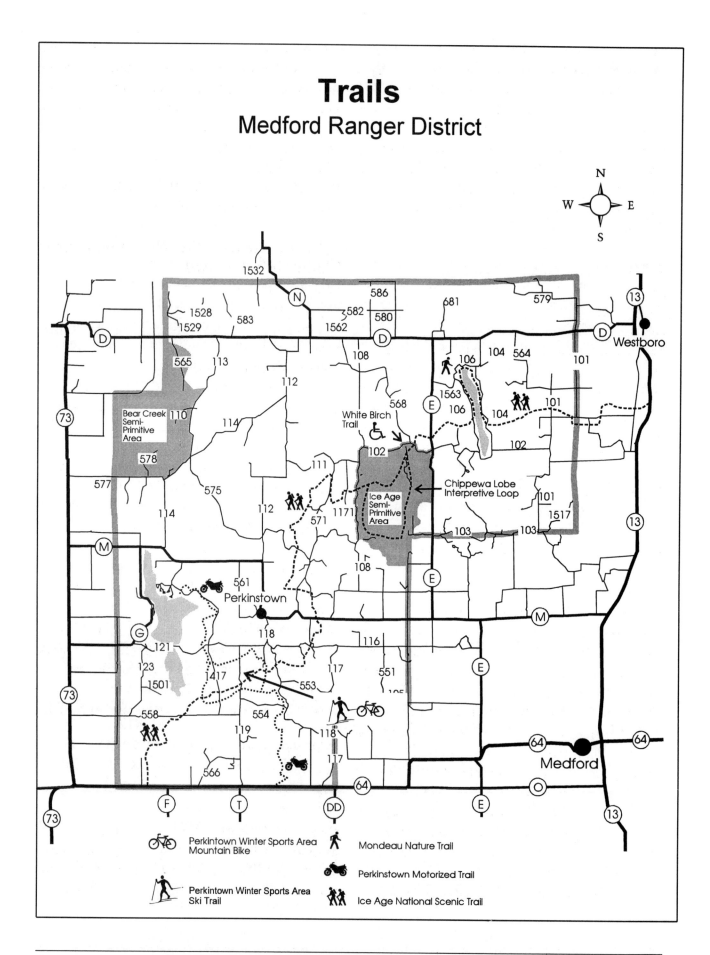

Perkintown Winter Sports Area Mountain Bike

Perkintown Winter Sports Area Ski Trail

Mondeau Nature Trail

Perkinstown Motorized Trail

Ice Age National Scenic Trail

rivers of melt water and debris beneath the glacier. Kettles are depressions in the earth's surface caused by melting ice chunks. Some of these filled with water to form small, deep lakes. Erratics are small rocks to 100+ ton boulders that were carried for many miles and left behind as glaciers melted. They derive their name from the erratic way they are scattered about the countryside.

Type of Landscape: Northern hardwood forest with gently rolling hills.

◆ Mondeaux Nature Trail

Length: 1.25 miles
Type: Hiking
Degree of Difficulty: Moderate
Trailhead: Start at the parking area at the Pines Picnic Area on the west side of the Mondeaux Flowage.
Description: This is a self-guided nature trail that follows an esker. There with signs along the way. It will take approximately 45 minutes to one hour to hike.
Points of Interest: Scenic overlooks and informative signs
Type of Landscape: Northern hardwood forest with scattered wetlands.

◆ Perkinstown Motorized Trail

Length: 20 miles
Type: ATV, horse, and mountain bike
Degree of Difficulty: Easy to moderate
Trailhead: The southern trailhead is located on Hwy 64, fourteen miles west of Medford. There is a small parking lot, vault toilet, and loading ramp. The northern trailhead is off FR 1417 at the Chippewa Campground boat landing parking lot on the Chequamegon Waters Flowage. Forest roads where the trail crosses also serve as trailheads.
Description: If you are interested in exploring the forest, the Perkinstown Motorized Trail is it. It is suitable for ATVs, snowmobiles, motorcycles, mountain biking, horseback riding, and foot travel. The trail, eight feet wide, has several interconnecting trails marked with orange diamonds and crosses several wooden bridges. The terrain ranges from

flat, low marsh areas and beaver ponds to upland forests with some relatively steep hills. A scenic overlook in the west provides a view of the Chequamegon Waters Flowage. Traffic travels both ways on the trail; caution is advised.

Points of Interest: Scenic vistas and wooden bridge crossings
Type of Landscape: Flat, low marsh areas to upland forests with some relatively steep hills.

◆ Perkinstown Winter Sports Area Mountain Bike Trail

Length: .7 to 2.5 miles long
Type: Mountain biking
Trailhead: Located at the Perkinstown Winter Sports Area Chalet.
Degree of Difficulty: Moderate
Description: Portions of the trail are open for mountain bikes. These include Trail Segments 361, 316, 318, and 318A.
Points of Interest: Scenic vistas
Type of Landscape: Flat, low wetlands to upland forests with some steep hills.

◆ Sitzmark Ski Trail

Length: .7 to 2.5 miles long
Type: Cross country skiing
Trailhead: Located at the Perkinstown Winter Sports Area Chalet.
Degree of Difficulty: Easy to Moderate
Description: One loop starts at the chalet and heads east, with several other loops west of FR 119.
Points of Interest: Scenic vistas
Type of Landscape: Low wetland areas to rolling hills.

◆ White Birch Trail

Length: 2 miles
Type: Hiking and hunter walking for the physically challenged
Degree of Difficulty: Easy to moderate
Trailhead: Take Cty E either north of Cty M or south of Cty D, then west on FR 102. The trail enters the north side of the Ice Age Semi-Primitive Area.

Description: While established as a hunter walking trail, it offers access to the forest for persons using wheelchairs. This trail has a slight grade, acceptable for motorized wheelchairs.
Points of Interest: Fourteen gravel turn-outs for hunting
Type of Landscape: Forest setting, with the trail having a slight grade.

Equestrian Trails

Horses can be ridden on the **Perkinstown Trail System**, the southern portion of the **Ice Age National Scenic Trail** below FR 116, and on **logging roads**. Horse trails are limited due to wet areas and easily-damaged soil types.

Mountain Bike Trails

Mountain bike trails are also limited in this District. Bikes can be ridden on the **Perkinstown Trail System**, **logging roads** and **selected trails at Perkinstown Winter Sports Area.**

The White Birch Hunter Walking Trail in the southeast corner of the Ice Age Semi-Primitive Area

Snowmobile Trails

The District has several developed snowmobile trails in the southwestern corner. The Forest maintains the land for the trails; local clubs are responsible for grooming, private property easements, and trail signage.

Information and trail maps are available from the Ranger District office, Taylor County Rec. Department, and the Medford Area Chamber of Commerce.

In general, snowmobile trails may change from year to year due to funding, private property easements, and other factors.

There are two state snowmobile corridors in this District:

◆ **State Trail 18** starts in Medford and heads west to enter the Forest just north of the intersection of Division and Center Avenues. The trail continues west until it joins the Perkinstown Trail System (Forest Trail 326) and State Trail 25.

◆ **State Trail 25** extends north of Clark County trails to Club Trail 73 just north of Hwy 64. It then travels west to connect to the Perkinstown Trail System just north of the Hwy 64 trailhead. It follows Forest Trail 326 until the Chippewa Campground, then continues around the north end of the flowage, where it turns west and exits the Forest as it heads to Hannibal.

Surrounding Area Facilities

Private Campgrounds

GILMAN

◆ **Miller Dam Resort:** Located east of Cty G on Memorial Drive at the dam; (715) 447-8274; 12 sites; on the Chequamegon Waters Flowage, 2,730 acres. There are electric hookups, and a boat landing. N4664 Cty G, Gilman, WI 54433.

Municipal Campgrounds

GILMAN

◆ **Gilman Village Campground:** Located on Cty B in Gilman; 15 sites; on the Yellow River. P.O. Box 157, Gilman, WI 54433.

MEDFORD

◆ **Medford Municipal Campground:** Located on River Road in Medford, on the west side of the mill pond, north of Hwy 64; on the Black River. There are RV hookups at the city park. 133 W State St., Medford, WI 54451; (715) 748-1187.

Boat Rentals

◆ **Miller Dam Resort**, (715) 447-8274, is located east of Cty G on Memorial Drive at the dam for the Chequamegon Waters Flowage.
◆ **Mondeaux Flowage Concession** is located at the north end of the flowage on FR 106.

Canoes and paddleboats are available for rent; (715) 427-5746.

Museums and Historical Sites

◆ **Taylor County Historical Society Museum** is located at the corner of Hwy 13 and Hwy 64 in the Multi-Purpose Building adjacent to the Taylor County Fairgrounds. Open Monday and Tuesday from 9 A.M. to 4 P.M. and Friday noon to 4 P.M. (715) 748-3808.

Scenic Drives

◆ **Rustic Road R-1** is a forest Rustic Road designated in Taylor County. From Westboro, go east on Cty D. The road is to the north, watch for signs.
◆ **Rustic Road R-62** is located east of Ogema (Hwy 13) on Hwy 86, then south on Cty C to Cty RR. It starts on Cty RR and extends to the east. This is also the road to Timm's Hill. The Rustic Road Board states "Although this rustic road is short in distance it is long in aesthetic quality."

Emergency Numbers

◆ **Sheriff**
Taylor County (715) 748-2200
Emergency 911, if prefix 748, 785, 678, 447, 668

◆ **Hospitals**
Memorial Hospital of Taylor County 135 S. Gibson St., Medford, WI 54451; (715) 748-2600

Other Information Contacts

◆ **County**
Taylor County Forestry Department, Courthouse, Medford, WI 54451; (715) 748-1486

◆ **State**
WI DNR, Medford Ranger Station, 660 Wheelock St., Medford, WI 54451; (715) 748-4955

◆ **Federal: U.S. Forest Service**
Medford Ranger District, 850 N. 8th, Hwy 13, Medford, WI 54451; (715) 748-4875, TTY (715) 748-4875

◆ **Chambers of Commerce**
Medford Area Chamber of Commerce, P.O. Box 172 Medford, WI 54451; (715) 748-4729
Taylor County Tourism Council, 224 Second Street South, Medford, WI 54451; (715) 748-3327

PARK FALLS

Ranger District

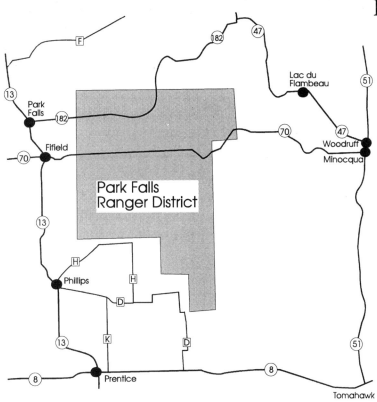

The **Park Falls Ranger District** covers more than 188,100 acres of land and water, of which 157,130 acres are federally owned. This is an area of low, rolling hills, wetlands, lakes, and the headwaters of several major river systems. The topography was formed by glaciers that passed this way some 10,000 years ago. Over time, great northern forests of aspen and birch, along with some stands of fir and pine, emerged. Several small areas of remnant virgin forest can still be seen today.

Notable points of interest are the South Fork of the Flambeau River, the historic Pike Lake Chain, Flambeau Trail System, Round Lake Log Driving Dam, Round Lake and Elk River Semi-Primitive Non-Motorized Areas, and Smith Rapids Covered Bridge.

The communities of Park Falls, Fifield, and Phillips lie to the west on Hwy 13. East of the District are the communities of Minocqua and Woodruff on Hwy 51, and Lac du Flambeau on Hwy 47.

FOR MORE INFORMATION ABOUT THIS AREA, CONTACT:

Park Falls Ranger District
1170 4th Avenue South
Park Falls, WI 54552
(715) 762-2461
TTY (715) 762-5701

THE FOREST

The **Park Falls Ranger District** is part of Wisconsin's Northern Highlands, formed when the Earth's bedrock rose to form a dome. This rise is the southern extent of what is called the Precambrian Canadian Shield. With elevations more than 1,400 feet above sea level, this region has the highest average elevation of land in the state. In some places, more than 100 feet of glacial till rests on top of the ancient bedrock, brought to the area during the Pleistocene Era—the Ice Age. Receding glaciers left an irregular landscape of gently rolling ground moraines, esker ridges, and sandy outwash areas. End moraines are delineated by hummocky hills and picturesque ridges.

At the end of the Ice Age, melting ice formed small depressions in the landscape and filled with water, creating hundreds of lakes and wetlands. Today, these lakes and wetlands support a wide variety of native flora and fauna, and have played an important role in providing recreational opportunities for Forest visitors. The majority of the lakes can be found north of Hwy 70 in pitted outwash areas.

The Park Falls Ranger District is north of the vegetation tension zone, where the warmer, southern forest gives way to the cooler northern hardwoods-conifers forest. The aspen, oak, and maple forests, along with scatterings of pine, hemlock, and other conifers, provide ideal conditions for observing nature and wildlife.

The headwaters of two river systems are found in the District. From the Pike Lake Chain, the South Branch of the Flambeau River extends westward toward Fifield. Further south, the Elk River has its headwaters in the Elk River Semi-Primitive Area. This river also extends in a westerly direction, where it joins with the Flambeau River.

Research Natural Areas

Research Natural Areas (RNAs) are designated to protect unique natural features or preserve examples of genetic diversity. RNAs are used primarily for research and education rather than public use.

◆ **Memorial Grove Research Natural Area**, 68 acres, can be reached by taking Hwy 70 east from Fifield or west from Minocqua to FR 143. An unmarked, roadside pull-off is on the north side of the highway, just east of Gerber (Turner Lake) Road. This old-growth hemlock forest is a small remnant of an ancient ecosystem. With its heavily shaded understory, large trees, downed logs, and abundant snags, it may provide visitors with their first close look at old-growth forest features. This is how northern Wisconsin looked before the clear-cutting and burning of the northern forest in the late 1800s and early 1900s.

Because this is a research natural area (RNA), and very sensitive to human impact, facilities are not provided. Easy access could lead to the area's demise. Visitors may catch a glimpse of these old hemlocks from the road, but are asked not to enter the area. Sites such as this represent a legacy that may never be repeated.

◆ **Tucker Lake Hemlock Research Natural Area**, 158 acres, can only be reached by foot. This RNA is surrounded by the Round Lake Semi-Primitive Non-Motorized Area. From Park Falls, travel east on Hwy 182 thirteen miles to FR 144, then south (right) five miles to FR 142, then north (left) three miles to FR 142C.

Special Forest Management Areas
Park Falls Ranger District

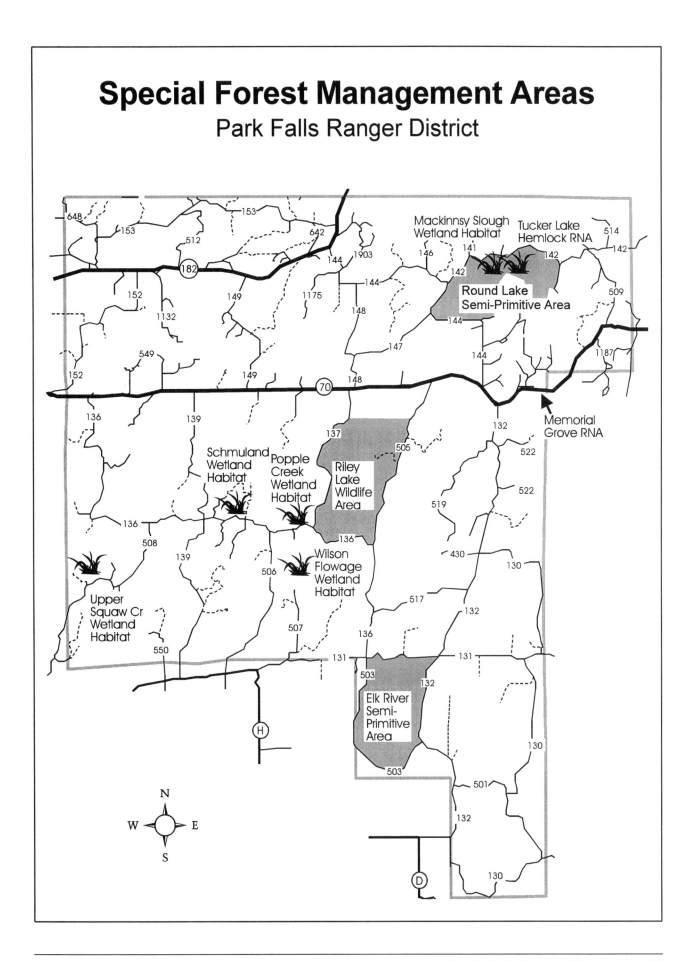

At the junction of FR 142 and the road leading into Twin Lakes Campground, there will be a hiking trail on the south side of the road that leads into the Round Lake Semi-Primitive Area. This Trail Segment (TS) connects with TS 175N. (*Please refer to the map on the Round Lake Semi-Primitive Area.*) Take this trail south and east to TS 175C, then south to Round Lake and TS 175. Follow TS 175 east to TS 175D. You are now at the southern end of the RNA. Trail segment 175D takes you through this crescent-shaped area of old-growth hemlock forest situated between two lakes. Tucker Lake can be reached by a canoe portage. Nesting eagles, loons, ospreys, waterfowl, and marsh birds frequent the region.

Semi-Primitive Non-Motorized Areas

◆ **Elk River Semi-Primitive Non-Motorized Area**, 4,350 acres, is a vast, lowland river valley bordered by ridges. Take Cty H east of Phillips about ten miles, then east on FR 131 four miles to FR 136. This is the northwestern corner of the semi-primitive area. The property is bordered by FR 131 on the north, FR 132 on the east, and FR 503 on the south and west.

This property is the least known and used semi-primitive area in the District. There is a dramatic change in elevation, in some places up to 200 feet. The Elk River—a Class I trout stream—forms a deeply dissected valley. The landscape is primarily old cedar and hemlock swamp, with some trees known to be more than 200 years old. Roads are unpaved and lined with an arched tree canopy, providing spectacular viewing of fall colors. In spring, visitors can look forward to an impressive display of wildflowers, such as trillium and spring beauty.

The Elk River Semi-Primitive Area provides a more challenging experience for Forest visitors. There are no facilities, so please come prepared.

◆ **Round Lake Semi-Primitive Non-Motorized Area**, 3,600 acres, is located in the northeastern corner of the District at the Vilas County line. Take Hwy 70 east from Fifield or west from Minocqua. At FR 144, travel north 2.5 miles to the southern edge of the semi-primitive area. The property is bordered by FR 144 on the south and west, FR 142 on the north and northwest, and FR 1182 on the east.

A host of recreational opportunities awaits visitors in a setting of extensive peat bogs interspersed with an aspen-birch forest. The area encompasses the northern half of Round Lake, along with three smaller lakes, Jupa, Oles, and Tucker. Also found here are the upper reaches of the South Fork of the Flambeau River and the Tucker Lake Hemlock RNA.

Eagles, ospreys, and loons are common nesters, giving ample opportunity for viewing by birdwatchers of all ages. Other recreational opportunities include primitive camping on Tucker Lake and the west shore of Round Lake, a picnicking area near the logging dam off FR 535, and canoeing the Flambeau River. Drinking water is not available. Ten miles of trails wind through the area, open to hiking and horseback riding in the summer, and cross-country skiing and snowshoeing in the winter. Being a non-motorized area, trails are not groomed.

In the past, this area was logged. As a result, this is a newer forest and some remnants of old logging roads remain. It does not offer as primitive an experience as the Elk River Semi-Primitive Area.

Wildlife Management Areas

◆ **Riley Lake Wildlife Management Area**, 5,000 acres, is located about twelve miles east of Fifield on Hwy 70, then south (right) on FR 137. The next six miles trace the western perimeter of the area to FR 136. Go east (left) for two miles to trace the southern perimeter to FR 505. Travel north (left) on FR 505 for six miles to circle the area and return to Hwy 70.

Round Lake Semi Primitive Area

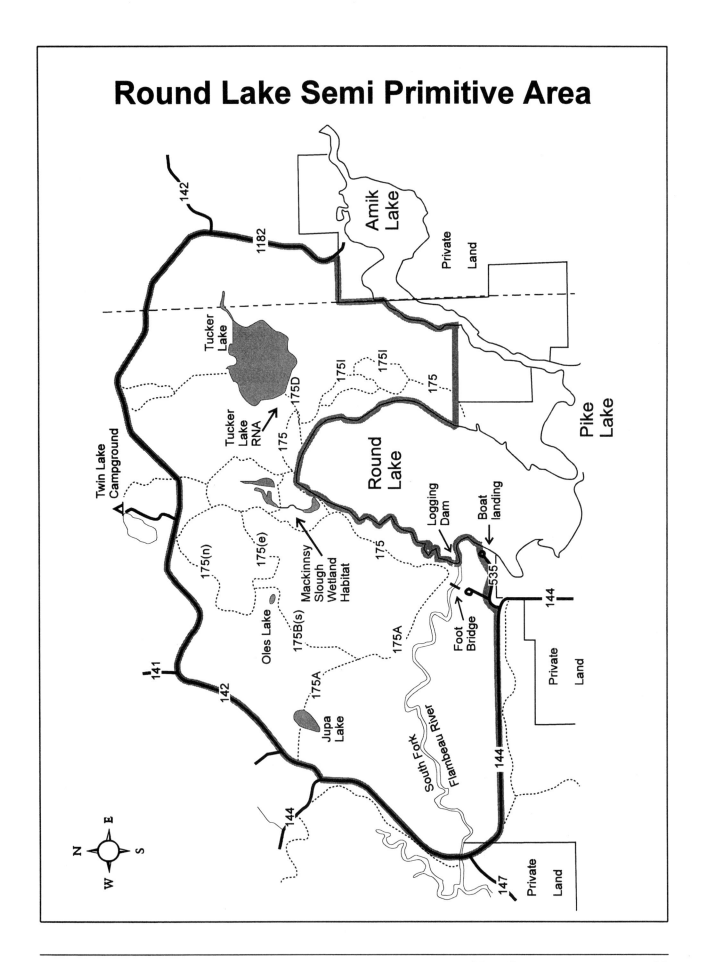

The Riley Lake Wildlife Area is an artifact of the logging era that is now managed as habitat for sharp-tailed grouse and other open-land wildlife species, such as northern harriers. The landscape is dominated by large, open space surrounded by a scattering of aspen, brush, and pioneer plants, such as blueberries and bracken fern. Open wetlands and peatlands contain black spruce, muskeg, and northern sedge meadows. Prominent hill-tops offer vistas of distant lakes and creeks.

The open landscape is maintained by controlled fires in the spring or fall, as conditions permit. A *very* rough (a true 4-wheel drive) road, FR 536, travels west of FR 505 to access the one interior lake (for which the area is named). FR 505 is a well-maintained gravel road open all year.

Because Forest roads encircle this area, there are ample opportunities for good wildlife observation from the comfort of your vehicle. Songbirds, hawks, court-ship rituals of sharp-tailed grouse, bear, deer, and other foragers can often be spotted. Its size and wild charac-ter also provide habitat for bobcat and timber wolves.

An information sign stands at the intersection of FR 137 and FR 136. There are no other facilities.

Wetland Habitat Areas

◆ **Mackinnsy Slough Wetland Area**, 89 acres, is located north of Hwy 70 on FR 144, then northeast on FR 142. Three impoundments are in the Round Lake Semi-Primitive Area, opposite the road to Twin Lake Campground. After parking at the Twin Lakes Campground, walk back to FR 142. Access to the area is by a short trail across the road, that leads to Trail Segment (TS) 175B, then east to TS 175C, then south. The three impoundments are to the east on a foot trail, about .5 miles from FR 142.

A 1.5-acre spring pond (originally developed in cooperation with Ducks Unlimited) and nearby stream were expanded into three small impound-ments. They are composed of marshy vegetation and open water, much like a beaver pond. A twelve-acre opening adjacent to the pond, offers an upland nesting area for migrating waterfowl.

◆ **Popple Creek Wetland Area**, 110 acres, is located south of Hwy 70 on FR 137, then just west (right) on FR 136 to the parking lot. The pond, located north of the parking lot, is a new impoundment on Popple Creek, which flows south from Riley Lake. While there is no de-veloped boat access, the impoundment is visible from the road and dam. The wetland is main-tained in a grass-scrub state surrounding open water and flooded timber. A watchable wildlife trail starts at the parking lot and travels south across a footbridge to Wilson Flowage. (*For more infor-mation on this trail, see the Trails section.*)

Popple Creek Wetland Area

◆ **Schmuland Wetland Area**, 81 acres, is located south of Hwy 70 on FR 139, then east about .5 miles on FR 136. This is a shallow, round lake surrounded by upland forests and approximately 30 percent marsh fringe. Carry-in access is on the west side. Aquatic vegetation is prominent throughout the lake. And as with other shallow lakes, there is a problem with fish kill conditions in the winter.

◆ **Upper Squaw Creek Flowage Wetland Area**, 150 acres, was built in 1960 in cooperation with the Wisconsin Department of Natural Resources. It is located south of Hwy 70 on FR 136, then south on FR 508, and then west on FR 518 to the containment dike. The flowage has a shoreline of tag alder-willow swamps and sedge meadows. A scenic point with large trees gives a sweeping view of the area. Dense, submerged vegetation can be found throughout the shallow flowage. Fish population is limited, due to the frequent winter kills caused by low oxygen levels.

◆ **Wilson Flowage Wetland Area**, 320 acres, is located south of Hwy 70 on FR 137, then just west on FR 136 to the Popple Creek parking lot. The flowage lies to the south. This long, narrow impoundment is a shallow, open-water lake, with abundant aquatic vegetation and a shoreline of tag alder-willow swamp. This new addition to the Forest was once under private ownership as a fish hatchery.

From the parking lot, a trail leads to the flowage. There are also several carry-in access points on the southeast shore. You will need to travel south on FR 506 to Cty H, then east until you reach FR 131. Travel east one mile on FR 131, then north about three miles on FR 507. The flowage will be to the west.

Wilson Flowage is managed for trophy northern pike, waterfowl, and associated wildlife. Bald eagles, otters, common loons, and other wildlife also benefit from the impoundment. Due to frequent winter kills, aerators are now installed to improve oxygen levels in the water, making trophy fishing possible.

Flickers—a type of large, spotted North American woodpecker—are common Forest visitors.

Wildlife

◆ **Birds**

Over 220 different species of birds may be found in the Forest at various times of the year. Birds may inhabit the Forest as permanent residents, migrate through the area each spring and fall, reappear every winter when the weather is too cold farther north in Canada, or reappear during the summer months to breed and raise their hatchlings.

To better your chance of seeing birds, it is important to understand their preferred habitat, food needs, and interaction with the environment. Binoculars, a bird guidebook, and a little luck all help.

◆ **Mammals**

The Forest is home to a variety of mammals, including fisher, white-tailed deer, black bear, bobcat, beaver, and snowshoe hare. Visitors may catch a rare glimpse of the eastern timber wolf or hear its calls at night.

An information sign at the Popple Creek Wetland Area provides visitors with an insight into beaver habitat.

Watchable Wildlife Areas

◆ **Popple Creek Wildlife Viewing Trail** (*Refer to the Trails section of this chapter for more information.*)

Hunting

Hunting is allowed on all National Forest lands, with the exception of developed campgrounds and special management areas. The District offers ideal habitat for ruffed grouse, common woodcock, white-tailed deer, and bear. Look for alder swamps interspersed with thick, pole-sized aspen during the early season. Proper identification of game animals is of the utmost importance, especially with coyotes. There is a pack of timber wolves in the area. It is easy to mistake a wolf for a coyote as the animals flash through the woods. Timber wolves are endangered in the State of Wisconsin and are a protected species.

Hunter Walking Trails

A number of hunter walking trails provide over seventeen miles of trails of quieter surroundings.

A popular hunting camp area is the **Elk River Semi-Primitive Non-Motorized Area**, a river valley bordered by ridges with access to vast lowlands. **No-trace camping is strongly encouraged at all hunting camps.**

◆ **East Fork of Hay Creek Hunter Walking Trail**, one mile long, is located one mile north of Hwy 182 on FR 512. This is a horseshoe-shaped trail that extends north to the creek.

◆ **Hay Creek Hunter Walking Trail**, one mile long, is located just east of Hay Creek on FR 152, east of Blockhouse Lake.

◆ **Lost Lake Hunter Walking Trail**, 1.3 miles long, is located south of Hwy 182 on FR 149 about 1.25 miles. The trail is to the southwest at a sharp, left-hand turn in the road.

◆ **Riley Creek Hunter Walking Trail**, 2.5 miles long, is located one mile east of FR 148 on Hwy 70, then south on Trail Segment 121. The trail extends to the southeast, where it ends in a large loop just west of the creek.

◆ **Sailor Creek Hunter Walking Trail**, two miles long, is located just south of Sailor Creek and west of FR 136, about one mile south of Hwy 70.

◆ **Squaw Creek Hunter Walking Trails**, seven miles long, are located south of Hwy 70 on FR 136. There are two trails, one on each side of Squaw Creek, which runs to FR 518.

◆ **Tracy Creek Hunter Walking Trail**, 1.3 miles long, is located about two miles south of Hwy 182 on FR 152. This lineal trail lies to the north and ends at a small-game opening.

◆ **Wintergreen Hike/Bike/Ski Trail** is located five miles east of Fifield on Hwy 70. Eight miles of trail are open to hunters.

Gathering of Forest Products

A woodland environment with forest openings is ideal for the growth and harvesting of numerous edible forest products. These include blackberries, raspberries, blueberries, mushrooms, and wintergreen. Berries and other pioneering plants are frequently found in large openings created by clear-cutting and prescribed burns, such as in the Riley Wildlife Area. Wintergreen can be found along shaded roads and trails.

Birdwatch:
Chequamegon's Winter Visitors and Spring/Fall Migrants

Listed below is a partial list of bird species that make their winter home in the Chequamegon National Forest.

Listed below is a partial list of bird species that migrate to the Chequamegon National Forest in the Spring and/or Fall.

Winter Visitors
Rough-legged Hawk
Golden Eagle
Snowy Owl
Northern Hawk-Owl
Great Gray Owl
Boreal Owl
Three-toed Woodpecker
Varied Thrush
Bohemian Waxwing
Northern Shrike
Snow Bunting
Pine Grosbeak
Common Redpoll
Hoary Redpoll

Spring/Fall Migrants
Horned Grebe
Great Egret
Black-crowned Night Heron
Tundra Swan
Snow Goose
Canada Goose
Northern Pintail
Northern Shoveler
American Wigeon
Canvasback
Redhead
Red-breasted Merganser
Ruddy Duck
Black-bellied Plover
Solitary Sandpiper

White-rumped Sandpiper
Pectoral Sandpiper
Ring-billed Gull
Herring Gull
Caspian Tern
Common Tern
Short-eared Owl
Grey-cheeked Thrush
Water Pipet
Philadelphia Vireo
Tennessee Warbler
Orange-crowned Warbler
American Tree Sparrow
Dark-eyed Junco
Rusty Blackbird
Pine Siskin

RECREATIONAL WATERS

Lakes

Within the border of the Park Falls Ranger District are 56 lakes, ranging in size from one to 806 acres. Most are north of Hwy 70. The northeast corner of the District is on the edge of the Northern Highland Lake District, including Round and Pike Lakes.

Below are some of the lakes within the District that have developed public boat launching facilities.

◆ Blockhouse Lake
Surface Area: 242 acres
Depth: Maximum 12 feet, mean 5 feet
Fishery: Northern pike and largemouth bass
Location: Six miles east of Park Falls on Hwy 182, then north on FR 153 to the boat landing on the northeast end of the lake.
Lake Conditions: The bottom is mainly sand and detritus; abundant vegetation can be found throughout the lake. Water is dark brown, with visibility down to two feet.
Shoreline: Seventy-five percent of the shore is mixed hardwoods and pine, and highly developed with many cottages. The remaining shoreline is wooded swamp and open marsh. Blockhouse Lake features an area of wild rice and nesting bald eagles.
Facilities: There is a boat landing, vault toilets, and a picnic table. An aerator helps prevent winter kill conditions.
Contour Map Available: Yes

◆ Emily Lake
Surface Area: 26 acres
Depth: Maximum 20 feet
Fishery: Northern pike, crappie, perch, and panfish
Location: Located in the extreme northeast corner of the District. From Hwy 70, take FR 509 north, then just east on FR 142 and north on FR 1178 to the lake.
Lake Conditions: The bottom is mainly sand with areas of mud. Water is dark brown, with visibility down to six feet.
Shoreline: The shoreline is a mix of forest and wetlands with no private development on the lake.
Facilities: There is a campground with drinking water and vault toilets near the landing.
Contour Map Available: Yes

◆ Newman Lake
Surface Area: 91 acres
Depth: Maximum 47 feet, mean 16 feet
Fishery: Largemouth bass, smallmouth bass, perch, and panfish
Location: From Hwy 182, take FR 144 southeast one mile, then north on FR 1903 to the lake.
Lake Conditions: The bottom is mainly sand and gravel with areas of detritus. Water is clear with visibility down to 16 feet. Aquatic vegetation is scattered along the shoreline.
Shoreline: Upland hardwoods and pine cover 65 percent of the shoreline; the remaining shoreline contains tamarack bogs. There are a number of private dwellings.
Facilities: There is a picnic area with drinking water, sandy swimming beach, playground and vault toilets. A large, T-shaped fishing dock can accommodate the physically challenged.
Contour Map Available: Yes

◆ Newman Springs
Surface Area: 7 acres
Depth: Maximum 15 feet, mean 6 feet
Fishery: Brook trout stocked annually
Location: Located just south of Hwy 182 and east of FR 645.

Lakes
Park Falls Ranger District

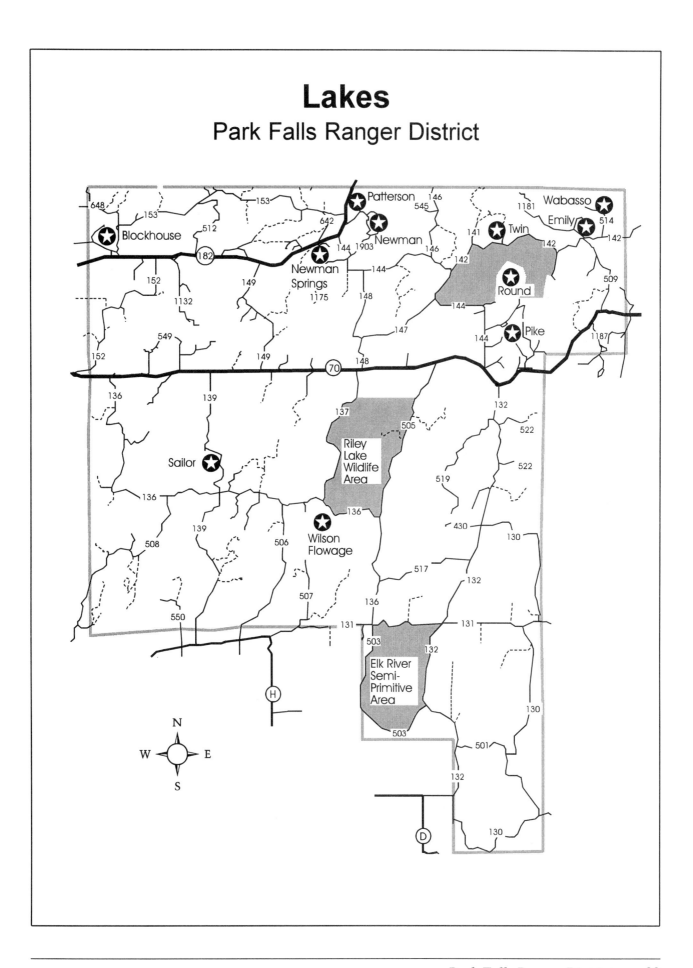

Lake Conditions: The bottom is about 12 percent gravel and rubble (north end), while the remaining bottom is made up of muck and detritus. Water is medium brown, with visibility to the bottom. Aquatic vegetation is scattered throughout the spring pond.

Shoreline: Except for the extreme south end, this spring pond is surrounded by tag alder-leatherleaf bog, with steep banks on the west and north sides behind the bog.

Facilities: A boat landing is on the north end, just off the parking lot on Hwy 182.

Contour Map Available: No

◆ Patterson Lake

Surface Area: 70 acres

Depth: Maximum 34 feet, mean 15 feet

Fishery: Trout and panfish stocked annually

Location: Located just east of Hwy 182, at the extreme north-central edge of the District.

Lake Conditions: The bottom is sand and gravel with small amounts of muck and rubble. Water is clear, with visibility down to ten feet. Aquatic vegetation is widely scattered throughout the lake.

Shoreline: Except for a small area of leatherleaf bog, the shoreline is made up of upland birch and aspen. There is one home visible from the lake on the north shore.

Facilities: A boat landing is on the northwest shore, east of Hwy 182

Contour Map Available: Yes

◆ Pike Lake

Surface Area: 879 acres

Depth: Maximum 17 feet, mean 11 feet

Fishery: Walleye, musky, northern pike, largemouth bass, smallmouth bass, crappie, and panfish

Location: From Hwy 70, travel 1.5 miles north on FR 144, turn right at Thorofare Road to the public landing on Round Lake. You need to go through Round Lake to get into Pike Lake.

Lake Conditions: Eighty percent of the bottom is sand, gravel and rubble, while the remaining twenty percent is muck. Water is medium brown, with visibility down to three feet. Aquatic vegetation is scattered along the shoreline.

Shoreline: Upland hardwoods, conifers, and several small tag alder-willow swamps make up 95 percent of the shore. The shoreline is well developed. Access to Pike, Turner, and Amik Lakes is through a small channel passing under Thorofare Road on the southeast corner of Round Lake.

Facilities: Several resorts on the lake may offer facilities.

Contour Map Available: Yes

◆ Round Lake

Surface Area: 726 acres

Depth: Maximum 24 feet, mean 16 feet

Fishery: Walleye, musky, northern pike, largemouth bass, smallmouth bass, crappie, perch, and panfish

Location: From Hwy 70, travel two miles north on FR 144, then right on FR 535 to the landing.

Lake Conditions: Bottom conditions are mainly sand and gravel, with minimal amounts of muck. Water is medium brown, with visibility down to five feet. Aquatic vegetation is common throughout the lake.

Shoreline: Ninety-eight percent of the lake is upland forest with mixed northern hardwoods and planted pines. The northern two-thirds of Round Lake lie within the Forest boundary. The southern third is privately owned and well developed. Access to Pike, Turner, and Amik Lakes is through a small channel passing under Thorofare Road, on the southeast corner of Round Lake.

Facilities: A boat landing, picnic area, and parking lot are located on FR 535. Several resorts on the lake may offer other facilities. A second, public owned boat landing can be found on the east shore, off Thorofare Road.

Contour Map Available: Yes

◆ Sailor Lake

Surface Area: 170 acres
Depth: Maximum 7 feet, mean 5 feet
Fishery: Northern pike, largemouth bass, perch, and panfish
Location: Located in the west central area of the District off Hwy 70. Travel three miles south on FR 139.
Lake Conditions: The bottom is a mix of muck, sand, gravel and boulders. Water is medium brown, with visibility down to three feet. Aquatic vegetation can be found throughout the lake. To help improve the fishery, trees have been cut and dropped in the water along the shore. An aerator was added to minimize winter kill conditions.
Shoreline: Seventy percent upland forest of mixed hardwoods with many large trees. The majority of the shoreline is publicly owned.
Facilities: Facilities include a campground, picnic area, drinking water, and vault toilets. There is also a sandy swimming area, but no marked beach.
Contour Map Available: Yes

◆ Twin Lakes

Surface Area: 19 acres
Depth: Maximum 16 feet, mean 7 feet
Fishery: Largemouth bass, crappie, perch, and panfish. Trout are stocked annually.
Location: Located in the northeast corner of the District. From Hwy 70, travel north on FR 144, then east on FR 142 about two miles.
Lake Conditions: The bottom is muck, sand, gravel, and rubble. Water is clear, with visibility down to ten feet. Aquatic vegetation can be found throughout the lake.
Shoreline: Except for three small leatherleaf bogs, ninety percent of the shore is lined with upland hardwoods and pines. The lake has a sandy edge and is very scenic.
Facilities: A boat landing is next to a campground with vault toilets and drinking water. A solar-powered aerator helps to prevent winter fish kills.
Contour Map Available: Yes

◆ Wabasso Lake

Surface Area: 49 acres
Depth: Maximum 18 feet
Fishery: Northern pike, largemouth bass, perch, and panfish
Location: Located in the northeast corner of the District. From Hwy 70 travel north on FR 509, then east on FR 142 about one mile, then north on FR 514 to the lake.
Lake Conditions: The bottom is sand with small amounts of rock and mud. Visibility is down to eleven feet.
Shoreline: A mix of upland forest and wetlands with no development on the lake, except for the campground.
Facilities: A boat landing is at the day use picnic area. No internal combustion engines allowed on this lake.
Contour Map Available: Yes

◆ Wilson Flowage

Surface Area: 289 acres
Depth: Maximum 11 feet, mean 6 feet
Fishery: Perch, trophy northern pike, and black crappie
Location: Located in the south central area of the District. Travel about five miles south of Hwy 70 on FR 137, and just west on FR 136.
Lake Conditions: The bottom is muck with abundant aquatic vegetation. Water is dark brown, with visibility down to four feet.
Shoreline: The shoreline is tag alder-willow swamp.
Facilities: Carry-in boat access on the northwest and southeast ends of the lake. An aerator was added to help prevent winter fish kills.
Contour Map Available: No

South Fork of the Flambeau River

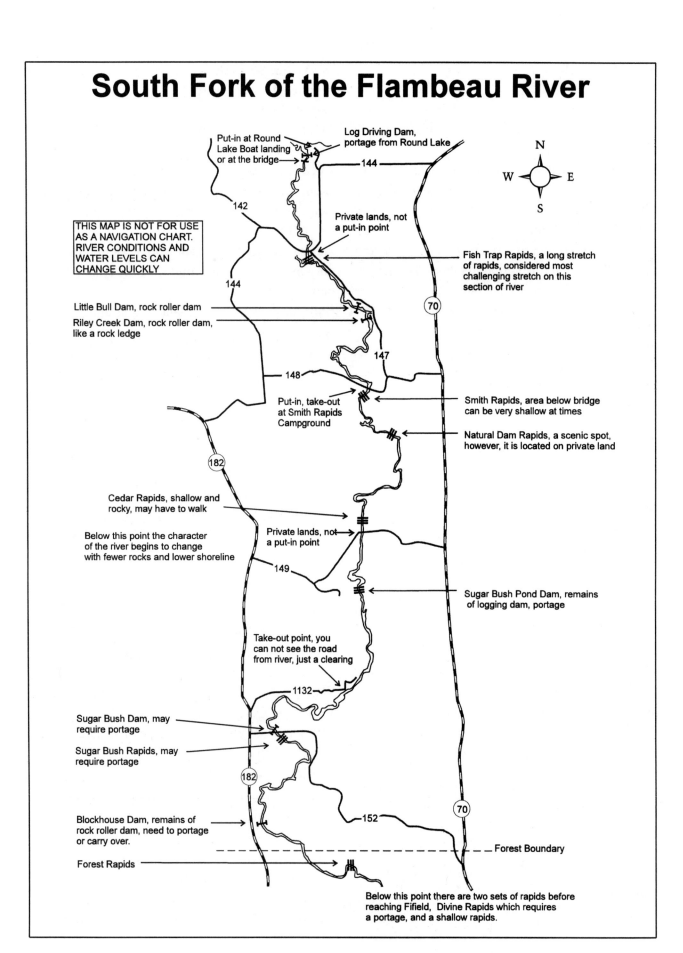

THIS MAP IS NOT FOR USE AS A NAVIGATION CHART. RIVER CONDITIONS AND WATER LEVELS CAN CHANGE QUICKLY

Put-in at Round Lake Boat landing or at the bridge

Log Driving Dam, portage from Round Lake

144

142

Private lands, not a put-in point

Fish Trap Rapids, a long stretch of rapids, considered most challenging stretch on this section of river

144

Little Bull Dam, rock roller dam

Riley Creek Dam, rock roller dam, like a rock ledge

70

147

148

Put-in, take-out at Smith Rapids Campground

Smith Rapids, area below bridge can be very shallow at times

Natural Dam Rapids, a scenic spot, however, it is located on private land

182

Cedar Rapids, shallow and rocky, may have to walk

Below this point the character of the river begins to change with fewer rocks and lower shoreline

Private lands, not a put-in point

149

Sugar Bush Pond Dam, remains of logging dam, portage

Take-out point, you can not see the road from river, just a clearing

1132

Sugar Bush Dam, may require portage

Sugar Bush Rapids, may require portage

182

Blockhouse Dam, remains of rock roller dam, need to portage or carry over.

152

70

Forest Boundary

Forest Rapids

Below this point there are two sets of rapids before reaching Fifield, Divine Rapids which requires a portage, and a shallow rapids.

Walk-In Lakes

Below are two lakes in the District which only have walk-in access.

◆ Jupa Lake

Surface Area: 9.5 acres
Depth: Maximum 13 feet
Fishery: Largemouth bass, perch, pike, and panfish
Location: Located north of Hwy 70 on FR 144 in the Round Lake Semi-Primitive Non-Motorized Area. Continue north on FR 142 for .12 miles. Take Trail Segment 175A to the east for .12 miles to reach the lake.
Lake Conditions: Bottom conditions are muck with little aquatic vegetation. Visibility is down to three feet. The lake has experienced winter kills.
Shoreline: The shore is spruce-tamarack bog.
Facilities: Carry-in access
Contour Map Available: No

◆ Tucker Lake

Surface Area: 118 acres
Depth: Maximum 32 feet, mean 14 feet
Fishery: Largemouth bass, black crappie, and bluegill
Location: Located north of Hwy 70 on FR 144 in the Round Lake Semi-Primitive Non-Motorized Area. Continue northeast on FR 142 to the trailhead opposite the road to Twin Lake Campground. You will need to follow Trail Segment (TS) 175C southeast, then TS 175 to TS 175D. It is about .75 miles to the lake.
Lake Conditions: Bottom conditions are mostly gravel with 15 percent muck. A shallow gravel bar lies in the middle of the lake. Water is light brown, with visibility down to ten feet. Aquatic vegetation is scattered throughout the lake.
Shoreline: Upland forest with some large trees make up 84 percent of the shore with spruce, tamarack, leatherleaf, tag alder bogs making up the rest.
Facilities: Carry-in access, no motors permitted. Tucker Lake can be reached by canoeing Tucker

Creek for those willing to portage over beaver dams.
Contour Map Available: No

Rivers

◆ South Fork of the Flambeau River

Length: 55 miles, about 24 miles lie within the Forest boundary
Gradient, Average: Three foot drop per mile
Fishery: Walleye, northern pike, musky, smallmouth bass, perch, and panfish
Description: Located in the northern half of the Forest and flows from the west side of Round Lake. Approximately twenty- four miles of the river wind through the Chequamegon National Forest. Along the route, you will encounter many points of interest, including the newly constructed Smith Rapids Covered Bridge, nesting and feeding bald eagles, a memorable trip through Fishtrap Rapids, remnants of the Sugar Bush Dam, scenic tree-lined shores, and islands of grass.

This river provides a rustic experience for canoeists. There are a number of Class I and Class II rapids and old logging river structures require some skill to navigate. There are six rapids and six dams along the way. Several old logging dams can be navigated. The character of the river changes with fluctuating water levels and can sometimes be dangerous, especially during spring thaw, when water levels are at their peak. Canoeists will pass along private property, and need to be respectful of docks and shorelines when choosing rest stops. Please use *low-impact camping*, (packing out what you packed in and leaving the area as you found it). There is an established picnic area at Round Lake Semi-Primitive Area. A campground, drinking water, and vault toilets are provided at Smith Rapids.
Access Points: Round Lake is the headwaters of the South Fork. Canoeists may access the river from the Round Lake Boat Landing, or carry in from the Round Lake Dam parking lot, both located along FR 535. To reach the access points from

Fifield, travel seventeen miles east on Hwy 70, then north (left) on FR 144 two miles, and then east on FR 535. There will be a dirt road to the north that takes you near the river, below the dam. You can also continue east on FR 535 to the boat landing on Round Lake. (Those who launch at Round Lake Boat Landing have to portage around the Round Lake Logging Dam.)

For a shorter trip, you can also launch at the Smith Rapids Campground. From Fifield, travel east thirteen miles on Hwy 70, then north on FR 148 for 2.5 miles to the Smith Rapids Campground. The river can also be accessed off FR 152 and FR 1132.

*Historical Note: During the late 1800s, the South Fork of the Flambeau was used to float pine logs to waiting sawmills downstream.

◆ **Squaw Creek**
Length: 6.5 miles
Gradient, Average: Two feet drop per mile
Fishery: Northern pike, largemouth bass, smallmouth bass, perch, and panfish
Description: This is a wide, deep, slow-moving, warm water stream that drains Squaw Lake into Pike Lake, and eventually enters the South Fork of the Flambeau River. The stream bank has a natural cover and averages 40 feet wide. Wild rice patches can be found along sections of the creek. Some obstructions, such as beaver dams, may be encountered.

The creek starts at the north end of Squaw Lake. After passing over a two foot dam, the creek travels north about 1.5 miles, where it passes over a small rock dam, then under Hwy 70. Squaw Creek then turns in a southwesterly direction and roughly parallels Hwy 70 for the next four miles before turning in a northwesterly direction for one mile until it enters Pike Lake. While the creek is within the Park Falls District, only a small portion of the shore is publicly owned. This route provides a more rustic and primitive experience.
Location: Located in the northeast section of the District. Squaw Creek flows from the north end of Squaw Lake north and west to Pike Lake.
Access Points: The creek can be accessed from Pike Lake, FR 143, Hwy 70, and the Squaw Lake boat landing on West Squaw Lake Road.
Facilities: Boat landings on Squaw Lake and Round Lake.

Trout Streams

The Park Falls District has sixteen streams (six Class I trout waters). Ten have access by road crossings. The main fish species of these streams is brook trout. Two of the more noted streams are **Elk River** and **Foulds Creek**.

POINTS OF INTEREST

Auto Tours

◆ **Fall Color Tour** covers 28 miles of rustic forest through the Park Falls District, with trees forming a canopy over the road. The fall colors of the northern hardwoods are spectacular. Bright red maples are a highlight.

Take Hwy 70 about fifteen miles east of Fifield, then south on FR 505. FR 505 will be along the eastern edge of the Riley Lake Wildlife Management Area. Continue south on FR 136 to FR 503.

This is the boundary road along the Elk River Semi-Primitive Area. This road will loop around to the east, joining FR 132. Continue north on FR 132. You will leave the Elk River Semi-Primitive Area when you cross FR 131. Continue north on FR 132 to Hwy 70. From here you can turn right to Minocqua or left to Fifield.

◆ **South Fork of the Flambeau River Auto Tour** covers twenty miles of paved state and county highways, and graveled Forest roads to link key attractions in the Park Falls District.

QUICK REFERENCE
Auto Tour Highlights
Within the Park Falls Ranger District

Fall Color Tour
Length: 28 miles
Highlights
    Fall Colors in Rustic Forest
    Riley Lake Wildlife Management Area
    Elk River Semi-Primitive Area

South Fork of the Flambeau River Auto Tour
Length: 20 miles
Highlights
    Riley Creek CCC Camp
    Garden Club Plantation
    Memorial Grove Research Natural Area
    Round Lake Semi-Primitive Area
    Round Lake Logging Dam
    Newman Lake Picnic Area

    Smith Rapids Campground
    Smith Rapids Covered Bridge

Wetlands and Wildlife Auto Tour
Length: 30 miles
Highlights
    Wilson Flowage
    Upper Squaw Creek Wetland Area
    Schmuland Wetland Area
    Popple Creek Wetland Area
    Riley Lake Wildlife Management Area
    Twin Lakes Campground
    MacKinnsy Slough Wetland Area
    Tucker Lake

Points of Interest
Park Falls Ranger District

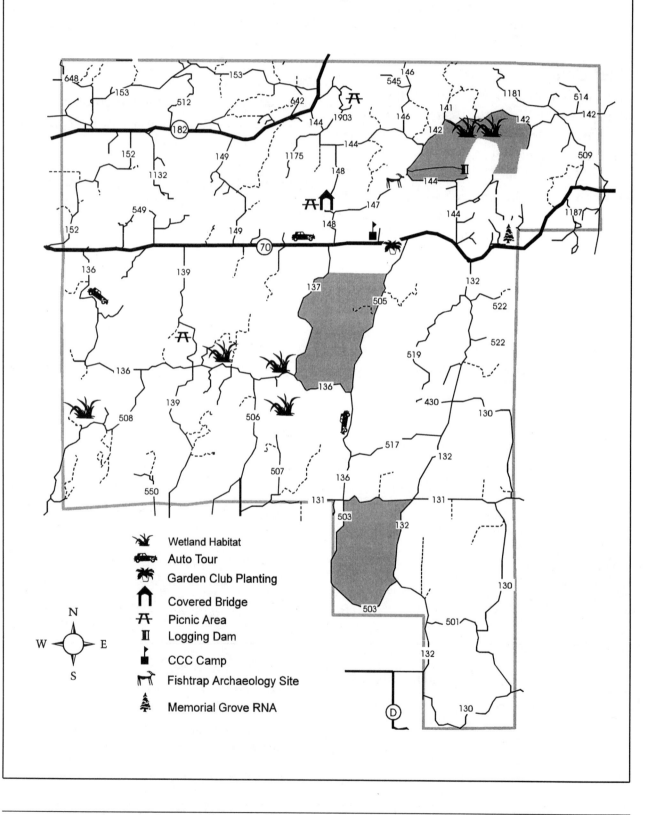

Wetland Habitat
Auto Tour
Garden Club Planting
Covered Bridge
Picnic Area
Logging Dam
CCC Camp
Fishtrap Archaeology Site
Memorial Grove RNA

N
W   E
S

Visitors may begin at any point and use the tour to become familiar with the history, recreational areas, and activities available in the District. The tour also gives visitors a scenic look at the fall colors and breathtaking winter scenery of the Chequamegon National Forest. For a longer tour, this can be easily combined with the Wetlands and Wildlife Auto Tour.

The suggested starting point is the corner of FR 148 and Hwy 70, located about thirteen miles east of Fifield. Proceed east on Hwy 70 for about 1.5 miles. You will pass the site of the Riley Creek CCC Camp on the north side of the road. There is a sign commemorating this historic site. Just east of the creek on the south side of the road is the Garden Club Plantation, which was planted with red pine in 1985.

Continue east about 4.5 miles to Memorial Grove Research Natural Area turn-off. This is located just east of Gerber (Turner Lake) Road on the north side of road. An old hemlock stand is visible from the road. You are asked to observe these beautiful trees from your vehicle and not tread into the forest.

Retrace your route on Hwy 70 west two miles to FR 144. Turn north (right) two miles to Round Lake Semi-Primitive Area and Round Lake Logging Dam. Turn right on FR 535, then take the first gravel road north to the trailhead, which leads to the dam and the headwaters of the South Fork of the Flambeau River. You can continue east on FR 535 to the boat landing for a view of expansive Round Lake.

Retrace your route to FR 144, turn north (right) and travel three miles to FR 148. At this point you can continue one mile west to FR 1903, which leads to Newman Lake Picnic Area, or turn south (left) to Smith Rapids Campground, and the unique Smith Rapids Covered Bridge on the Flambeau River. From this point continue south on FR 148 2.5 miles to your starting point on Hwy 70.

◆ **Wetlands and Wildlife Auto Tour** follows graveled and paved Forest roads for thirty miles to five developed wetlands and one wildlife management area in the heart of the Park Falls District. Created by the placement of a small dam, these wetland impoundments provide valuable habitat for a variety of wildlife. Visitors have driving access to Squaw Creek and Schmuland Impoundments, and a short walking trail to reach Wilson Flowage. Riley Lake Wildlife Management Area is accessible by a road along the western edge. Visitors will also be treated to scenic views and glimpses of migrating waterfowl, great blue herons, kingfishers, furbearers and other wetland users. The chance of seeing wildlife is high in these quiet, well-forested areas.

From Fifield, travel east about four miles on Hwy 70, then south on FR 136 seven miles, then south (right) onto FR 508, then west (left) on FR 518 to Upper Squaw Creek Wetland Area. Retrace your route to FR 136. Turn east (right) on FR 136 and continue east about 2.5 miles. Schmuland Wetland Area is on the north side of the road.

Continue east for about three miles to the parking lot on Popple Creek, which is just west of FR 137. Popple Creek Wetland Area will be visible to the north. The watchable wildlife trail goes to the south along the creek to Wilson Flowage.

Continue east on FR 136, then north on FR 137. Riley Lake Wildlife Management Area will be on the east for the next four miles. When FR 137 reaches Hwy 70, turn east (right) and travel to FR 144. Then turn north and continue on FR 144 two miles to FR 142. Follow FR 142 north three miles to Twin Lakes Campground. There is a trail at the junction of Twin Lake Campground Road and FR 142 that leads south into the semi-primitive area to MacKinnsy Slough Wetland Area and Tucker Lake. Retrace your route to Hwy 70. You can either turn west (right) to Fifield, or turn east (left) to Minocqua and Woodruff.

A Forest road map, binoculars, and a bird guidebook are helpful aids and are highly recommended.

Civilian Conservation Corps Camps

There were a number of CCC camps in the Park Falls Ranger District. These include:

◆ **Camp Riley Creek F-3, Company 642**, Fifield, is located on the west side of Riley Creek, about one mile east of FR 148, and on the north side of Hwy 70. A sign along Hwy 70 commemorates the men who lived at the camp from 1933 to 1942.

◆ **Camp Sailor Lake F-7, Company 651**, Fifield

◆ **Camp Sheep Ranch F-4, Company 644**, Phillips

Picnic Areas

◆ Newman Lake Picnic Area

Location: From Park Falls, travel east on Hwy 182 thirteen miles, then one mile southeast (right) on FR 144 to FR 1903. Turn northeast (left) and follow FR 1903 one mile to Newman Lake Recreation Area.

Description: Newman Lake's clear water makes it one of the most popular picnic and beach sites in the District. It was renovated in 1993-94. The picnic area stretches along the southern end of the lake.

Facilities: Facilities include forested picnic sites, sand beach, marked swimming area, vault toilets, changehouses, historic picnic shelter (built by the CCC in the 1930s), horseshoe and volleyball areas, playground, shoreline trail, fishing pier (*accessible to the physically challenged*), boat landing, and seasonal drinking water. The picnic shelter may be reserved for group use by contacting the Ranger District Office at (715) 762-3294.

◆ Sailor Lake Picnic Area

Location: From Fifield, travel Hwy 70 east eight miles, then three miles south (right) on FR 139 to the entrance of Sailor Lake Picnic Area.

Description: Adjacent to the Flambeau Multi-Purpose Trail System and Sailor Lake Campground, this picnic area is popular with mountain bikers, ATV riders, and fall hunters. A spur off the main trail leads to the Flambeau Trail System.

Facilities: A large, open shelter has a scenic view of Sailor Lake and may be reserved for group use by contacting the Ranger District Office at (715) 762-3294. Other facilities include a boat landing, shady open space, seasonal drinking water, vault toilets, ATV ramp, and an unmarked, sandy swimming area.

◆ Smith Rapids Picnic Area

Location: From Fifield, travel east on Hwy 70 about thirteen miles, then 2.5 miles north (left) on FR 148 to Smith Rapids Campground and Day Use Area.

Description: Smith Rapids is a popular spot for picnicking because of its scenic view of the South Fork of the Flambeau River and its unique covered bridge, one of only two in Wisconsin. An open picnic shelter is located within the campground.

Facilities: Smith Rapids is specifically tailored to accommodate horseback riders. Facilities include seasonal drinking water, picnic sites with tables and grills, vault toilets, and the River Saddle Trail that begins along the river, north of the covered bridge.

Spots off the Beaten Path

With hundreds of square miles of space in the Park Falls Ranger District, there are countless places that would make an ideal spot for a quiet, picnic outing. Picnic tables are provided. Here are just a few.

◆ **Blockhouse Lake Boat Landing**

◆ **Elk River Semi-Primitive Area**

Round Lake Logging Dam. Ongoing efforts are being made to restore this historic log driving dam on the South Fork of the Flambeau River.

◆ **Patterson Lake Boat Landing**

◆ **Round Lake Boat Access** at the south end of Round Lake Semi-Primitive Area

◆ **Wintergreen Trailhead**

◆ **Wabasso Lake Boat Landing**

Structures and Landmarks

◆ **Fishtrap Archaeology Site 4** is located on the corner of FR 144 and FR 147, just west of Round Lake. This Flambeau-Springstead prehistoric site was first recorded in 1978, when reported to the Forest by local collectors. There have been three "digs" at the site, uncovering many interesting facts about the people who once lived in the area. Projectile points, which appear to date back to late Paleo-Indians around 9,000 B.C. to 5,000 B.C., are among the artifacts found so far. Other

items, including pottery shards, native copper artifacts, quartz cores, animal bones, and hundreds of quartz flakes, were also unearthed. Radiocarbon dating of soil sediments and animal remains indicate the site was also occupied between 1,000 and 1,100 years ago. These dates point at the Middle Woodland Period of the western Great Lakes prehistory.

Another very interesting fact was the discovery of the type of stone used to make artifacts. The raw material came from Minnesota siltstone, North Dakota flint, and Hixton silicified sandstone from southern Wisconsin. This supports the theory that an extensive trade network existed between tribes thousands of years ago.

As with any archaeological site, collecting by the public is not permitted and is a federal offense. If you are interested in participating as a volunteer in the Passport in Time excavation program, contact the Forest Headquarters.

◆ **Garden Club Planting** is located on the south side of Hwy 70, 1.5 miles east of FR 148. The trees in this area had been harvested, and in 1985, the Wisconsin Garden Club Federation donated funds to replant the area in red pines. Today, you are able to see a young, growing forest, replacing the harvested trees.

◆ **Round Lake Logging Dam** is located about seventeen miles east of Fifield on Hwy 70, then north 2.5 miles on Round Lake Dam Road

(FR 144), then turn east (right) on FR 535. About .25 miles in is a gravel road to the north, that will lead you to a trailhead and a route to the dam. There is a walking bridge over the Flambeau River and a trail that goes to the dam.

This dam was built in 1878 so that Round Lake could be a reservoir for spring logging drives. During the winter, trees were cut, hauled by sleigh to the lake, and stacked on the ice above the dam. When spring breakup came, the dam would be opened to sluice (flush) the logs through the dam and down the river on a wall of water. This was an economical way to move needed logs to sawmills downstream.

The dam was last used between 1909-14. Nominated in 1981 to the **National Register of Historic Places**, the dam serves as a reminder of our culture and the difficulty of moving timber to market in the 19th century. Today, the Round Lake Logging Dam is being restored through a Challenge Cost Share program. The dam was dismantled by hand in September, 1992. Individual pieces were inspected for historical significance and structure soundness for reuse in the restoration. The project is expected to be completed in 1995 by volunteers and Park Falls Ranger District personnel.

Smith Rapids Covered Bridge, the favorite spot of many Forest visitors, is one of the most picturesque sites in the Chequamegon National Forest.

◆ **Smith Rapids Covered Bridge** is located about thirteen miles east of Fifield on Hwy 70, then two miles north on FR 148. It is the first authentic, covered vehicle bridge constructed in the state in the 20th century. Smith Rapids Bridge is over 80 feet long, creating a clear span over the river and permitting unobstructed flow of the river for recreational canoeists. The bridge replaced an old, three-span, timber-girder bridge.

Modern materials were used in the construction of this 100 year-old design. The **Town Lattice Truss design** was chosen to give an aesthetically pleasing, yet functional bridge for the rural, wooded setting. This was an important consideration because of the status of the river as a candidate for a National Scenic Riverway. In the construction of bridge components, glued-laminated, CCA and Penta-treated wood was used. The lamination process helps eliminate flaws that may occur in dimensional timbers and creates a strong, stable framework.

CAMPGROUNDS

Established Campgrounds

There are four campgrounds in the Park Falls Ranger District. Except for Sailor Lake, all Forest campgrounds are north of Hwy 70. Campground hosts are available at some of the campgrounds during the summer months to welcome you and answer questions.

◆ Emily Lake Campground
Location: From Hwy 70, on the eastern edge of the District, take FR 509 north three miles, then turn east (right) on FR 142 for one-fourth mile to FR 5178, then north to the campground.
Number of sites: Ten rustic sites
Facilities: Picnic tables, parking spurs, fire grills, boat landing, vault toilets, and drinking water are provided. There is an unmarked swimming area.
Description: This is a quiet, more rustic setting. Emily Lake Campground is often used by people visiting the Lac du Flambeau Reservation, since it is only a few miles west of Lac du Flambeau.
Reservations and Fee: All sites are on a first-come, first-serve basis with a $6 fee. Open from the end of May to mid-October.

◆ Sailor Lake Campground
Location: Located in the southwestern part of the District. Take FR 139 three miles south of Hwy 70.
Number of Sites: Twenty moderately developed sites that can accommodate RVs up to 35 feet
Facilities: These shady sites each have a parking spur, fire grill, and picnic table. There is also a developed boat landing, picnic area, scenic picnic shelter, a trail spur to the Flambeau Trail System, an ATV ramp, and an unmarked swimming area.
Description: This campground gets a lot of use from fall hunters and people using the Flambeau Trail System.
Reservations and Fees: All sites are on a first-come, first-serve basis with a $6 fee. Open from the end of May to mid-October.

◆ Smith Rapids Campground
Location: Located in the middle of the District. Take FR 148 two miles north of Hwy 70. The campground is to the west, just before the covered bridge.
Number of Sites: Thirteen, nine of which are specially designed for equestrian campers
Facilities: Each site has a hitching rail, picnic table, and fire grill along with boat access to the South Fork of the Flambeau River, vault toilets, picnic shelter, and drinking water.
Description: Located in view of the covered bridge, this is an ideal focal spot for horseback riding, fishing the river, hiking, and canoeing.
Reservations and Fees: All sites are on a first-come, first-serve basis with a $6 fee. Open from the end of May to mid-October.

◆ Twin Lakes Campground
Location: From Hwy 70, on the eastern edge of the District, take FR 509 north three miles, then three miles west (left) on FR 142 to the campground.
Number of sites: Seventeen moderately developed sites (two designed for the physically challenged)
Facilities: Parking spurs, picnic tables, fire grills, boat landing, small sandy beach, vault toilets, and drinking water are provided.
Description: This is a family campground that has been upgraded with a paved road and new toilets. All facilities are designed to be accessible.

Campgrounds
Park Falls Ranger District

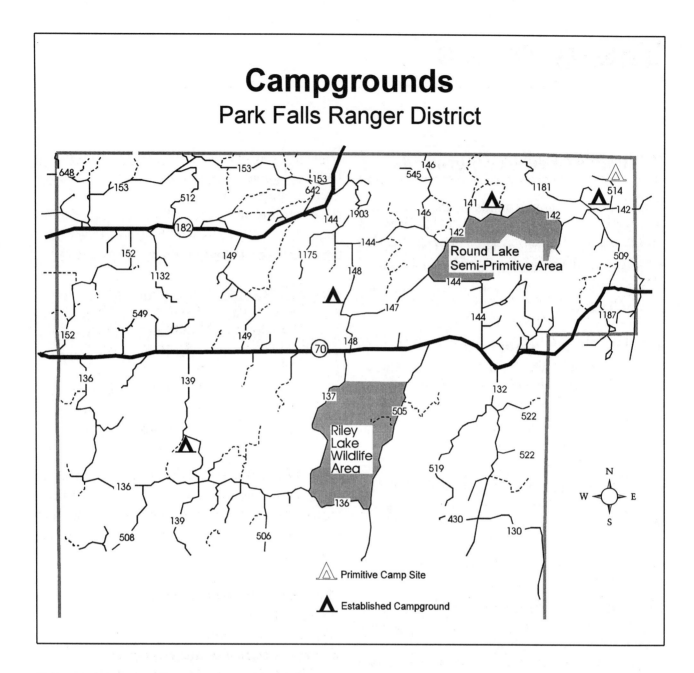

648 153 153 512 182 153 642 144 1903 545 146 146 141 1181 142 514 142
152 149 1175 144 144 142 509
1132 148 Round Lake Semi-Primitive Area 144 1187
549 147 144
152 149 70 148 132
136 139 137 522
505 519 522
Riley Lake Wildlife Area
136 130 430
136 508 139 506

⌂ Primitive Camp Site

▲ Established Campground

N W E S

Reservations and Fees: All sites are on a first-come first-serve basis with a $6 fee. Open from the end of May to mid-October.

Dispersed Camping

If you are looking to find an ideal out-of-the-way campsite for a more primitive experience, all Forest lands are open for dispersed camping except established campgrounds and other designated areas. Several of the more popular areas for dispersed camping include: **Elk River Semi-Primitive Non-Motorized Area**, **Patterson Lake** at the boat landings, and the **Round Lake Semi-Primitive Non-Motorized Area**, one site on the west shore and one spot on the south shore of Tucker Lake.

◆ **Wabasso Lake Campground** will be converted to a "new" primitive camping area in 1995, with two undeveloped sites accessible by canoe or walk-in. It is an excellent panfish lake.

TRAILS

◆ Flambeau Trail System

Length: 60 miles open to ATV, motorcycle, snowmobile use

Type: Multiple-use, motorized and non-motorized. Trails are closed to 2- and 4-wheel drive vehicles.

Degree of Difficulty: Easy to moderate

Trailheads:

Blockhouse Lake Access is located 1.5 miles north of Hwy 182 on FR 153.

Highway 182 Access is nine miles east of Park Falls on Hwy 182 to FR 523.

Round Lake Boat Access is north of Hwy 70 on FR 144 approximately two miles, then east (right) on FR 535.

Sailor Lake Access is south of Hwy 70 on FR 139 three miles.

Wintergreen Access is five miles east of Fifield on Hwy 70.

Description: The Flambeau Trail System offers a scenic tour of much of the Park Falls Ranger District. Two adjoining loops of different lengths (one north of Hwy 70 and the other south) offer access to visitors of all ages and experience levels.

This trail system is highlighted by scenic beauty and is rich with natural and cultural history. Sixty miles are maintained for ATV, motorcycles, and snowmobiles. Portions of selected trails are seeded and mowed for wildlife cover and food. Because trail segments intersect other trails, watch for posted signs. Most trailheads have a parking area and vault toilets. Wintergreen—the main trailhead—has drinking water, chalet, and information board.

Points of Interest: This trail system connects many of the attractions in the Park Falls Ranger District, including Sailor Lake Campground, South Fork of the Flambeau River, Round Lake Logging Dam, Smith Rapids Covered Bridge, Fifield Fire Tower, Newman Lake Day Use Area, Riley Creek Wildlife Management Area, and Popple Creek Watchable Wildlife Trail.

FLAMBEAU TRAIL SYSTEM SEGMENTS		
TRAIL	LENGTH	USE
101(most)	19.2 miles	Multi
102 (part)	10.5 miles	Multi
103 (part)	3.0 miles	Multi
105	6.0 miles	Multi
107	1.5 miles	Multi
111	23.5 miles	Multi
121	16.0 miles	Multi

Type of Landscape: Trails wind through rolling terrain, lined with towering green forests of northern hardwoods and pine-scented woodlands. Trails cross five wooden bridges over rushing rivers and meandering stream beds.

◆ Hogsback Hiking Trail

Length: 1.5 miles

Type: Family-oriented hiking

Degree of Difficulty: Easy to moderate

Trailhead: Hogsback Trail begins at the Wintergreen trailhead, five miles east of Fifield on Hwy 70.

Description: The trail heads west for about a hundred feet on a segment of the Flambeau Trail System before it turns left and crosses Hwy 70.

Once across the highway, the trail passes around a gate and up a short but steep esker which may be slow going with small children. Hogsback Trail then follows the top of the esker and has views of scenic wetlands and forests—especially nice during fall colors. The trail surface is cobbly, with glacially-rounded

Trails
Park Falls Ranger District

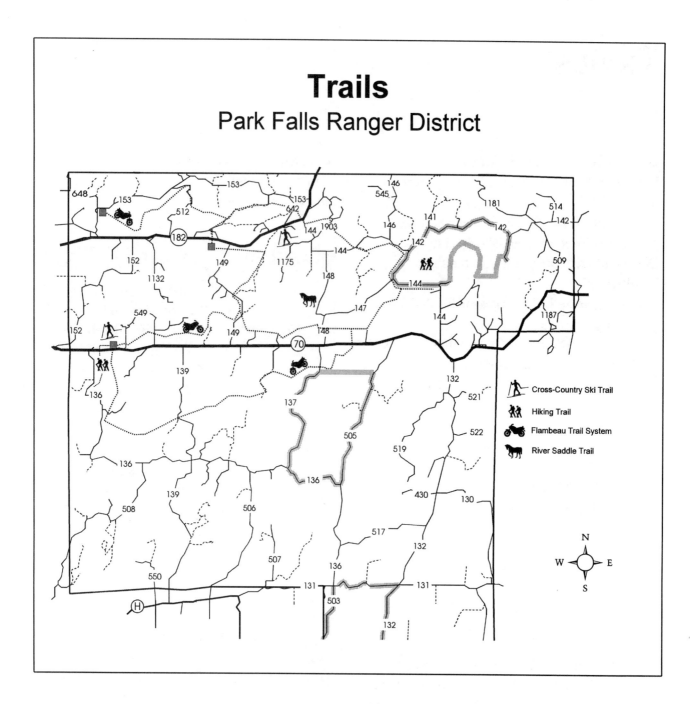

stones, and there is a canopy of hardwood trees overhead. Near the trail's end, you will skirt the edge of a bog to reach the Spur Lake Access. You may retrace your route, or at Spur Lake, travel west a short distance to FR 136, then north to return to Hwy 70.

Facilities include a chalet, vault toilets, parking lot, seasonal drinking water, and information board.

Points of Interest: The trail follows the top of an esker, a glacial ridge of stratified sands and gravels deposited long ago by a stream beneath the glacial ice sheet. The trail is narrow and tree-lined, providing ample opportunities for viewing birds and scenic vistas.

Type of Landscape: This is a forested, rolling landscape, with a series of hills connected by dips or depressions.

◆ Newman Spring Hike/Bike/Ski Trail

Length: 6.8 miles

Type: Hiking, biking, cross-country skiing

Degree of Difficulty: Easy to moderate

Trailhead: Travel twelve miles east of Park Falls on Hwy 182.

Description: There are two one-way trail segments leaving the parking lot and one returning. These trails form a number of interlocking loop trails. Trail segments range from .1 to one mile in length, offering the hiker, skier, and biker a variety of routes through glaciated terrain in upland ridges and lowland marshes. The trail passes through areas of lowland conifers, marshes, red-pine plantations, northern hardwoods, and white birch stands. The diversity of the trail provides a pleasant and unique tour for both the beginner and experienced skier.

Facilities include a parking lot, vault toilet, and information board.

Points of Interest: A loop recently added to the trail system crosses several scenic streams via wooden bridges. Newman Spring offers year-round scenic charm and is known for good brook trout fishing.

Type of Landscape: Rolling glaciated terrain with scenic vistas of wetlands.

◆ Popple Creek Watchable Wildlife Viewing Trail

Length: 0.5 miles

Type: Family-oriented hiking

Degree of Difficulty: Easy to moderate

Trailhead: From Fifield, travel east on Hwy 70 thirteen miles to FR 137, then south (right) six miles to FR 136, then west (right) .25 miles to the parking area.

Description: This trail partially follows an esker that traces the western shore of the Wilson Flowage. The trail extends south from the parking lot on FR 136. (*The path can be hard to follow in places.*) It crosses a quaint bridge over the Popple Creek that links the Popple Creek Impoundment with the Wilson Flowage. After crossing the bridge, the trail will bend to the left, passing through an open area. It continues to the left, passing through an area with remnants of past activities. After following a tall ridge, the trail opens on to a beaver pond. The trail continues along the north edge of the pond, where it ends with a panoramic view of Wilson Flowage and an osprey nesting platform. This wildlife viewing trail offers a close-up look at spring and autumn waterfowl migrations. Interpretive exhibits focus attention on several trail highlights.

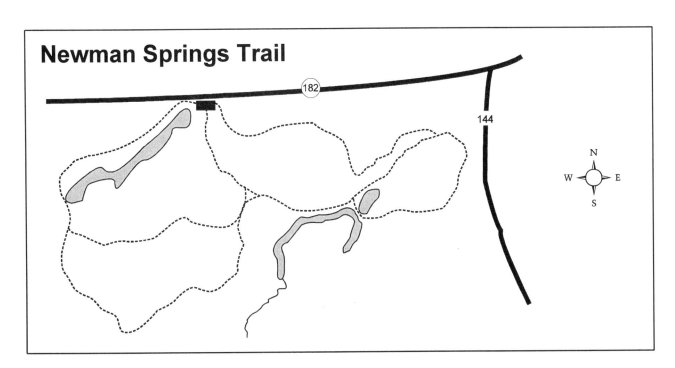

Newman Springs Trail

River Saddle Trail (East)
Trail # 126

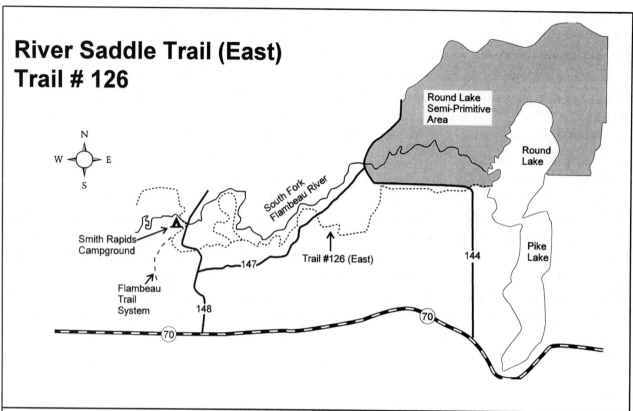

River Saddle Trail (West)
Trail #126

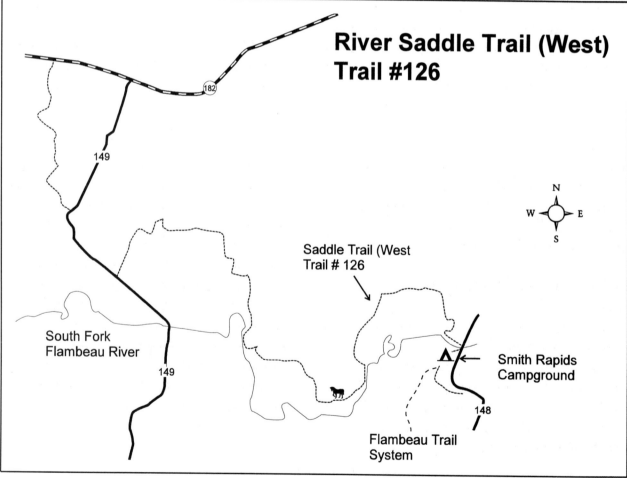

Facilities include a parking lot and interpretive exhibits.

Points of Interest: Visitors walk alongside a beaver dam, and may encounter a variety of wildlife. An osprey nesting platform is also visible.

Type of Landscape: Glaciated terrain, punctuated by ridges of pine and expansive views of wetlands.

◆ River Saddle Trail

Length: 18.5 miles

Type: Horseback riding on a primitive trail

Degree of Difficulty: Easy to moderate

Trailhead: From Fifield, travel thirteen miles east on Hwy 70, then north (left) on to FR 148 two miles to Smith Rapids Campground. The trail can also be accessed from the Round Lake Logging Dam parking area, located on FR 535.

Description: This trail starts at Round Lake and follows Trail Segment 126 along the scenic South Fork of the Flambeau River as it heads westward. At Smith Rapids, it crosses to the north side of the river. It also follows an old logging road that crosses open fields, wildlife openings, pine plantations, and young upland and lowland forests. The trail continues to Hwy 182, where there is a pull-off.

Facilities include a campground, drinking water, vault toilets, and hitching posts.

Points of Interest: This trail system is highlighted by views of the South Fork of the Flambeau River and the Smith Rapids Covered Bridge.

Type of Landscape: Relatively level uplands and pine plantations interspersed with narrow, wooded paths, lowlands, and openings.

◆ Round Lake Trail System

Length: 10.8 miles

Type: Rustic trail system for hiking, biking and cross-country skiing

Degree of Difficulty: Easy to moderate

Trailhead: From Fifield travel twenty miles east on Hwy 70, then north (left) on FR 144 two miles, and then east (right) on FR 535. Other trailheads can be found on FR 142.

Description: This trail provides access to the Round Lake Semi-Primitive Non-Motorized Area, about 3,600 acres in size. The area is closed to motorized vehicles. As such, none of the trails are groomed during winter months. There are several looping trails, a trail along the northern half of Round Lake, and walking trails to Jupa and Tucker Lakes. This unique area has numerous foot trails and old road grades. Facilities include a vault toilet at the boat landing; no water.

Points of Interest: At the origin of the Flambeau River, a late-1800s logging dam is under restoration. The dam is listed on the National Register of Historic Places and is surrounded by large pines, once common to the area. A stand of old-growth hemlock, approximately 160 years old, lies to the north between Round Lake and Tucker Lake.

Type of Landscape: Trail terrain varies from fairly gentle slopes and steeper ridges to occasional low, wet spots. Wet feet are possible.

◆ Wintergreen Hike/Bike/Ski Trail

Length: 7.9 miles of interlocking loops

Type: Hiking, biking, and cross-country skiing

Degree of Difficulty: Moderate to difficult

Trailhead: The trailhead is approximately five miles from Fifield on Hwy 70.

Description: This trail offers the hiker, skier and biker a variety of routes through rolling glacial terrain, ranging from upland ridges to lowland marshes. The trail winds through a mixture of forest types, some ideal for spotting wildlife. There are four loops that extend to the north. Loops A, B, and C are for intermediate level skiing and loop D is for expert. The trails are groomed during the ski season.

Facilities include a parking lot, vault toilets, seasonal drinking water, chalet, and information board.

Points of Interest: Scenic vistas overlooking several ponds and bogs dot the trail, with a picnic site on the segment just east of Loop C. The trail system may also be used as a fall hunter walking trail.

Type of Landscape: Rolling glacial terrain dotted with low wetland areas, common to this area.

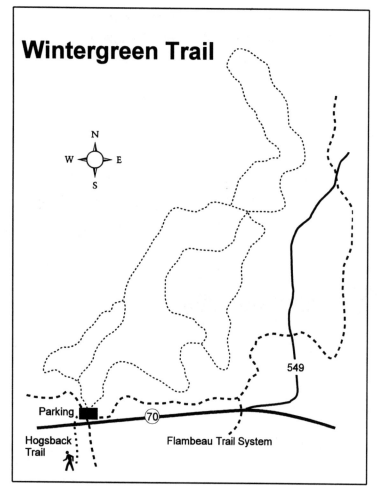

Wintergreen Trail

N
W E
S

549

Parking

Hogsback
Trail

70

Flambeau Trail System

Snowmobile Trails

The Park Falls District is criss-crossed by snowmobile trails. While the Forest provides the land for the trails, local clubs are responsible for grooming, private property easements, and trail mapping. Price County is known for some of the best-groomed trails in Wisconsin. Information and maps are available from the **Price County Snowmobile Association**, 225 South Lake, Phillips, WI 54555. Trail information is also available by calling (715) 339-3575 or the local chamber of commerce.

Snowmobile trails may change from year to year due to funding, easements, and other factors. Before using a trail for the first time, contact the County Trail Coordinator for an up-to-date map.

There are three state snowmobile corridors in this District:

◆ **State Trail 10**, Fifield to Minocqua, enters the District just north of Hwy 70 on TS 101 and continues east to Round Lake, where it turns southeast, crosses Hwy 70, and enters Oneida County. State Trail 19 crosses this trail several miles east of FR 148. There is a parking lot at the Wintergreen trailhead, five miles east of Fifield.

◆ **State Trail 12**, Hwy 13 to Minocqua, enters the southern end of the District from the west, travels 3.3 miles east through the District on TS 109, and leaves the east side of the District, where it enters Oneida County.

◆ **State Trail 19**, Hwy 8 to the Flambeau Flowage, enters the District from the south. From Hwy 8 to the District boundary is about six miles. The trail continues on TS 120 twenty-two miles, when it joins up with TS 121, which goes north 1.5 miles, over Hwy 70, to State Trail 10. The trail turns east (right) on TS 101 about 1.5 miles, then turns north on TS 111. It follows this segment northwest about twelve miles. After crossing Hwy 182, the trail turns north on TS 106 1.4 miles, where it leaves the District. State Trail 19 continues to follow Hwy 182 north into Iron County.

There are also a number of local and club trails that use portions of the Flambeau Trail system. These include:

◆ **State Trail 13** runs from Park Falls to TS 111. There is a trailhead at Blockhouse Lake. The trail continues eastward ten miles on TS 111, where it joins State Trail 10.

◆ **Trail Segments 103** and **102** run north and south in the far west end of the District, connecting TS 111 with the trails at Solberg Lake.

For other segments open to snowmobiling, please see the Flambeau Trail System.

Snowmobilers enjoying some of the many miles of trails in the Chequamegon National Forest

SURROUNDING AREA FACILITIES

Private Campgrounds

FIFIELD/PARK FALLS

◆ **Hicks Landing:** East 1.5 miles on Hwy 70, then south on Hick's Landing Road; (715) 762-5008; 10 sites; on Sailor Creek Flowage, 170 acres; N12855 Hicks Road, Fifield, WI 54524.

◆ **Moose Jaw Lodge Campground:** East of Hwy 13 on Hwy 70, north on FR 144; (715) 762-3028; 20 sites; on Round Lake, 726 acres; N15098 Shady Knoll Drive, Park Falls, WI 54552.

◆ **Trefil's Pike Lake Campground and Resort:** Located east of Hwy 13 on Hwy 70, north of FR 144 and east on Thorofare Road; (715) 762-3058; on the Pike Lake Chain; N15014 Thorofare Road, Park Falls, WI 54552.

MINOCQUA/LAC DU FLAMBEAU

◆ **Broken Bow Campground:** Located 12 miles west of Minocqua on Hwy 70, turn on Old Prairie Road; (715) 588-3844; 50 sites; on Broken Bow Lake, 134 acres; 14855 Deer Trail Road, Lac du Flambeau, WI 54538.

◆ **Lazy L Campground:** (715) 588-3883; 21 sites; 8208 Bo-Di-Lac Drive, Minocqua, WI 54548.

◆ **Patricia Lake Campground:** Take Hwy 70 west from Minocqua for 2.5 miles, then go south on Pinemere Road; (715) 356-3198; 85 sites; 8505 Camp Pinemere Road, Minocqua, WI 54548.

◆ **Tee Pee Campground:** (715) 356-5609; 50 sites; on Shishebogama Lake, 716 acres; 8938 E. Minch Road, Minocqua, WI 54548.

◆ **Tribal Campground and Marina:** On Hwy 47 in Lac du Flambeau; (715) 588-3310; 71 sites; Lac du Flambeau, WI 54538.

PHILLIPS

◆ **Comfort Cove:** Located east of Hwy 13 on Cty H, north on Solberg Lake Road, and north on East Solberg Road; (715) 339-3360; 25 sites; on Solberg Lake, 859 acres; HCR 4 Box 801, Phillips, WI 54555.

◆ **Musser Lake Cabins/Campground:** Located east of Phillips on Cty H and south on Musser Road; (715) 339-3577; 10 sites; on the Musser Flowage, 563 acres, and Elk River; Rt 1, Musser Road, Phillips, WI 54555.

◆ **Roll-in Point:** Located on Solberg Lake; (715) 339-4585; 21 sites; on Solberg Lake, 859 acres; HCR 4 Box 987, Phillips, WI 54555.

Municipal & County Campgrounds and Parks

FIFIELD/PARK FALLS

◆ **Hines Park:** located on Sherry Ave, north of Hwy 182, within the city of Park Falls; (715) 762-2436; 10 sites with electric/water hookups; flush toilets, boat landing; on the Flambeau River; 400 S. 4th Ave., Park Falls, WI 54552.

PHILLIPS

◆ **Solberg Lake County Campground:** Cty H east, Solberg Lake Road, then north on West Solberg Lake Road to campground; (715) 339-4505; 31 sites, nominal fee; first come-first serve; picnic shelter, boat landing, fishing pier, drinking water, vault toilet; on Solberg Lake, 859 acres; Normal Building, Phillips, WI 54555.

State Campgrounds

◆ **Northern Highland-American Legion State Forest**, the Department of Natural Resources operates this 200,000-acre State Forest. Camping is available northeast of the Park Falls Ranger District. Additional information is available at the DNR-Woodruff Area Headquarters, Cty J, P.O. Box 440, Woodruff, WI 54568; (715) 356-5211.

Attractions

◆ **Scheer's Lumberjack Shows**, located on Hwy 47, in downtown Woodruff. See World Champion lumberjacks doing trick and fancy log rolling, buck sawing, canoe jousting, and more; (715) 356-4050.

Canoe/Mountain Bike Rentals

◆ **BJ's Sportshop:** located one block north of downtown Minocqua on Hwy 51, offers bike rentals; (715) 356-3900.
◆ **Minocqua Sport Rental:** rents bikes, canoes and much more. Located three blocks from the Hwy 51 stoplights on Hwy 70 West; (715) 356-4661 or 356-4125.
◆ **Oxbow Resort:** canoes and mountain bikes available for rent; Rt. 1, Box 250, Park Falls, WI 54552; (715) 762-4786.

Hatcheries/Wildlife Centers

◆ **Lac du Flambeau Fish Hatchery:** Walleye, trout, and musky fish-rearing facility, trout pond for fishing, tours; P.O. Box 67, Lac du Flambeau, WI 54538; (715) 588-3307.

◆ **Northwoods Wildlife Center Wildlife Hospital:** Located on Hwy 70 West, .5 miles west of Hwy 51. It is a non-profit organization dedicated to wildlife conservation. Tours available; 8683 Blumstein Road, Hwy 70 West, Minocqua, WI 54548; (715) 356-7400.

Museums and Historical Sites

◆ **Lac du Flambeau Chippewa Museum and Cultural Center:** features cultural exhibits of the Chippewa, pow wows, tours, workshops, and gift shop; P.O. Box 804, Lac du Flambeau, WI 54538; (715) 588-3333.
◆ **Old Town Hall Museum:** open June through Labor Day, Fridays and Sundays from 1 P.M. to 5 P.M. Artifacts from logging days, 1879 to 1930s. For information contact: Director, Old Town Hall Museum, Fifield, WI 54524.

Petting Zoo

◆ **Jim Peck's Wildwood:** Located two miles west of Hwy 51 on Hwy 70 in Minocqua. Petting zoo, nature walks, trout and musky ponds, adventure boats, and gift shop; (715) 356-5588.

Emergency Numbers

◆ **Sheriff**
Oneida County (715) 362-6212
Emergency 911
Price County (715) 339-3011
Vilas County (715) 479-4441, 1-800-472-7290

◆ **Hospitals**
Flambeau Medical Center 98 Sherry Ave, Park Falls, WI 54552; (715) 762-2484

Howard Young Medical Center 240 Maple St. Woodruff, WI 54568; (715) 356-8000

Other Information Contacts

◆ County
Oneida County Forester, Courthouse, Rhinelander, WI 54501; (715) 369-6140
Price County Recreation Department, Normal Building, Phillips, WI 54555; (715) 339-4505
Vilas County Forester, Courthouse, Eagle River, WI 54521; (715) 479-3680
Vilas County UWEX, P.O. Box 369, Eagle River, WI 54521; (715) 479-3648

◆ State
WI DNR, Park Falls Area Headquarters, 875 South 4th Ave, P.O. Box 220, Park Falls, WI 54552; (715) 762-3204. Covers Price County.
WI DNR, Woodruff Area Headquarters, Cty J, P.O. Box 440 Woodruff, WI 54568. (715) 356-5211. Covers Forest, Oneida and Vilas Counties.

◆ Federal: U.S. Forest Service
Park Falls Ranger District, 1170 4th Avenue South, Park Falls, WI 54552; (715) 762-2461

◆ Chambers of Commerce
Arbor Vitae-Woodruff Chamber of Commerce, P.O. Box 266, Woodruff, WI 54568; (715) 356-6171 or (800) 876-8818.
Lac du Flambeau Chamber of Commerce, P.O. Box 804, Lac du Flambeau, WI 54538; (715) 588-3333.
Minocqua Chamber of Commerce, P.O. Box 1006, Minocqua, WI 54548; (715) 356-5266 or (800) 44-NORTH.
Park Falls Chamber of Commerce, 4th Ave, P.O. Box 246, Park Falls, WI 54552; (715) 762-2703.
Phillips Area Chamber of Commerce, 104 S. Lake Street, P. O. Box 155, Phillips, WI 54555; (715) 339-4100 or (800) 526-2417.
Prentice Tourist Information, P.O. Box 98, Prentice, WI 54556; (715) 428-2811.

CHAPTER 7

WASHBURN

Ranger District

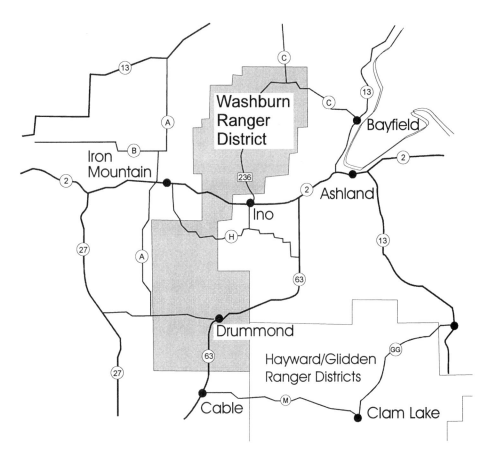

There is over 238,720 acres of land and water in the **Washburn Ranger District**, of which 190,000 acres are federally owned. The area has been shaped by the mountain building process of wind, rain, and glaciation.

Notable points of interest are Flynn Lake Semi-Primitive Non-Motorized Area, Rainbow Lake Wilderness, Moquah Barrens, CAMBA Trail System, Mt. Valhalla, and the North Country National Scenic Trail.

Area communities can provide needed supplies and services. Ashland, Washburn, and Bayfield lie to the northeast on Hwy 2 or Hwy 13, Iron River is to the west on Hwy 2, and Cable, south on Hwy 63. Drummond and Delta are in the middle of the District on Hwy 63 and Cty H, respectively.

FOR MORE INFORMATION ABOUT THIS AREA, CONTACT:

Washburn Ranger District
113 East Bayfield St.
P.O. Box 578
Washburn, WI 54891
(715) 373-2667

THE FOREST

The **Washburn Ranger District** is located in the Northern Highlands of Wisconsin, ancient by even geological times. This was at the leading edge of continental plate movements several billion years ago. It has seen violent volcanic activities by plates colliding, a rift valley formed by forces ripping the crust apart, and mountains built as the plates came back together again. Then, for two and one-half million years, the landscape was shaped by four continental glaciers. Today, the District has a diverse landscape of highlands in the north, outwash plains, rolling hills, and kettle lakes through the center, and a mix of glacial outwash plains and terminal moraines surrounding the Lake Owen area. To the west are rolling sand barrens covered with pines. Much of the District is covered with scattered conifers and pines, northern hardwoods, and wetlands.

Lakes predominate two areas, the old glacial lake basin and terminal moraine near Delta, and pitted outwash areas near Lake Owen.

Surface water flows in two directions. A Great Divide was formed by ancient mountains that extended east to west. Although the mountains have been reduced to rolling hills, the divide remains. Waters north of the divide flow into Lake Superior, then through the Great Lakes to the Atlantic Ocean. Waters to the south flow through the Chippewa River System into the Mississippi River and south to the Gulf of Mexico.

The weather in the northern part of this district is cold and wet enough to have small patches of boreal forest. However, Lake Superior, acting as a large heat (cold) storage basin, moderates the temperature near the lake. The result is more frost-free days in fall and cooler days during the summer. The Bayfield area benefits from this, with excellent apple-growing weather.

Research Natural Areas

Research Natural Areas (RNAs) are designated to protect unique natural features or preserve examples of genetic diversity. RNAs are used primarily for research and education rather than public use.

◆ **Moquah Barrens Research Natural Area**, one square mile, is located in the northern third of the District on the eastern edge of the Moquah Barrens Wildlife Area. From Iron River, travel east on Hwy 2, or from Ashland, travel west on Hwy 2. At Ino, turn north on FR 236 and travel about seven miles. FR 236 will take you through the middle of the property. Prescribed burns, as on adjacent lands, are not permitted here. The Forest Service has set aside this one square mile area to determine what occurs when man-made fires are prevented. Different types of vegetation can already be seen, and trees are slowing reclaiming the area.

Semi-Primitive Non-Motorized Areas

◆ **Star Lake Semi-Primitive Non-Motorized Area**, 5,076 acres, is located four miles north of Drummond on Forest Highway (FH) 35, then east (right) on FR 224 and travel two miles along the southern boundary of the Star Lake area to the Star Lake Boat Landing. Continue one more mile on FR 224, then north (left) on Little Star Lake Road (FR 293) and travel one mile to a small parking/boat landing area to access the trails. Other trails can be accessed by continuing on FR 224 one mile to the trailhead parking area.

Special Forest Management Areas

Washburn Ranger District

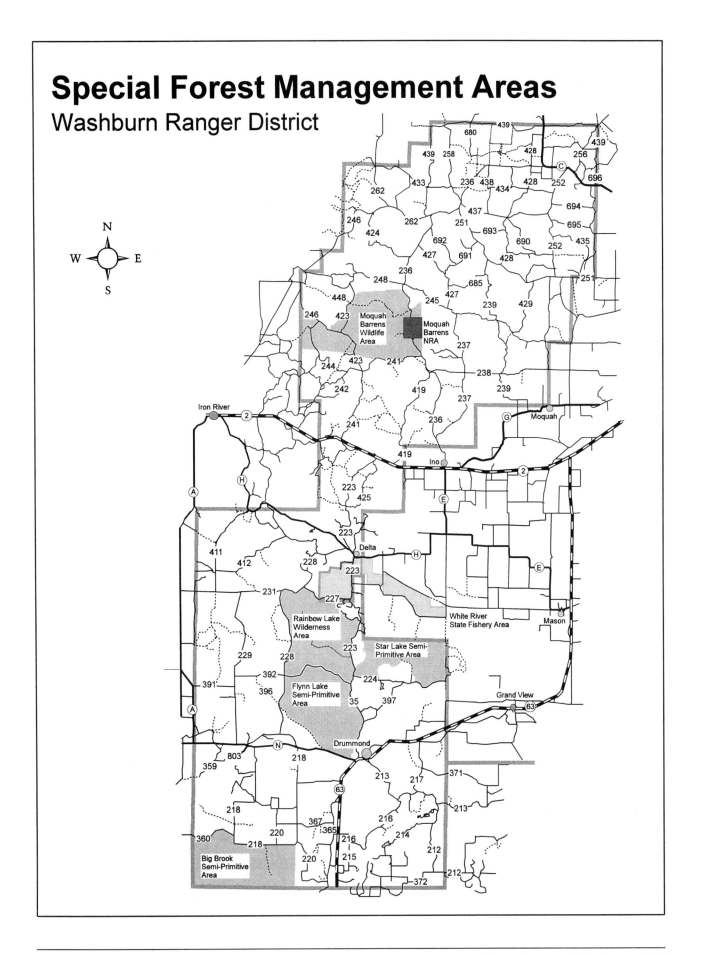

As a non-motorized area, it offers visitors a more secluded, back-country experience. There are hunter walking trails which provide access. There are some private lands in the northeast corner of the property.

Features include low wetland bogs and marshes, with a variety of vegetation and wildlife and fishing on Little Star, Bog, and Nymphia Lakes, which are adjacent to the southern boundary. Additional walk-in access is via a hunter walking trail to Cranberry Lake. Take Trail Segment 403 (north of FR 224 and across from Anodanta Lake) north one mile. The trail to the east leads to the lake. Area landscape has changed due to flooding by beaver dams.

◆ **Flynn Lake Semi-Primitive Non-Motorized Area**, 6,655 acres, is located just west of Drummond on Cty N. The boundaries include Cty N, FR 396 and FR 228 on the south and west sides, FR 392 on the north, and FH 35 on the east.

This area features mixed hardwood and northern conifer forests, rolling glacial terrain, kettle lakes, and numerous trails. The North Country National Scenic Trail cuts across the northeast corner, with old logging and railroad grades scattered throughout. Many trails are unmarked and overgrown with vegetation. Popular lakes for panfish fishing are Wabigon, Stratton Ponds, Nelson, Balsam Pond, Armstrong, Jorgenson, and Flynn Lakes. This semi-primitive area is popular for hunting, snowshoeing, hiking, and wildlife viewing.

◆ **Big Brook Semi-Primitive Non-Motorized Area**, 4,740 acres, is located north of Cable on Hwy 63 to Blue Moon Road (FR 365). Turn northwest (left) onto Blue Moon Road and travel 1.5 miles, then west (left) on FR 222 five miles, then turn west (left) on FR 218, which is the northern boundary of the property. Continue west 2.5 miles to reach the access road, FR 380, to Big Brook Lake. FR 360 and FR 218 make up the northern boundary, with the Forest border making up the south and west sides.

This area features upland hardwoods in the west. There are more wetlands in the east that are part of the headwaters and upper watershed for the Totagatic River.

Parking is available at Camp Lake near the junction of FR 362 and FR 218. There are numerous gated roads along the northern boundary, that provide parking and walk-in access for those wishing a back-country experience. FR 380 is open for vehicle traffic to the north end of Big Brook Lake.

Wildlife Management Areas

◆ **Moquah Barrens Wildlife Management Area** (*See Watchable Wildlife Areas*)

Wetland Habitat Areas

No specific work to develop wetland habitat impoundments has been done in this District. However, there are numerous natural areas that provide valuable habitat and wildlife viewing opportunities.

Wilderness Areas

◆ **Rainbow Lake Wilderness**, 6,583 acres, is located between Hwy 2 and Hwy 63. From Drummond, travel west on Hwy 63, then north on FH 35 about four miles. This will bring you to the intersection of FH 35 and FR 392, the southeast corner of the wilderness.

The wilderness is encompassed by FR 392 on the south, FR 228 on the west, FR 227 on the north and FH 35 on the east. Bellevue Lake, on the northeast corner, is just outside the wilderness area.

This wilderness has a lot to offer, with lakes and trails among the rolling hills of the terminal moraine. Forest cover is a well-established mix of

Rainbow Lake Wilderness

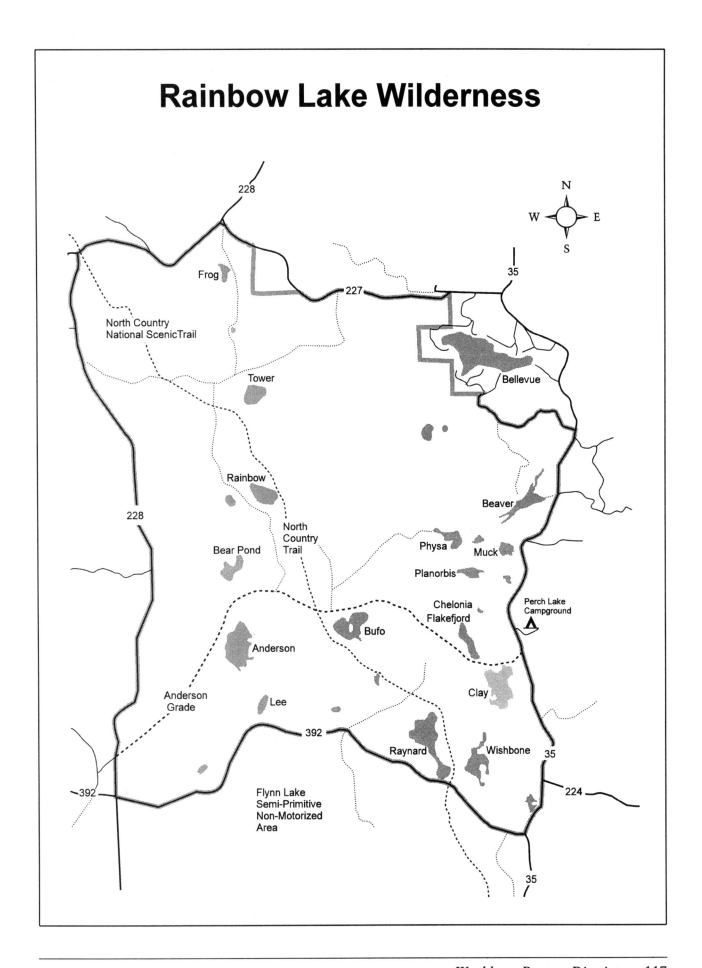

228

Frog

227

35

North Country
National ScenicTrail

Tower

Bellevue

228

Rainbow

Beaver

North
Country
Trail

Physa

Muck

Bear Pond

Planorbis

Chelonia
Flakefjord

Perch Lake
Campground

Bufo

Anderson

Clay

Anderson
Grade

Lee

392

Raynard

Wishbone

35

392

224

Flynn Lake
Semi-Primitive
Non-Motorized
Area

35

Badgers, foxes, and other small animals make their home by burrowing into the sides of hills and along roads.

bluebirds, indigo buntings, cardinals, warblers, upland plovers, and brown thrashers. Many are neotropic, birds that fly to the tropics in the winter.

◆ **Mammals** The Forest has an abundance of white-tailed deer and black bear, along with badgers in the sand country and fishers in the woodlands.

northern hardwoods (oak, birch, basswood, and maple) along with stands of balsam fir, hemlock, and red and white pine. The North Country National Scenic Trail and the Anderson Grade Trail crisscross the area, giving easy access.

There are twenty-four lakes and ponds, many close to the edge of the wilderness, that offer a variety of experiences. These include Reynard for canoeing and wildlife watching, and Beaver Lake for trout fishing and wildlife watching. For those who wander off established trails, an enjoyable wilderness experience awaits—come prepared.

Wildlife

There is an abundance of wildlife throughout the Washburn Ranger District.

◆ **Birds** Birds of prey abound, including kestrels, broad-winged and redtail hawks, and barred and saw-whet owls. In the winter, you may see snow and great gray owls. Songbirds in the area include

Watchable Wildlife Areas

◆ **Moquah Barrens Wildlife Management Area**, 8,900 acres, is located in the northern third of the District. From Iron River, go east on Hwy 2, or from Ashland, go west on Hwy 2. At Ino, turn north on FR 236 and travel about six miles to FR 241, which is the southeast corner of the area. This wildlife area is about three miles wide and six miles long. FR 241 extends along part of the southern boundary, with FR 236 passing through the eastern edge and FR 423 through the western edge. This property, in contrast to many other parts of the District and Forest, is a large expanse of open savanna landscape, typified by rolling hills of grass and scrubs, and islands of jack pine, aspen, and scrub oak.

It is home to sharptail grouse, black bear, badgers, fisher, fox, coyote, white-tailed deer, and many songbirds like the bluebird and upland plover. The badgers' oval-shaped burrows can be seen in sandy hillsides or road cuts. Remember, these can be dangerous animals if disturbed. Viewing can be done from your car along the roads that border or pass through the area. The word *moquah* means "bear" in the Ojibwa language.

Besides wildlife, there is an abundance of wildflowers, such as the trailing arbutus. This area is noted for its blueberries, sand cherries, blackberries, and hackle berries.

The reasons for this area's diverse environment are its sandy outwash soils and wildfires that eliminate woody plants such as trees and shrubs. With modern fire protection, wildfires have been mostly eliminated. To maintain this unique environment, prescribed burns are periodically set under controlled conditions.

Hunting

Hunting is allowed throughout the Forest, except in campgrounds and special-use areas. It is important to keep in mind that you will encounter others who will be using the Forest for hiking, nature watching, and other recreational pursuits.

Hunter Walking Trails

There are a variety of hunter walking trails on the Washburn Ranger District. These trails have interconnecting loops of varying lengths, with many timber types and age classes. Hunters are encouraged to write, phone, or visit the Ranger District office to obtain up-to-date trail maps. These trails provide a more secluded hunting experience. All trails are gated, with small parking areas, and have limited maintenance and signage.

◆ **Drummond Hunter Walking Trails**, ten miles long in two loops and several lineal sections, is located just south and east of Drummond and is part of a cross-country ski trail. There are two parking areas on Hwy 63 and five on FR 213.

◆ **Everett Lake Hunter Walking Trail**, .9 miles long, is located north of Drummond on FH 35 to Delta, then west on Cty H .75 miles, then west (left) on Old Cty H about .5 miles. After crossing the east fork of the White River, there will be a dirt road to the south (left) that takes you to the gated trail.

◆ **Pigeon Lake Hunter Walking Trails**, 7.9 miles long, are located about three miles west of Drummond on Cty N. The trails are south of Cty N, west of FR 222, and east of FR 218. There are two parking areas on Cty N and two on FR 218.

◆ **Star Lake Hunter Walking Trails, A and B**, 9 miles long, are located north of Drummond on FH 35, then east (right) on FR 224. The Nymphia Lake Trail runs north on FR 293 to Boggy Pond. There is a parking lot with the trail running straight east. The second trail, a large loop, is located at Boggy Pond.

Gathering of Forest Products

One of the best locations to pick berries in the Chequamegon National Forest is the Moquah Barrens Wildlife Management Area and the adjoining open pine barrens. This area has raspberries, blueberries, and blackberries.

Seasons for berries vary with the weather. Raspberries generally ripen in July, blueberries the end of July and August, and blackberries in August, September, and October.

Gathering other items such as pines cones, pine boughs, and trees, may require permits. Some permits require a fee, depending on usage and whether it is a commercial operation.

RECREATIONAL WATERS

Lakes

Within the borders of the Washburn Ranger District are more than 15 lakes, ranging in size from one to 1,323 acres. Most are in the southern two-thirds of the District. Much of the lake property is privately owned; however, 102 lakes have some or all of the shoreline in Forest ownership. The lakes listed below provide public access and offer a range of recreation opportunities, including fishing and wildlife watching.

◆ Bass Lake (Two Lakes Campground)
Surface Area: 59 acres
Depth: Maximum 35 feet, mean 15 feet
Fishery: Northern pike, largemouth bass, and panfish
Location: From Drummond, travel southeast on FR 213. After passing over the northern end of Lake Owen, take FR 214 south to Two Lakes Campground.
Lake Conditions: The bottom is mostly sand with scattered areas of gravel and rock. Water is clear with visibility down to twelve feet.
Shoreline: The shore is entirely owned by the Forest. It is 60% open meadow or marsh, with the remaining area upland forest.
Facilities: Two Lakes Campground and related facilities
Contour Map Available: Yes

◆ Bass Lake
Surface Area: 84 acres
Depth: Maximum 43 feet, mean 15 feet
Fishery: Northern pike, largemouth bass, black crappie, perch, and panfish
Location: From Drummond, travel north on FH 35 past Perch Lake Campground and Mud Lake. Take FR 1866 to the east.

Lake Conditions: The bottom is a mix of sand and muck, with scattered gravel areas. Water is medium brown, with visibility down to five feet.
Shoreline: The shore is upland forest with scattered spruce and tamarack. There is a leatherleaf-black spruce bog adjacent to the lake on the southern end.
Facilities: There is an area for dispersed camping, along with vault toilets and a boat landing.
Contour Map Available: Yes

◆ Camp Nine Lake
Surface Area: 10 acres
Depth: Maximum 12 feet
Fishery: Panfish
Location: From Drummond, go west on Cty N, then northwest on FR 396. Continue on FR 230, then west on FR 392, then south on FR 229, then west on FR 391, and finally north on FR 395 to the lake.
Lake Conditions: The bottom is sand and gravel with scattered areas of muck. Water is clear with visibility down to ten feet.
Shoreline: The shore is a wetland fringe of grass and leatherleaf with an upland hardwood backdrop. It is entirely owned by the Forest Service.
Facilities: Unimproved landing for small boats
Contour Map Available: No

◆ Cisco Lake
Surface Area: 95 acres
Depth: Maximum 105 feet, mean 29 feet
Fishery: Walleye, northern pike, largemouth bass, smallmouth bass, black crappie, perch, panfish, and bullhead
Location: North two miles from Drummond on FH 35, then east on FR 397 to the landing.
Lake Conditions: The bottom is a mix of 55% rock, 30% sand and gravel, and 15% muck. Aquatic

Lakes
Washburn Ranger District

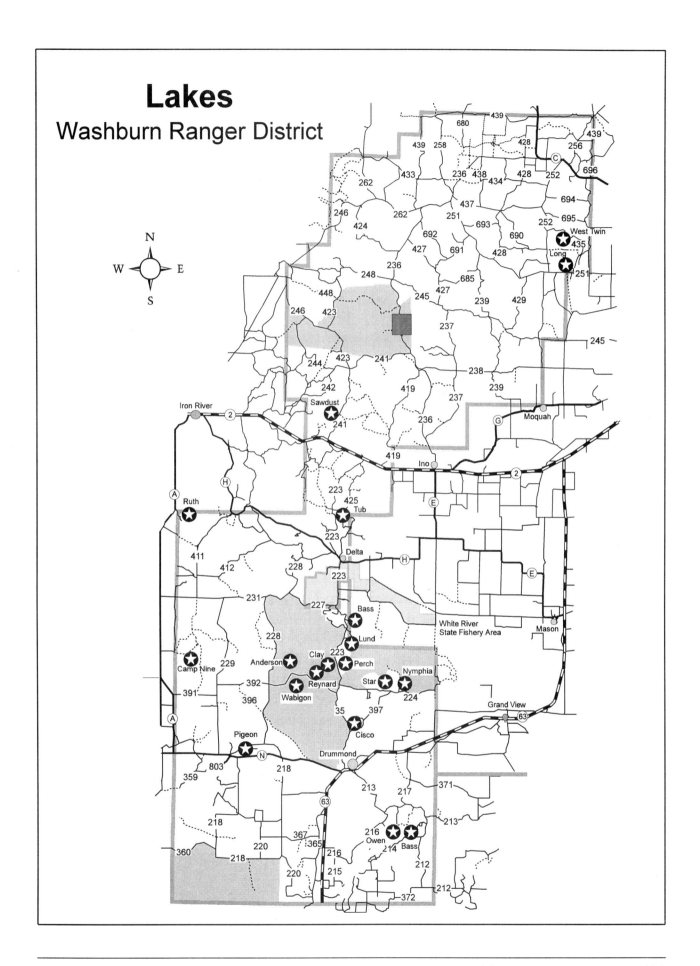

vegetation is sparse. The water is clear, with visibility down to fifteen feet. Fish cribs have been added to improve fish habitat.

Shoreline: The shoreline is upland hardwood of birch, maple and oak with scattered hemlock. It is partially owned by the Forest Service.

Facilities: Developed boat landing

Contour Map Available: Yes

◆ Lake Owen

Surface Area: 1,323 acres

Depth: Maximum 95 feet, mean 27 feet

Fishery: Walleye, northern pike, largemouth bass, smallmouth bass, black crappie, perch, trout, and panfish

Location: From Drummond, travel three miles southeast on FR 213, then south on FR 216 to the landing at the Lake Owen Outlet Area. There is also a landing at the Two Lake Campground, which is south of FR 213 on FR 214.

Lake Conditions: The bottom is a mix of sand, gravel, rubble, and boulders, with small areas of muck. Fish cribs have been added to improve fish habitat. Water is clear, with visibility down to 26 feet.

Shoreline: The entire shoreline is made up of mixed hardwoods and pine. This is a long, narrow lake with two large bays on the north end. Three-quarters of the shoreline is privately owned and well developed. Federal lands can be found on the north and west sides.

Facilities: Federal campground and separate picnic area plus private facilities

Contour Map Available: Yes

◆ Lake Ruth

Surface Area: 66 acres

Depth: Maximum 27 feet, mean 15 feet

Fishery: Largemouth bass, black crappie, perch, and panfish

Location: From Iron River (Hwy 2), take Cty A south four miles to the Forest boundary and the lake.

Lake Conditions: Sand and gravel make up the bottom with muck near wetland areas on the southern end of the lake. Water is clear, with visibility down to 13 feet.

Shoreline: The south and east shores are marsh wetlands, with the remaining shoreline forested uplands.

Facilities: Unimproved boat landing on the southwest end, off Cty A

Contour Map Available: Yes

◆ Long Lake

Surface Area: 36 acres

Depth: Maximum 16 feet

Fishery: Northern pike, largemouth bass, and perch

Location: From Washburn (Hwy 13), travel west about five miles on Wanebo Road, which turns into FR 251. Take FR 1890, at the picnic area entrance, around the north side of the lake to the landing.

Lake Conditions: The bottom is all sand. Water is clear, with visibility down to 16 feet. The lake experiences winter kill conditions.

Shoreline: The shore is a mix of birch, aspen, oak, jack pine, and Norway pine. It is entirely owned by the Forest Service.

Facilities: Picnic area on the north end

Contour Map Available: Yes

◆ Lund Lake

Surface Area: 22 acres

Depth: Maximum 36 feet, mean 11 feet

Fishery: Largemouth bass and panfish

Location: From Drummond, travel north on FH 35 about six miles. The landing is to the south of FR 801.

Lake Conditions: The bottom is a mix of sand, gravel, muck, and scattered areas of rubble. Water is clear, with visibility down to ten feet.

Shoreline: The entire shore is upland hardwoods with scattered pines.

Facilities: Parking and carry-in boat landing

Contour Map Available: Yes

◆ Nymphia Lake

Surface Area: 10 acres
Depth: Maximum 41 feet
Fishery: Trout
Location: From Drummond, travel north about four miles on FH 35, then east on FR 224, and continue one mile past Star Lake. The landing is to the north.
Lake Conditions: The bottom is muck. Water is light brown, with visibility down to eight feet.
Shoreline: This is an acid bog lake surrounded by black spruce-tamarack bog with an adjacent wetland.
Facilities: Carry-in boat landing
Contour Map Available: Yes

◆ Perch Lake

Surface Area: 75 acres
Depth: Maximum 75 feet, mean 19 feet
Fishery: Largemouth bass, trout, and panfish
Location: Located about five miles north of Drummond on FH 35. The landing is to the east at Perch Lake Campground.
Lake Conditions: The bottom is mostly sand, rock, and gravel. Fish cribs have been added to improve habitat. Water is clear, with visibility down to eight feet.
Shoreline: The shore is 40% soft marsh and leatherleaf bogs, with the remaining shore a mix of upland hardwoods and a scattering of pines.
Facilities: Moderately developed boat landing
Contour Map Available: Yes

◆ Pigeon Lake

Surface Area: 213 acres
Depth: Maximum 21 feet, mean 12 feet
Fishery: Northern pike, largemouth bass, black crappie, perch, and panfish
Location: Located about four miles west of Drummond on Cty N. The landing is to the north.
Lake Conditions: The bottom is mainly sand, with scattered areas of rubble, gravel, and silt. Fish cribs have been added to improve habitat. Water is clear, with visibility down to sixteen feet.

Shoreline: The shore has a grassy edge with mixed upland hardwoods and scattered pines. One-third of the shore is publicly owned with a number of homes along both shores.
Facilities: Developed boat landing
Contour Map Available: Yes

◆ Sawdust Lake

Surface Area: 17 acres
Depth: Maximum 36 feet
Fishery: Largemouth bass and panfish
Location: From Iron River, travel east on Hwy 2 about six miles, then 1.75 miles north on FR 241. The landing is to the west.
Lake Conditions: Water is light brown, with visibility down to six feet.
Shoreline: The shore is a mix of upland hardwoods and pines.
Facilities: Carry-in boat landing
Contour Map Available: No

◆ Star Lake

Surface Area: 201 acres
Depth: Maximum 52 feet, mean 10 feet
Fishery: Northern pike, largemouth bass, perch, panfish, and bullhead
Location: From Drummond, travel north on FH 35, then two miles east on FR 224. The landing is on the north side of road.
Lake Conditions: The bottom is a mix of sand and muck. Sand can be found mainly in the east bay with muck in the west bay. The water is clear, with visibility down to twenty-two feet. Aquatic vegetation is common, especially in areas of muck.
Shoreline: Except for a few tag-alder swamps, the shore is upland hardwood and scattered white spruce and pine. The lake is made up of two connected bays, each with small islands. Except for the southern portion of the east bay, the entire lake is federally owned. There are several homes in the area.
Facilities: Improved boat landing
Contour Map Available: Yes

◆ Tub Lake

Surface Area: 11 acres
Depth: Maximum 31 feet
Fishery: Largemouth bass and panfish
Location: From the corner of Cty H and FR 35 in Delta, travel 2.5 miles north on FR 223. The lake is to the east at the junction of FR 426.
Lake Conditions: Water is clear, with visibility down to twenty-seven feet.
Shoreline: The shoreline is upland forest, with a narrow strip of grass wetland bordering part of the lake. It is surrounded by Forest lands.
Facilities: Unimproved boat landing on the north end of the lake
Contour Map Available: Yes

◆ West Twin Lake

Surface Area: 18 acres
Depth: Maximum 47 feet, mean 12 feet
Fishery: Largemouth bass, smallmouth bass, and panfish
Location: From Washburn (Hwy 13), travel west on Wanebo Road about five miles to FR 251. Continue on FR 251 for 1.75 miles into the Forest, then north on FR 252 for .75 miles, then east on FR 435 to the landing at the campground.
Lake Conditions: The bottom is sand when associated with the uplands and muck near the bogs. Water is clear, with visibility down to 10 feet.
Shoreline: Shoreline is entirely within the Forest. It is 80% upland forest with 20% bog wetland.
Facilities: Boat landing is at the campground and is a little rocky.
Contour Map Available: Yes

Walk In Lakes

There are many other treasures among the Forest lakes. We have detailed a number of the more noted lakes. There are also many walk-in lakes on Forest property. Access is by dragging or carrying your watercraft some distance. There are no facilities. Listed below are several primitive lakes you may want to explore.

◆ Anderson Lake

Surface Area: 33 acres
Depth: Maximum 46 feet
Fishery: Largemouth bass
Location: From Drummond, travel west on Cty N, then northwest on FR 396, then north on FR 228. The Anderson Grade Trail to the lake is just north of FR 392.
Lake Conditions: The bottom is 65% sand, gravel, and rock, with the remaining area muck. Water is clear, with visibility down to sixteen feet.
Shoreline: Except for a small black-spruce swamp, the shoreline is made up of northern hardwoods. The lake is entirely federally owned.
Facilities: None
Contour Map Available: No

◆ Clay Lake

Surface Area: 31 acres
Depth: Maximum 59 feet, mean 22 feet
Fishery: Largemouth bass and panfish
Location: From Drummond, travel five miles north on FH 35. The lake is in the Rainbow Lake Wilderness, just west of Perch Lake Campground.
Lake Conditions: The bottom is mainly rock, with scattered areas of sand and gravel. Water is light brown, with visibility down to eight feet.
Shoreline: The shore is upland hardwoods and conifers and completely owned by the Forest Service.
Facilities: None
Contour Map Available: Yes

◆ Reynard Lake

Surface Area: 32.6 acres
Depth: Maximum 55 feet
Fishery: Largemouth bass and panfish
Location: From Drummond, travel north three miles on FH 35, then west (left) one mile on FR 392. The lake, located in the Rainbow Lake Wilderness, is to the north.

Lake Conditions: Aquatic vegetation is abundant especially in the small bays. Water is clear, with visibility down to seventeen feet.

Shoreline: About half the shore is leatherleaf wetland and tamarack bogs, and is entirely owned by the Forest Service.

Facilities: None

Contour Map Available: No

◆ Wabigon Lake

Surface Area: 35 acres

Depth: Maximum 72 feet

Fishery: Northern pike, largemouth bass, panfish, and trout

Location: From Drummond, travel north three mileson FH 35, then about 2.5 miles west on FR 392. The lake is to the south in the Flynn Lake Semi-Primitive Area.

Lake Conditions: Water is clear, with visibility down to nine feet.

Shoreline: Wooded uplands make up about 70% of the shoreline with the remainder wetlands. The shore is completely owned by the Forest Service.

Facilities: None

Contour Map Available: Yes

Rivers

This District, being part of the headwaters for several river systems, has only small streams and creeks. For the most part, they are not canoeable. However, there is one river next to the District that may be of interest to some—the White River System.

◆ White River

Length: 50 miles

Gradient, Average: Ten-foot drop per mile

Fishery: Brown and brook trout

Description: The White River starts near Delta, with Lake Two its headwaters. It extends eastward 34 miles, then northward 21 miles, joining the Bad River before entering Lake Superior. The canoe route is from Pike River Town Park to Hwy 63, just south of Mason, covering a distance of about 14 river miles.

Starting at the park, the river runs eastward to Town Line Road at Sutherland, about four river miles. You can continue east through Bibon Marsh for another ten miles. Once you enter the marsh there are no take-out points until Bibon Road, just west of Hwy 63 and across from Cty E. From here, you can continue for another two miles into Mason. The river is mostly flat water with riffle areas.

Access Points: From Drummond, travel north on FH 35 to Delta (Cty H). Turn east (right) on Cty H and travel 1.5 miles, then south (right) at the town hall. The park and river will be one mile to the south. The take-out point is on Bibon Road, .5 miles west of Cty E/Hwy 63.

◆ Lake Owen Log Flume (Long Lake Branch)

Length: 3 miles

Gradient, Average: 31 foot drop per mile

Fishery: Minimual fishery in upper stretch

Description: This is a second stream, that is canoed at times. It extends northwest from Lake Owen through Rodger Lake and Rust Flowage to the mill pond at Drummond. This is a short trip of about three miles through secluded country. There is a portage around the Rust Flowage dam.

Access Points: South of Drummond on FR 213, continue a short distance on FR 216 to Lake Owen Outlet.

Trout Streams

While Bayfield County has 102 trout streams nearby, there are a very limited number of trout streams within the Washburn Ranger District. **Long Branch Creek and its tributaries** are the only trout streams within the District. They are located just northeast of Drummond.

POINTS OF INTEREST

Auto Tours

◆ **Fall Color Tour 3** is part of the Cable Area Chamber of Commerce and Chequamegon National Forest Fall Color Program. It is 46 miles long, covering the southern part of the District. This tour highlights the fall colors of the northern hardwoods in the Chequamegon National Forest and surrounding area. Oak, maple, and birch splash color against a backdrop of evergreen conifers. You will travel along both wide, paved highways and more intimate, canopied gravel roads.

The tour starts at Cable. Travel north on Hwy 63 about two miles, then west (left) on Blue Moon Road, then west (left) on FR 222 (Tri-Lake Road). This road will take you straight north through glaciated forests of maple and oak. When you reach Cty N, continue north on FR 228, passing the Rainbow Lake Wilderness to Delta Road. Continue east on FR 228. Turn east (right) on Scenic Drive and travel to Cty H. At Cty H, turn right and travel a short distance to Delta, then south (right) on FH 35. This will take you past the wilderness area back to Hwy 63. Along the way, you will pass Perch Lake Campground, a nice spot for a break. At Hwy 63, you can go west (right) back to Cable or go east (left) to Drummond.

QUICK REFERENCE

Auto Tour Highlights
Within the Washburn Ranger District

Fall Color Tour 3
Length: 46 miles
Highlights
    Fall Colors of Northern Hardwoods
    Cable
    Glaciated Oak and Maple Forest
    Rainbow Lake Wilderness
    Perch Lake Campground
    Drummond

Moquah Barrens Auto Tours
—The Barrens Tour
Length: 20 miles

Highlights
    Restoration of Moquah Pine Barrens
    Flora and Fauna of Endangered
      Ecosystem

—The Valhalla Tour
Length: 21 miles
Highlights
    Mt. Valhalla Recreation Area
    Scenic vistas
    Historical sights

Points of Interest
Washburn Ranger District

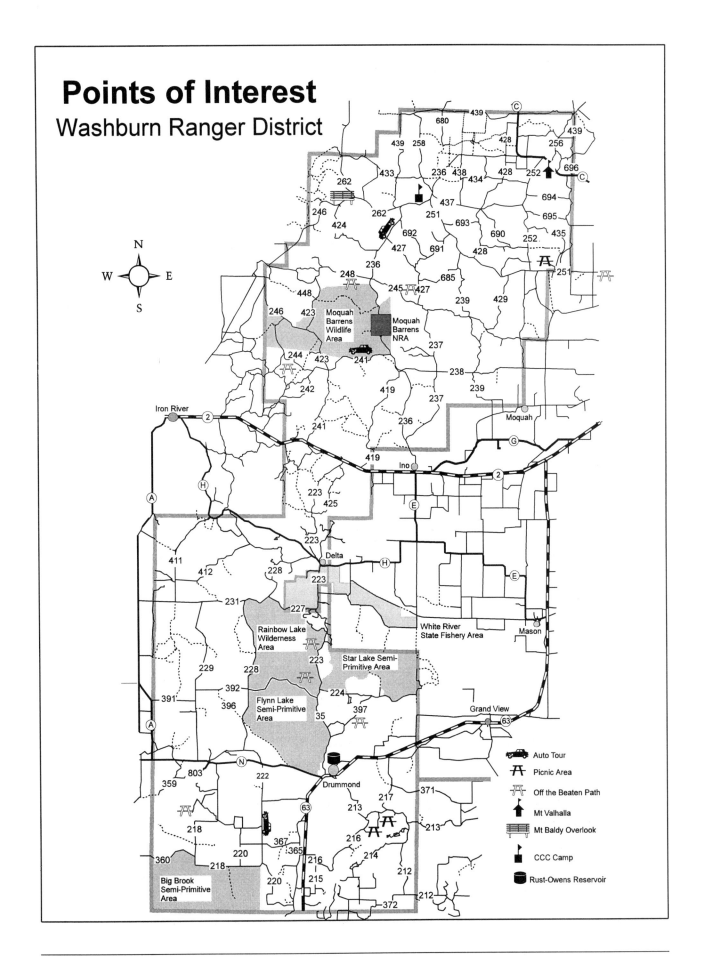

N
W E
S

Iron River

Moquah

Ino

Delta

Mason

White River
State Fishery Area

Rainbow Lake
Wilderness
Area

Star Lake Semi-
Primitive Area

Flynn Lake
Semi-Primitive
Area

Grand View

Drummond

Big Brook
Semi-Primitive
Area

Moquah
Barrens
Wildlife
Area

Moquah
Barrens
NRA

Auto Tour
Picnic Area
Off the Beaten Path
Mt Valhalla
Mt Baldy Overlook
CCC Camp
Rust-Owens Reservoir

A picturesque stop at the Lake Owen Outlet Picnic Area.

◆ Moquah Barrens Auto Tours

These auto tours feature the Moquah Barrens Wildlife Management Area and the restoration of a pine barrens ecosystem. A detailed brochure has been developed by the Forest Service for both routes.

The Barrens Tour, 20 miles, focuses on the management and restoration of the Moquah pine barrens and the wildlife and vegetation that inhabit this endangered ecosystem. The trail starts at Ino (Hwy 2). Proceed north on FR 236, then west (left) on FR 241, continue west on FR 244. At FR 245, turn east (right) on to FR 423. This loops you back to FR 241. Take FR 241 south, back to Ino.

The Valhalla Tour, 21 miles, focuses on past and present land management activities, highlighting historical sites and vistas of scenic wetlands. Visitors will begin this auto tour just north of Ino (Hwy 2) on FR 236. Stay on FR 236, traveling north through the District, to Cty C. Take Cty C east to Mt. Valhalla Recreation Area and Washburn (Hwy 13).

Civilian Conservation Corps Camps

There were a number of CCC camps established throughout the Washburn Ranger District. Many camps started in 1933, and all camps phased out in 1942. Camps did not always stay in one place. They were moved to other local sites or other parts of the state depending on need. (Federal camps are designated with the letter "F.")

◆ **Camp Brinks F-5, Company 640 and 3653,** is located west of Washburn (Hwy 13) on Cty C, then 5.5 miles west on FR 236. A dedication sign and several building sites are located nearby. The men originally had to walk the fourteen miles from Washburn to the camp site, which was established in April, 1933.

◆ **Camp Delta F-101, Company 2622,** Drummond

◆ **Camp Horseshoe F-35, Company 3653,** Ashland

◆ **Camp Pigeon Lake F-42, Company 640,** Drummond

◆ **Camp Twin Lakes F-6, Company V-1676,** Iron River, Wisconsin

Picnic Areas

◆ Lake Owen Outlet Picnic Area

Location: From Drummond, travel southeast on FR 213 for 2.5 miles to FR 216, then .25 miles south to the entrance.

Description: This picnic area is located on the northwest bay of Lake Owen, at the outlet and dam that form the lake. One of the interesting features is the old flume that was used to move logs several miles to the mill pond at Drummond.

Facilities: This picnic area has a play area, picnic tables, drinking water, vault toilets, and improved boat landing.

◆ Lake Owen Picnic Area

Location: From Drummond, travel south on FR 213 three miles to the entrance.

Description: This is a day use area, located on the north end of Lake Owen. One of the trailheads for the Drummond Trail System starts at the shelter.

Facilities: This picnic area is equipped with a shelter, picnic area, marked swimming beach, play area, seasonal drinking water, and vault toilets. Firewood is stocked at the chalet for winter use.

◆ Long Lake Picnic Area

Location: From Washburn, travel south one mile on Hwy 13, then west (right) on Wanebo Road six miles to FR 435. Turn north (right) to the entrance of the Long Lake Day Use Area.

Description: This picnic area is located on the eastern shore of Long Lake. It has a scenic view of Long Lake and access to local trails.

Facilities: There is a picnic area for the mobility impaired, grills, accessible vault toilets, paved parking lot, boat launch, drinking water, large sandy beach, and marked swimming area. An interpretive trail and associated boardwalk provide an opportunity to learn more about the area.

Spots off the Beaten Path

◆ **Bearsdale Springs** is located west of Drummond on Cty N, then south on FR 218 at Pigeon Lake, then west and south on FR 1807, which ends at the spring. This is a fresh-water spring in a forest setting.

◆ **Beaver Lake** is located north of Drummond on FH 35. It is in the Rainbow Wilderness, about one mile north of Perch Lake Campground. This is a nice setting among white pines.

The Lake Owen Day Use Area, located on the north end of Lake Owen.

◆ **Bladder Lake** is located east of Iron River on Hwy 2, then north on FR 241, and west on FR 244 to the north end of the lake.

Clay Lake is located north of Drummond on FH 35. This lake is in the Rainbow Lake Wilderness, southwest of Perch Lake Campground.

◆ **Horseshoe Lake** is located west of Washburn (Hwy 13) on Wanebo Road, continue west on FR 251, then south (left) on FR 239, then west (right) on FR 685, and finally south (left) one mile on FR 427. The lake is on the west (right) side of the road.

◆ **Johnson Springs** is located two miles north of Drummond on FH 35, then east (right) on FR 397 about two miles. After crossing the North Country Trail, there will be a road to the right that goes to the spring.

◆ **Pine Lake** is located west of Washburn (Hwy 13) on Wanebo Road; continue west on FR 251, then south (left) on FR 236, and west (right) on FR 245. Continue west on FR 248 for .75 miles. The road to the lake will be to the south.

Structures and Landmarks

◆ **Mt. Baldy Overlook** is located nine miles northwest of Washburn on Cty C, then west (left) on FR 236 six miles, then west (right) on FR 262 four miles. Finally turn west (left) on FR 262A and travel one mile to the parking area. It is about 600 feet up a moderate-grade path to the top. The overlook offers scenic views of northern forests on the Bayfield Peninsula, Lake Superior, and the north shore of Minnesota. To the west, Two Harbors can be seen. Facilities include accessible vault toilet, parking area, and interpretive wayside exhibit. The exhibit focuses on the glacial history, maritime history, and views on the horizon across Lake Superior.

◆ **Mt. Valhalla Recreation Area** was a former alternate Olympic ski jumping practice site from the 1950s to 1969. From Washburn, travel northwest on Cty C seven miles to the Mt. Valhalla Recreation Area. Interpretive displays, located inside the chalet, describe this historic Olympic ski jumping hill. The chalet was rebuilt in 1974 after a fire destroyed the original structure.

There are scenic vistas of glacial terrain and dramatic views of hardwood and pine forests. Facilities include vault toilets, drinking water, information boards, parking area, and well-marked, groomed trails. The chalet is open in the winter. Appointments are necessary for off-season use. There are a number of hiking and ski trails. There is a campground at Birch Grove and a picnic area farther south at Long Lake.

◆ **Rust-Owen Reservoir** is located just west of Drummond on Hwy 63, then north (right) on FH 35 for .25 miles to the parking area on the left. Facilities include parking area and trail.

This small reservoir was once a reliable source of water for fire protection to the lumber mill and town below. The structure is 46 feet in diameter with a 20-foot-high interior. The walls are over three feet thick and are made of native fieldstone. The interior is lined with cement and could hold over 180,000 gallons of water. Piping to carry the water was made of cedar strips held together with spiral-wrapped steel bands covered with coal tar or creosote. Water for the reservoir was pumped uphill by two steam-powered pumps.

When you visit this site, you will be treated to a scenic view of Drummond Lake and the surrounding hills. **Please use caution**—loose rocks from this structure are scattered around the area. Visitors are encouraged to stay on the trail to prevent additional erosion of the hillside.

Other points of interest in this area include the **Valhalla Overlook, Ridge Top Trail** and the **Sun Bowl,** a large, open valley.

CAMPGROUNDS

Established Campgrounds

◆ Birch Grove Campground

Location: From Washburn, travel south one mile on Hwy 13, then west eight miles on Wanebo Road, then north (right) on FR 252 two miles, and then east (right) one mile on FR 435. The campground is between East and West Twin Lakes.

Number of Sites: Sixteen rustic sites that accept RVs up to 35 feet long

Facilities: Each site has a fire grill, parking spur, picnic table, and tent pad. There are vault toilets, drinking water, a boat landing to each lake, a small picnic area, fishing pier, and an interpretive trail. A campground host is present to greet visitors. Mt. Valhalla Trail System is about two miles to the north.

Description: This campground is popular with families and is moderately busy.

Reservations and Fee: All sites are on a first-come, first-serve basis, $6 fee. Open from May 1 to November 1.

◆ Perch Lake Campground

Location: From Drummond, travel north on FH 35 for five miles. The campground will be to the right.

Number of Sites: Sixteen rustic sites on two loops separated by the lake. Most sites accept 35-foot RVs. Six sites are available for group camping and can be reserved.

Facilities: Each site has a fire grill, parking spur, picnic table, and tent pad. There are vault toilets, drinking water, and a boat landing to Perch Lake. There is a campground host to greet visitors.

Description: This campground is just east of Rainbow Lake Wilderness and north of the North Country National Scenic Trail. It has moderate use by fishermen, mountain bikers, and hikers using the wilderness area. It is family-orientated and quiet.

Reservations and Fee: All sites are on a first-come, first-serve basis, $6 fee. Open from May 1 to November 1. For group camping reservations, call (715) 373-2667.

◆ Two Lakes Campground

Location: From Drummond, travel five miles southeast on FR 213, then turn onto FR 214 and follow it to the campground, located between Lake Owen and Bass Lake.

Number of Sites: Ninety moderate sites, on two lakes, that can accept RVs up to 50 feet long. There are also seven walk-in campsites. Barrier-free campsites can also be reserved.

Facilities: Each developed site has a fire grill, parking spur, picnic table, and tent pad. There are accessible vault toilets, drinking water, pay phone, fishing pier, boat landings on Lake Owen and Bass Lake, sanitary dump station, two marked swimming beaches, and an interpretive trail.

Description: This is one of the more popular campgrounds due to its location on Lake Owen and its access to the North Country National Scenic Trail and Porcupine Lake Wilderness near the campground.

Reservations and Fee: Campsite reservations can be made by calling 1-800-280-2267; TTY 1-800-879-4496. To reserve barrier-free sites, call (715) 373-2667.

Campgrounds
Washburn Ranger District

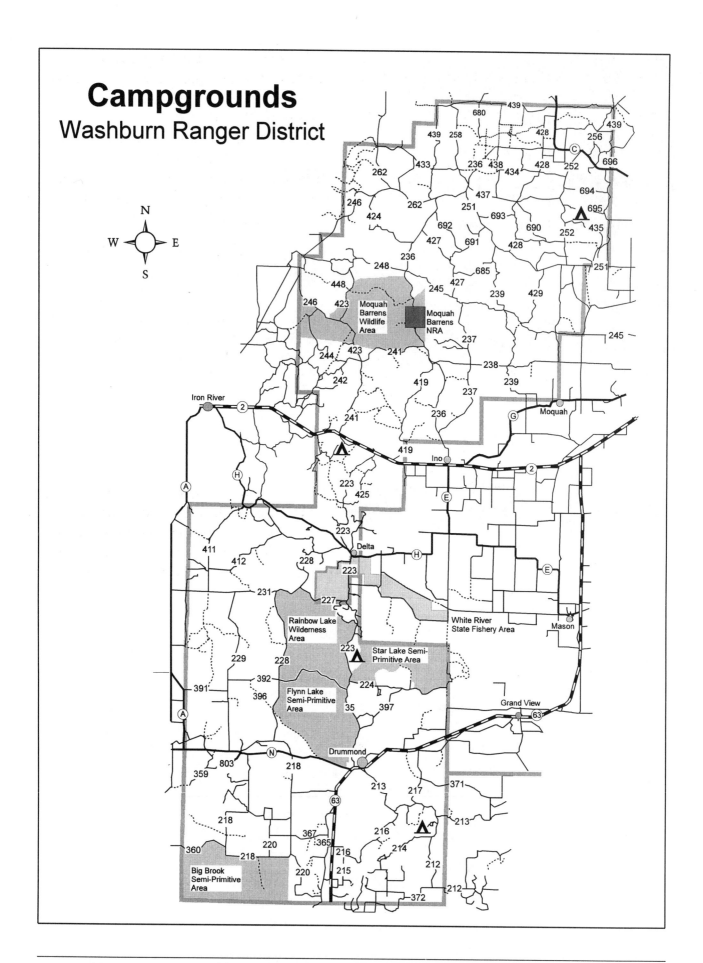

The Two Lakes Campground is a popular destination for Forest visitors, due to its location on scenic Lake Owen, and easy access to the North Country National Scenic Trail and Porcupine Lake Wilderness.

◆ Wanoka Lake Campground

Location: Located about seven miles east of Iron River on Hwy 2, then south (right) a short distance on FR 234.

Number of Sites: Twenty rustic sites that accept RVs up to 35 feet long

Facilities: Each site has a fire grill, parking spur, picnic table, and tent pad. There are vault toilets, drinking water, and a carry-in boat access to Wanoka Lake. A campground host is present.

Description: The Tri-County Trail is just north of Hwy 2. This campground, with its setting of mature pines, is popular with ATV users and those wanting an overnight stop along Hwy 2.

Reservations and Fee: All sites are on a first-come, first-serve basis, $6 fee. Open from May 1 to November 1.

Dispersed Camping

While dispersed camping is permitted in many areas throughout the District, popular spots include **Bass Lake**, **Pine Lake**, **Horseshoe Lake**, **Camp Nine Lake**, **Johnson Springs**, and **Bearsdale Spring Pond**. For directions, see Recreational Waters.

TRAILS

◆ **Anderson Grade Trail**

Length: 4 miles

Type: Hiking and cross-country skiing

Degree of Difficulty: Easy to moderate

Trailhead: From Drummond, travel north on FH 35 five miles to the Anderson Grade Trailhead parking area (near Perch Lake Campground).

Description: This trail follows an historic railroad grade that extends from FH 35 westward to FR 228, through the Rainbow Lake Wilderness. Motorized vehicles and mechanical devices such as mountain bikes are not permitted. The grade is flat and easy. Anderson Lake is also easily reached from the west (FR 228). The parking area is on FR 392.

Points of Interest: Clay, Bufo, and Anderson Lakes are excellent places for back country, low-impact recreational experiences.

Type of Landscape: A mix of northern hardwood and conifers on flat topography.

◆ **Bass Lake Interpretive Trail**

Length: 1.5 miles

Type: Hiking and interpretive

Degree of Difficulty: Easy to moderate

Trailhead: This trail is located at the Two Lakes Campground. From Drummond, travel south on FR 213 five miles to FR 214. Turn south and continue .5 miles to the campground entrance.

Description: This is a loop trail that interprets the natural history and biological processes of the lake community. Beaver dams and aspen stumps are evidence of beaver activity. Fire scars left from the turn-of-the-century logging era can be found along the trail. Facilities include vault toilets, parking area, pay phone, seasonal drinking water, and campsites.

Area wildlife include waterfowl, porcupine, small mammals, songbirds, birds of prey, coyote, and fox.

Points of Interest: This trail features both ecological processes and forest management practices.

Type of Landscape: It is a hardwood and conifer forest covering rolling glacial terrain. Scenic views of the lake run the entire length of the trail.

◆ **Beaver Lake Trail**

Length: .1 mile

Type: Hiking

Degree of Difficulty: Easy to moderate

Trailhead: This trail is two miles north of Perch Lake Campground on FH 35. From Drummond, travel north on FH 35 seven miles to the parking lot on the west side of the highway.

Description: This trail features a carry-in point to Beaver Lake, which is stocked with rainbow trout, and provides an opportunity to view wildlife. Located in the Rainbow Lake Wilderness, motorized vehicles and mechanical devices such as mountain bikes are not permitted. No facilities are provided.

Points of Interest: Wildlife viewing

Type of Landscape: Glacial terrain blanketed with mature hardwood and conifer mixed forests.

◆ **Birch Grove Interpretive Trail**

Length: .9 miles

Type: Hiking and interpretive

Degree of Difficulty: Easy to moderate

Trailhead: From Washburn, travel south on Hwy 13 one mile, then west (right) on Wanebo Road and then seven miles to FR 252. Turn northeast (right) and travel three miles to FR 435. Turn east (right) and travel one mile to Birch Grove Campground. This trail is on the north and west sides of the lake. It is accessed from the parking lot at the entrance to the campground.

Trails
Washburn Ranger District

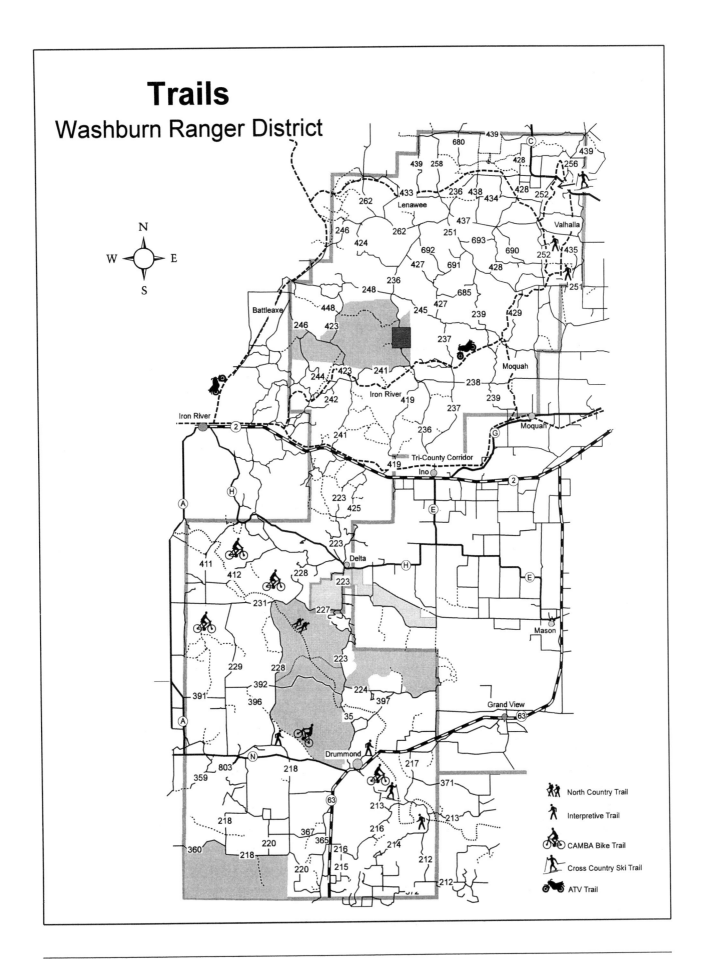

N
W E
S

680
439
C
439 258
428
256
439
433
236 438
434
428
252
Lenawee
262
437
Valhalla
262
251
693
690
435
246
692
252
424
691
428
251
427
236
248
685
Battleaxe
448
245
427
429
246
423
239
237
Moquah
423
241
238
239
244
Iron River
419
242
237
236
G
Iron River
Moquah
2
241
419
Tri-County Corridor
Ino
2
223
425
E
223
Delta
H
E
411
228
412
223
Mason
231
227
229
228
223
392
224
391
396
397
Grand View
35
63
A
N
Drummond
217
803
218
371
359
213
63
213
218
216
367
365
214
360
218
216
212
220
215
220
212

North Country Trail

Interpretive Trail

CAMBA Bike Trail

Cross Country Ski Trail

ATV Trail

Drummond Cross-Country Ski Trail

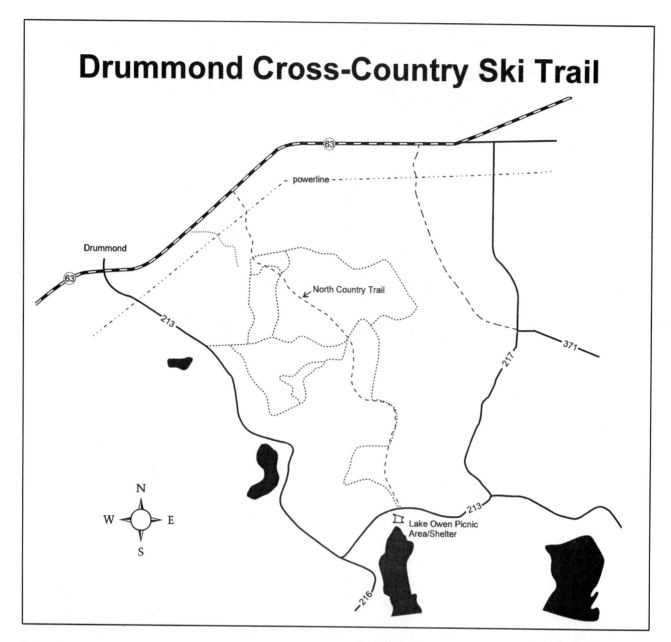

Description: This trail interprets the area's natural history and forest management practices. Facilities include vault toilets, parking area, seasonal drinking water, campsites, boat ramp, information board, interpretive signs, and fishing pier.

Points of Interest: Featured attractions are scenic overlooks with benches.

Type of Landscape: Glaciated terrain is punctuated with hardwood forests and lowland hardwood swamps.

◆ Drummond Cross-Country Ski Trail

Length: 9.9 miles

Type: Hiking, cross-country skiing, and mountain biking

Degree of Difficulty: Easy to moderate

Trailhead: From Drummond, travel south on FR 213 one mile to the trailhead.

Description: Skiers can choose from three main loops of varying lengths. The main trail, Boulevard, runs from the parking lot to the Lake Owen Picnic Shelter (4.6 km). Four loop trails branch off this main trail. These trails are 2.6 km to 7.1 km long. The North Country National Scenic Trail also connects with this trail between FR 217 and Hwy 63. These trails are part of the CAMBA mountain biking trail system.

At the Lake Owen Picnic Area, there is parking, shelter, fireplace, firewood stocked in the winter, seasonal drinking water, vault toilets, and access to the North Country National Scenic Trail.

Points of Interest: North Country National Scenic Trail passes through the area, leading to the Lake Owen Picnic Area and Shelter.

Type of Landscape: Rolling hills with conifer forests.

◆ Drummond Woods Interpretive Trail

Length: .7 miles

Type: Hiking and interpretive

Degree of Difficulty: Easy to moderate

Trailhead: From Drummond, travel north on Hwy 63 for .8 miles to FR 235. Turn west (left) into the parking area.

Description: This trail features logging and railroad history. Old-growth white pine and white pine stumps are visible, along with fire scars from the logging era. The trail follows a former railroad grade and is a spur on the North Country National Scenic Trail (NCT). This trail starts at the NCT trailhead. Travel a short distance north on the NCT. The Drummond Woods Trail will branch off to the west (left) to form a loop. A parking area is provided.

Points of Interest: Old-growth virgin white pine and hemlock, historic logging railroad grade, and the North Country National Scenic Trail.

Type of Landscape: Glaciated terrain cloaked with white pines and northern hardwoods, including yellow birch.

◆ Long Lake Interpretive Trail

Length: 1.2 miles

Type: Hiking and interpretive

Degree of Difficulty: Easy to moderate

Trailhead: From Washburn, travel one mile south on Hwy 13 to Wanebo Road. Turn west (right) and travel six miles to FR 435. Travel 100 feet to the entrance of Long Lake Picnic Area.

Description: This trail features lake views, bog vegetation, and upland hardwoods and pines. The jack pine is in a climatic (mature) stage. The trail starts in the picnic area on the north end or at the beach on the south end. It loops around the lake and has a boardwalk over wetlands on the western end of the lake. Facilities include accessible vault toilets, paved trails through the picnic area, picnic tables, grills, swimming area, beach, drinking water, and interpretive signs.

Points of Interest: Lowland bog vegetation, board walk, mature jack pine forests, and easy access to the snowmobile/ATV trail system.

Type of Landscape: Glacial terrain, low wetland-sphagnum bog environment, and upland hardwood forests.

◆ North Country National Scenic Trail

Length: 28 miles of the 3,200-mile North Country National Scenic Trail system

Type: Hiking, cross-country skiing, snowshoeing, and mountain biking, except in Rainbow Lake Wilderness

Degree of Difficulty: Easy to moderate

Trailhead: You can access the trail at any of the road crossings. These include Cty A south of Iron River, FR 231 at the west border of the wilderness area, FR 392 just west of FR 35 and on the southeast end of the wilderness area, Hwy 63 east of Drummond, Lake Owen Picnic Area, and Two Lakes Campground.

Description: This the western half of the 60.5-mile NCT trail segment through the Forest. Starting at Cty A south of Iron River, the trail angles southeast to Lake Owen. It travels through a mix terrain of rolling sand barrens, along terminal moraines to the glacial outwash at Lake Owen. There are many scenic overlooks and deep forests of hardwoods and pines.

North Country National Scenic Trail

Forest Boundary

A

N
E
W
S

Ruth Lake

2.1

411

4.4

412

231

0

A'

228

7.1

231

228

Tower Lake

Rainbow Lake

10.2

Rainbow Lake
Wilderness

Bufo Lake

Anderson Lake

392

Clay Lake

Perch Lake
Campground

35

Wishbone
Lake

Raynard
Lake

13.5

15.3

Armstrong
Lake

Flynn Lake
Semi-Primitive Area

B

N
E
W
S

B'

16.8

Minnow
Lake

Essox
Lake

Cisco
Lake

397

223

N
E
W
S

63

19.6

Drummond
Interpretive
Trail

213

C

C'

23

213

26

368

27.5

213

Hayward Ranger District

216

Lake Owen

Bass
Lake

214

N
E
W
S

Mileage from Cty A is posted at
key points along the trail. It is
27.5 miles from Cty A to FR 213
just west of Lake Owen

From the Cty A trailhead five miles south of Iron River, the trail extends seven miles southeast over FR 411 and FR 412 before ending at the parking area on FR 231. This is the northwest corner of the Rainbow Lake Wilderness. The trail continues its southeast direction for another six miles, passes near Tower, Rainbow, Bufo, and Reynard Lakes. About two-thirds through the Wilderness, NCT crosses Anderson Grade Trail, a remnant logging railroad grade. This segment ends at the southern border of the wilderness area at the FR 392 parking lot, just west of FR 35.

From the Rainbow Lake Wilderness, the trail continues south, then east through the Flynn Lake Semi-Primitive Area and crosses FH 35. It continues its eastward trek, passing between Arrowhead Lake and Cisco Lake and then crossing FR 397. At this point the trail turns south to Hwy 63. NCT joins Drummond Woods Interpretive Trail on FR 235, just north of Hwy 63. There is a small grocery store in Drummond, one mile to the west on Hwy 63. This segment is about six miles long.

From Hwy 63, the trail heads south, where it shortly joins the Drummond Cross-Country Ski Trail. NCT follows the Boulevard Loop south to the Lake Owen Picnic Area, where there is water, vault toilet, and a shelter. This segment is about eight miles long.

After leaving the picnic area, the final segment heads south, following Lake Owen first south, then east, and then looping around the north end of the lake to reach Two Lakes Campground. Along the way, the trail crosses FR 213 twice before reaching Hayward Ranger District and the Porcupine Lake Wilderness. From FR 213 you can travel west, then south on FR 214 to the Two Lakes Campground. There is also a spur trail from the registration station at the campground that leads you back to the trail and into the Porcupine Lake Wilderness.

There will be no drinking water along most of this trail. You need to bring your drinking water or water-purification equipment. There are several established campgrounds and picnic areas along the way. Supplies can be found in Drummond.

Points of Interest: Rainbow Lake Wilderness, Porcupine Lake Wilderness Area, and Flynn Lake Semi-Primitive Area

Type of Landscape: A mix terrain of rolling sand barrens, terminal moraines, and glacial outwash

◆ Pigeon Lake Interpretive Trail
Length: 1.8 miles
Type: Hiking and interpretive
Degree of Difficulty: Easy to moderate
Trailhead: From Drummond, travel west on Cty N three miles to FR 228. Turn north (right) and travel one mile to the trailhead.
Description: This trail system adjoins the Pigeon Lake Field Station for the Natural Resources College, University of Wisconsin. The trail loops to the north. This trail highlights ecosystems management and forest land management practices. Facilities include a parking lot, interpretive signs, and information board.
Points of Interest: Visitors will view a northern bog environment and associated wildlife.
Type of Landscape: Upland and lowland glacial terrain features conifers and bog vegetation.

◆ Teuton Cross-Country Ski Trail System
Length: 12.8 miles
Type: Hiking and cross-country skiing, classical and skating
Degree of Difficulty: Moderate to difficult
Trailhead: From Washburn, travel northwest on Cty C for seven miles to the Mt. Valhalla Recreation Area.
Description: This trail system is located southwest and behind the Mt. Valhalla chalet. There are three major loops of 1.7 miles, 2.8 miles and 3.5 miles. The glacial terrain provides scenic overlooks of hardwood and pine forests. A number of cutoff loops have been added to Loop A. This loop travels uphill for the first mile, which can be stressful.

Facilities include the chalet, vault toilets, drinking water, trail brochure, parking area, and well-marked, groomed trails. Appointments are necessary for off-season use.

Valkyrie and Teuton
Cross-Country Ski Areas

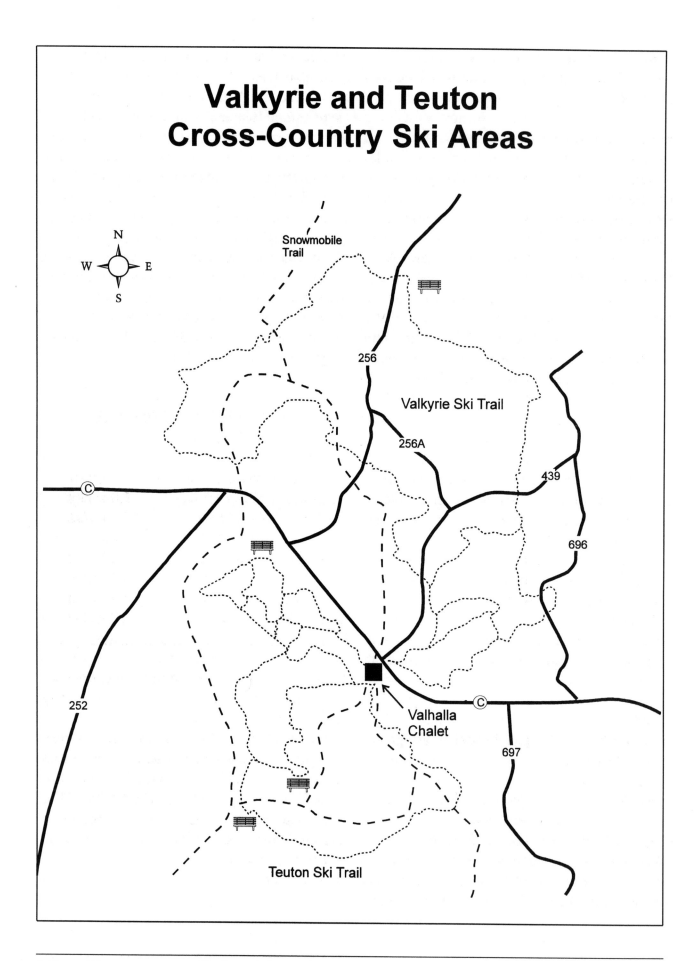

Points of Interest: Scenic vistas
Type of Landscape: Glacial terrain with harwoods and pines.

◆ Valkyrie Cross-Country Ski Trail

Length: 14.7 miles
Type: Hiking and cross-country skiing, classical and skating
Degree of Difficulty: Moderate to difficult
Trailhead: From Washburn, travel northwest on Cty C seven miles to the Mt. Valhalla Recreation Area.
Description: This trail system is adjacent to the Mt. Valhalla Recreation Area, north of the chalet and Cty C. Parking is available at Mt. Valhalla. There are three trail loops of varying lengths and experience levels passing through glacial landscaped terrain covered with hardwood and pine plantations. Loop C brings skiers or hikers to the dramatic vista at the Sun Bowl. Rest stops can be found on the 6.1-mile Loop C and the 2.3-mile Loop B. Loop A is 1.9 miles long. With all the hills on the longest trail, it is best to bring food and water. Forest management practices to provide open areas are evident along the trail.

Facilities include the chalet, vault toilets, drinking water, trail brochure, parking area, and well-marked, groomed trails. Appointments are necessary for off-season use.
Points of Interest: Scenic views
Type of Landscape: Glacial terrain with hardwoods and pine.

◆ Washburn Ranger District Multiple-Use Trail System

Length: 105.4 miles
Type: Multiple-use trails, with snowmobiling and ATV being the prevalent activities
Degree of Difficulty: Easy to difficult
Trailheads: The chalet at the Mt. Valhalla Recreation Area northwest of Washburn, is a popular access point. Other trailheads are near the communities of Washburn, Ashland, Bayfield, Cornucopia, Port Wing, Herbster, Iron River, Ino, Delta, Drummond, Cable, Grand View, and Barnes.
Description: This trail system is composed of fifteen interconnecting trails that crisscross the Washburn Ranger District. They traverse a variety of forest habitats, including pine plantations, hardwoods, and open barrens. Forest management practices are evident along the trails. Selected trails are groomed for snowmobile use, and are part of county and state trail systems. For trail segments open to snowmobiles, refer to current snowmobile maps. Facilities include area campgrounds and the chalet at the Mt. Valhalla Recreation Area.

Most trail segments open for ATV use are in the northern third of the District.

WASHBURN MULTIPLE USE TRAIL SYSTEM		
TRAIL	NAME	LENGTH
504	Moquah Spur	3.8 miles
505	Iron River	18.5 miles
515	Lenawee	12 miles
516	Battleaxe	4.2 miles
522	Valhalla	15.3 miles
522A	Ridgetop	1.1 miles
522B	Tower	.07 miles

Obtain a copy of the up-to-date trails either from the Ranger District office or from Bayfield County (1-800-777-7558).
Points of Interest: Mt. Valhalla Recreation Area, Mt. Baldy, Moquah Barrens Wildlife Management Area, Moquah Barrens Research Natural Area, Apostle Islands National Lakeshore, Northern Wisconsin Interpretive Center, and Lake Superior
Type of landscape: Rolling hills with hardwood and pine plantations.

Equestrian Trails

There are no established horseback riding trails in the District. People who ride the Multiple-Use Trail System and the forest roads meet at Mt. Valhalla Chalet and disperse camp at Pine Lake and Horseshoe Lake.

Mountain Bike Trails

These are a number of trails established especially for mountain bikes by the Chequamegon Area Mountain Bike Association (CAMBA), P.O. Box 141, Cable, WI 54821 (715) 798-3833.

◆ Delta Cluster Trails

Length: 72 miles
Type: Mountain bike
Degree of Difficulty: Easy to difficult, mostly moderate
Trailhead: Any of the road crossings or area parking lots can act as a trailhead. A major trailhead is on Cty A south of Iron River, which is also the trailhead for the North Country National Scenic Trail.
Description: This is a series of interconnecting loops located in 46 square miles of forest, north and west of Rainbow Lake Wilderness. These trails follow Forest roads, dirt roads, and Forest trails. Terrain varies from sandy pine barrens in the west to the glacial outwash area in the east. Each route offers a variety of sights.

South Fork and East Fork Loops are the easiest trails in the cluster. They follow paved, improved, and dirt roads. The moderately difficult routes, Pine Barrens and West Fork Loops, offer more variety of road types. Tall Pines and Buckskin Loops are almost entirely off-road. The most challenging is the scenic and hilly Delta Loop.
Points of Interest: Scenic vistas
Type of Landscape: Hilly glacial terrain with sandy rolling hills in the west.

◆ Drummond Cluster Mountain Bike Trails

Length: 82 miles
Type: Mountain biking
Degree of Difficulty: Easy to moderate
Trailhead: The main trailhead is at the town park on Drummond Lake. From Hwy 63 in Drummond, take Wisconsin Street north to Superior Street, then west (left) on Superior to the park. The park offers bathrooms, picnic pavilion, and parking. There are other facilities in town.
Description: This is a series of loop trails that center around the town of Drummond. These trails use existing town and forest roads, and ski/hiking trails to offer a wide variety of experiences. There are two main loops. From the trailhead, go south to Hwy 63. From here you can go east and south on Lake Owen Drive to the Drummond Ski Area, or west to Cty N, or north to FH 35. Longer trails are to the north and west of town with shorter trails to the southeast.

The Drummond loops offer a forest experience without fear of being lost in the deep woods. These routes, on paved or well-maintained county and Forest roads, travel over level or slightly rolling terrain that is ideal in wet or dry conditions. Facilities inlcude bathrooms, shelter, and parking at the town park.
Points of Interest: North Country National Scenic Trail passes through the area, leading to the Lake Owen Picnic Area and Shelter at the southern end of the trail.
Type of Landscape: Rolling hills with conifer forests.

Snowmobile Trails

There are seven state snowmobile corridors in this District. They include:

◆ **State Trail 2**, Superior to Hurley, is the Tri-County Trail corridor. It follows the north side of Hwy 2 about four miles through the Forest.

◆ **State Trail 7**, Drummond to Barnes, starts at the junction of State Trail 63 and heads west on TS 510 (Bear Paw) 13.2 miles. About two-thirds of the way TS 511 (Totagatic) will leave this segment and head toward the southwest 4.6 miles before leaving the Forest. TS 510 continues northwest over Cty N before leaving the Forest and heading to Barnes. State Trail 31 joins State Trail 7 near the Forest boundary.

◆ **State Trail 31**, Barnes to Iron River to Bayfield, enters and leaves the Forest in a number of places. Starting east of Barnes and just north of Cty N, State Trail 31 joins State Trail 7 near the Forest boundary. It then heads north on TS 513 (Buckskin) 11.5 miles before leaving the Forest to head to Iron River. After leaving Iron River, the trail heads east-northeast into the Forest on TS 505 (Iron River). The trail runs 18.5 miles to Long Lake. Here it uses TS 522 (Valhalla) and heads north 15.3 miles to the northeast corner of the District. The trail then uses TS 520 two miles, where it leaves the Forest and heads to Bayfield.

There are also a number of local and club trails that use portions of the Washburn Ranger District trails. These include:

◆ **Trail 3** (Battleaxe), Iron River to Port Wing, is mostly outside the Forest. TS 516, along the northwest border, is used for 4.2 miles before it heads west.

◆ **Trail 4** (Lenawee), Port Wing to Washburn, enters the Forest in the northwest corner and travels eastward on TS 515 (Lenawee) 12 miles where it joins with State Trail 31.

◆ **Trail 16** (Delta Trail) leaves Trail 2 approximately six miles east of Iron River and travels south to connect with the Mason Trail.

◆ **Trail 63** (Moquah Spur Trail Segment) enters the Forest west of Moquah off Cty G and travels 4.5 miles north to connect with Trail 31.

◆ **Trail 63** (Wildcat Trail Segment) At Drummond, travel east of Hwy 63, then south to Cable. The trail also goes north from downtown Drummond, then east to Grand View.

In general, snowmobile trails can change from year to year due to funding, easements and other factors. For up-to-date trail conditions, call 1-800-GRANDFUN.

SURROUNDING AREA FACILITIES

Apostle Islands National Lakeshore

This National Park lies at the northern tip of Wisconsin. It contains 21 of the 22 islands north and east of the Bayfield Peninsula. Madeline Island, located just east of Bayfield, is mostly privately-owned and not part of the park system. There is a 12-mile-long section of mainland west of Red Cliff Indian Reservation that is part of the park as well.

The islands are accessible by water taxi and private boat. Caution must be used at all times, for the cold water and sudden storms of the area can be very dangerous.

The Visitor Center at the Old County Courthouse in Bayfield has interpretive films, slides, artifacts, information, and restrooms. The center is open from 8 A.M. to 4:30 P.M., (715) 779-3397. There is a second visitor center at Little Sand Bay. Take Hwy 13 west of Red Cliff, then Cty K north, then north on Park Road.

Private Campgrounds

BAYFIELD/WASHBURN AREA

◆ **Apostle Islands View Campground:** Located .5 miles south of Bayfield on Hwy 13 and west on Cty J, follow signs; (715) 779-5524; Star Rt, P.O. Box 8, Bayfield, WI 54814.
◆ **Red Cliff Recreation Complex:** Three miles north of Bayfield on the Red Cliff Reservation; (715) 779-3743; P.O. Box 529, Bayfield, WI 54814.

◆ **Trail'er Inn:** Eleven miles west of Ashland on Hwy 2; (715) 682-4658; Rt 3, P.O. Box 353, Ashland, WI 54806.

IRON RIVER

◆ **Ranch Park:** Four miles north of Mason on Hwy 63; (715) 746-2424: Rt 2 Ashland, WI 54806.
◆ **Tri Lake Timbers Campground:** Three miles east of Iron River on Hwy 2, one mile north on East Long Lake Road, junction with FR 242; (715) 372-4627; Rt 1, P.O. Box 282, Iron River, WI 54847.
◆ **Top O' The Morn Resort & Campground:** South of Hwy 2 on Cty A, then right on Iron Lake Road; (715) 372-4546; Rt 1, P.O. Box 21, Iron River, WI 54748.
◆ **Wild Wood Campground:** One-half mile east of Iron River. on Hwy 2, then south on Wayside Road, then .5 miles on Wildwood Drive; on Peterson Lake; (715) 372-4072; Rte 2, P.O. Box 18W, Iron River, WI 54847.

Municipal Campgrounds and Parks

BAYFIELD/WASHBURN AREA

◆ **Big Rock Campground:** Located three miles north of Washburn on Cty C, turn right on Big Rock Road, one mile; overlooks the Sioux River; Washburn, WI 54891.
◆ **Big Rock Park:** Located one mile northwest of Washburn on Cty C, then north on Big Rock Road.
◆ **Dalrymple Campground:** Located .75 miles north of downtown Bayfield on Hwy 13; 30

wooded lakeshore sites; city water, picnic tables; overlooking Lake Superior; (715) 779-5712.

◆ **Memorial Park:** Located on Lake Superior in Washburn; 52 tent and trailer sites, electric, flush toilets, showers, firewood, playground, picnic tables, swimming beach, freezer service, cable TV hookup, pets allowed; (715) 373-5440; Washburn City Hall, P.O. Box 638, Washburn, WI 54891.

◆ **West End Park:** Located on Lake Superior in Washburn; 45 tent and trailer sites, dump station, electric, flush toilets, showers, firewood, playground, picnic tables, boat launch, swimming beach, pets allowed; (715) 373-5440; Washburn City Hall, P.O. Box 638, Washburn, WI 54891.

IRON RIVER

◆ **Delta Lake Park:** Located south of Iron River on Cty H, then west one mile on FR 228, then north to Delta Lake. Facilities include campground, beach, and boat landing.

◆ **Moon Lake Park:** Located .5 miles south of Iron River on Cty H to Moon Lake; camping, beach, and boat landing.

◆ **Twin Bear Park:** Located five miles south of Iron River on Cty H to the Pike Lake Chain; toilet, beach, camping, and boat landing.

ASHLAND

◆ **Prentice Park:** City of Ashland; campground, observation tower to observe wild swans, playground, walking trails, pavilion, picnic facilities.

Attractions

◆ **Big Top Chautauqua:** The old canvas tent-show stage, offering a variety of quality entertainment: theater, comedy, music, magic, and historical narratives. P.O. Box 455, Washburn, WI 54891; (715) 373-5851.

◆ **Blue Water Maritime Center:** Displays on small-craft tradition in the Apostles, commercial fishing, lighthouse tending, boat building demonstrations; 2nd St. and Maypenny Ave., Bayfield, WI 54814.

Bike Rentals

◆ **Bay City Cycles:** Mountain bike rentals; 412 2nd St. West, Ashland, WI 54806; (715) 682-2091.

◆ **Bodin's On The Lake:** Bike and sailboard rental; 121 Rittenhouse Ave, Bayfield, WI 54814; (715) 779-3400, and Lakeshore Dr, Ashland, WI 54806; (715) 682-6441.

Boat Rentals

◆ **Bear Country:** Sporting goods, boat, motor, pontoon rental; Drummond, WI; (715) 739-6645.

◆ **Cable Service Center:** Pontoon boat sales & rentals; Cable, WI 54821; (715) 798-3444.

◆ **The New Telemark Resort:** Boat rentals; P.O. Box 277, Cable, WI 54821; (715) 798-3811 or (800) 472-3001.

◆ **Wagner's Port Sand Resort & Campground:** Rental of boats, pontoon, motors, and kayaks; Rt 2, P.O. Box 453, Webster, WI 54893; (715) 349-2395.

Canoe and Sea Kayak Rentals

◆ **Trek 'N Trail:** Sea kayak rentals, instructions and excursions; Rittenhouse Ave, Bayfield, WI 54814; (715) 779-3320.

Downhill Skiing

◆ **Mt. Ashwabay Ski Hill:** 11 downhill runs from beginner to expert, 30 km of cross-country ski trails, instruction available, night skiing, rentals; P.O. Box 928, Bayfield, WI 54814; (715) 779-3227.

◆ **Telemark Resort:** 11 downhill runs, 100 km of groomed and tracked cross-country ski trails, lodge, tennis, horseback riding, sleigh rides, more; P.O. Box 277B, Cable, WI 54821; (715) 798-3811.

Museums & Historical Sites

◆ **Bayfield Heritage Museum:** Located at 100 Rittenhouse Ave in Bayfield; exhibits illustrate the settlement, growth of industry, and agriculture of Bayfield; (715) 779-3272 or 779-5060.

◆ **Buffalo Art Center:** A museum and gift shop of the Lake Superior Chippewa. Festivals, workshops, and craft demonstrations throughout season. Red Cliff Reservation, P.O. Box 529, Bayfield, WI 54814; (715) 779-5858.

◆ **The Cooperage Museum & Gift Shop:** Watch a local cooper at work, assembling barrels around the huge open hearth, guided tours daily; P.O. Box 687, Bayfield, WI 54814; (715) 779-3400.

◆ **Drummond Museum:** Logging and lumbering industry artifacts, wildlife artifacts; (715) 739-6669, 739-6256 or 739-6260.

◆ **Washburn Area Historical Society Museum:** Located on Bayfield Street; artifacts from Washburn's past; (715) 373-5345 or 373-2289.

◆ **Western Bayfield County Museum:** Located one block south of Main St and US Hwy 2, across from the post office; display of logging tools and markers, 300 other artifacts; (715) 372-4359 or 372-4456.

Emergency Numbers

◆ **Sheriff**
Ashland County (715) 682-7023
Bayfield County (715) 373-6120

◆ **Hospitals**
Memorial Medical Center, 1615 Maple Lane, Ashland, WI 54806; (715) 682-4563

Other Information Contacts

◆ **Snow & Fishing Hot Line** for the Washburn Area (715) 373-5017
◆ **Weather Report:** 24 hrs/day in Apostle Island Area (715) 682-8822

◆ **County**
Bayfield County Forestry Dept, Courthouse, P.O. Box 445 Washburn, WI 54891 (715) 373-2191

◆ **State**
WI DNR, Brule Area Headquarters, Hwy 2, P.O. Box 125, Brule, WI 54820 (715) 372-4866, covers Ashland, Bayfield and Douglas Counties

◆ **Federal: U.S. Forest Service**
Washburn Ranger District, P.O. Box 578, 113 E. Bayfield St, Washburn, WI 54891 (715) 373-2667, Fax (715) 373-2878

◆ **Chambers of Commerce**
Ashland County Clerk's Office, Courthouse, Ashland, WI 54806
Ashland Chamber of Commerce, 320 4th Ave. West, P.O. Box 746, Ashland, WI 54806
Bayfield Chamber of Commerce, 42 Broad St., P.O. Box 138, Bayfield, WI 54814
Iron River Business Ass'n, P.O. Box 64, Iron River, WI 54847 (715) 372-4766
Washburn Marketing and Promotion Committee, P.O. Box 326, Washburn, WI 54891

INDEX